LET ME PREY UPON YOU

"Beware of false prophets, who come to you in sheep's clothing, but inwardly are ravenous wolves."

—MATTHEW 7:15

LET ME PRAY ~~PREY~~ ~~WITH~~ UPON YOU

BREAKING FREE FROM A MINISTER'S SEXUAL ABUSE

SANDY PHILLIPS KIRKHAM

ABSAM
CINCINNATI, OHIO
SandyPhillipsKirkham.com

Praise for
LET ME PREY UPON YOU

"Sandy's story draws you deeper and deeper into her world as a teen abused by her youth pastor and the years of pain as she struggled with the aftermath of his abuse. A compelling account of clergy abuse."

—DEBBIE MOTZ

"Sandy's book is a go-to resource for anyone wanting to understand the concepts of grooming and abuse of religious authority. Her story captures the pain, the shame and long struggle to heal from clergy abuse."

—DAN FRONDORF, CO-FOUNDER OF CINCINNATI SNAP CHAPTER

"Kirkham **lost** her youth, innocence, and her faith in the very place that she should have been safest—her beloved church, by a minister that she trusted. In *Let Me Prey Upon You*, however, she has **found** her voice!!"

—SUE TRAKAS, PROFESSOR EMERITA

"*Let Me Prey Upon You* is an important story of a minister who preyed upon and sexually abused several young women, while moving from church to church to church. But it is more than that, it is also the story of one courageous woman who, years later, finally dealt with and confronted her past to begin her journey of healing. Sandy Kirkham's story is one of lies, manipulation, coercion, and abuse, but it is also a story of courage, resilience, and bravery."

—SUSAN RANDALL, COUNSELOR

"Sandy does an amazing job describing the power imbalance of clergy, the spiritual confusion and destruction of clergy abuse by sharing her difficult story. She is an inspiration and an overcomer."

—KIM RUNG, CLERGY ABUSE SURVIVOR AND ADVOCATE

"In her book, *Let Me Prey Upon You*, Sandy Kirkham shares from her heart and own life, her tragic experience as a victim of pastoral abuse. She takes the reader along her entire journey of abuse, which began in her teen years, and reveals details of her suffering, her bondage, and eventually her path to freedom and recovery. This true story is told from an extremely personal perspective in a moving and powerful way and is well worth a read."

—ELLEN SMITH

"Sandy speaks truth in her story of clergy abuse and is an inspiration to all of us who have been abused by a church leader. While describing the extreme pain she experienced by her youth pastor and the church's rejection, she also offers hope. *Let Me Prey Upon You* is instrumental in understanding the dynamics when a spiritual leader crosses the boundaries of his profession with a member of his congregation."

—MARY JO NOWORYTA, CLERGY ABUSE SURVIVOR AND ADVOCATE

"*Let Me Prey Upon You* tells the too infrequently told story of a vulnerable teen betrayed by a pastor who should have been protector but was instead abuser. Sandy Kirkham describes with great clarity the emotional hemorrhaging from abuse that often goes undetected by others and even the victim as well. The good news is, after decades of hiding her past, Sandy found freedom by acting to set things straight. She writes from a passion to see victims restored as she has been and others protected from suffering her fate in the first place."

—HAROLD SWIFT, CHURCH ELDER

"A well-written book that provides first person narrative of a young, faith driven, over-achieving girl who is manipulated and then trapped in an abusive relationship by someone of power in the church. The book provides a window into the author's world and we can see how this occurs as well as the self-doubt fostered by the offender. It also shares the trauma that is caused when the offender is not only not held accountable, but moved into a new position that allows his abusive behavior to continue. Finally, it is a book of courage and survival and one that provides hope for victims."

—SHELLEY MARSHALL

Reviews and Awards for LET ME PREY UPON YOU

"I was gripped the entire time from cover to cover. Sandy brilliantly shows how complex abuse is and how abuse is anything but accidental."

—PASTOR JIMMY HINTON, JIMMYHINTON.ORG

"This book is incredible. I couldn't put it down until I read it from cover to cover. This is a must read resource for those interested in abuse within the church."

—CLARA HINTON

"This is Sandy's story. What began as a normal girl who loved her church family became an odyssey of evil for which she may very well be expected to shoulder all the blame. But this story is not without hope, it is not without healing and it is not without a survivor. If you or someone you love has been sexually abused, you need to read this book. If you even suspect this is so, you should read it."

—TALES FROM BOOK DRAGON REVIEW

"Sandy courageously tells her story of abuse. Her story is powerful and will have a profound impact on anyone who reads it."

—JILL RILEY POST TRAUMATIC FAITH PODCAST

2021 INDEPENDENT PRESS AWARD
Winner
Religion: NonFiction

Distinguished Favorite
Book Cover Design: Nonfiction
Women's Issues: Nonfiction

PODCAST TOUR
Tune in to listen

Speaking Out on Sex Abuse
Clara and Jimmy Hinton

Couples Synergy
Dr. Ray and Jean Kadkhodaian

Protector's Tool Kit
Warrior Wednesday—Guy Beveridge

Save Your Sanity
Dr. Rhoberta Shaler PhD

Preacher Boys Podcast
Eric Skwarczynski

Barbara and You Show
Barbara Foster

Resilient Hacks
Elizabeth Meyers

Survivor Sanctuary
Kelly Downing

Let Me Prey Upon You
Breaking Free from a Minister's Sexual Abuse
By Sandy Phillips Kirkham
Published by Absam, LLC, Cincinnati, Ohio

Copyright © 2019 Sandy Phillips Kirkham

sandyphillipskirkham.com

All rights reserved.

This publication is protected under the U.S. Copyright Act of 1976 and all other applicable international, federal, state, and local laws, and all rights are reserved, including resale rights: you are not allowed to reproduce, transmit, or sell this book in part or in full without the written permission of the publisher.

For permission requests, write to the publisher, addressed Attention: Absam, LLC, c/o Sandy Phillips Kirkham, 287 Sunny Acres Drive, Cincinnati, OH 45255

ORIGINAL FRONT COVER DESIGN: Bob Portune
INTERIOR DESIGN: Wendy Dunning, wendydunning.com
EDITORS: Peter Wietmarschen and Colleen Wietmarschen, https://YourLiteraryProse.com
BOOK CONSULTANTS: Peter Wietmarschen and Colleen Wietmarschen

ISBN: 978-1-7341952-0-0 (Hardback)
ISBN: 978-1-7341952-2-4 (Paperback)
ISBN: 978-1-7341952-1-7 (eBook)
Library of Congress Control Number 2019918017

Published in the United States of America
Printed on recycled paper
10 9 8 7 6 5 4 3 2 1

Dedication

To my husband Bill, my rock

ACKNOWLEDGMENTS

Deepest gratitude to Anne Badanes for giving so freely of her time and talents to help me tell my story. Anne kept me focused when my emotions threatened to go off the rails.

Thanks to my many beta readers who read and critiqued my first manuscript. Your input and encouragement were invaluable.

To Mary Ann Mayers and Karen Shoemaker, you helped me to understand the writing process and realize what was needed and not needed in my early manuscripts.

Thank you to my editors, Peter and Colleen Wietmarschen, who helped refine my manuscript for print and who helped guide this book through the publication process.

Thank you to designers Bob Portune for his excellent cover design and Wendy Dunning for expertly laying out the interior of this book and other design support.

A special thank you to my dear book club friends who stood by me, both in my early recovery and writing this book: Anne Miller, Su Randall, Sandy Hoover, Lynne Morris, Gail Gattas, Amy Groneman, Sue Trakas, Beth Swift, and Ellen Smith. I treasure our friendships.

How fortunate I am to have been blessed with the steadfast love and support of my two dearest friends, Teri Toepfert Hemmelgarn and Chris Reller Miller. You remind me every day what it means to be a friend.

TABLE OF CONTENTS

Acknowledgments
9

Preface
13

Foreword
David Pooler, PhD
Baylor University School of Social Work
14

PART ONE
VICTIM
17

Queensgate—Next Exit
A New Home
Youth Group
Sweet Sixteen
Number A36D _ _
Playing the Field
Strike One
By Their Fruits Ye Shall Know Them
Trapped
Lexington
Who Said It Was Over?
Number 40

PART TWO
SURVIVOR
113

Aftermath
Spiritual Wounds
Revelations
Don't Tell! Tell?
Now What?
For Better or Worse
Repeat Offender
The Wolf Exposed
Preparation
Confrontation
Seeking Justice
Obstacles
Restitution
The Elders

PART THREE
ADVOCATE
191

Silent No More
Deeper Understanding: Pastors
Deeper Understanding: Victims
Setting Things Right
Back in the Pulpit
What The Hell Just Happened?
Reflection

Epilogue: Using His Name
221

Appendix A
Resources: Healing and Understanding
223

Appendix B
Research on Clergy Abuse by David K. Pooler
225

Appendix C
Documentation and Letters
231

Appendix D
Photos
244

PREFACE

The idea of writing this book terrified me. I knew my story was important and needed to be shared, but I doubted my ability to appropriately express my fears, my sorrow, my pain, my hope, and finally my ability to rejoice. Would I be able to find the words and the strength to dig deep into the dark places where my pain and guilt was hidden for so long? Could I relive it all over again in black and white words? Would I be able to convey the devastation of my abuse? Would my story be met with criticism and doubt? Would I stay committed to the finish? My answer to all these questions was simple: just start to write.

I began to write my story, not at the beginning, but in the middle. Odd, but it was the middle of my story, my secret, which led me to write this book. The emotions of writing were overwhelming. Many times I simply stopped; it was too painful to recall those moments, to put my feelings on paper for all to read. When I needed a break, I took one. When I again felt strong enough, I returned to writing. In the end, my questions were answered and my doubts erased. With a supportive husband, family, and friends cheering me on, the finished line was reached.

"An untold story never heals."

—MARY DEMUTH

FOREWORD

David Pooler, PhD
Baylor University School of Social Work

Perhaps you are reading this because you have been profoundly affected by the failures of the church and its leaders. You may have been deeply hurt by a leader or may be close to someone who has. You may know of a pastor, priest, or spiritual leader who has been guilty of sexual misconduct. Grief, loss, and betrayal may be experiences with which you are intimately acquainted. Maybe you are reading this for a greater understanding of clergy abuse and how it happens.

This is Sandy Kirkham's story. Sandy has the extraordinary ability to take you deep into the inner world of what it is like to be sexually exploited by a trusted leader. She will take you along her journey of healing and being transformed by her pain into a flourishing survivor. I want to give you some guardrails for your journey along with her, to provide a backdrop and a better understanding of her experience.

I know Sandy, and I have seen what she has done with her life with the help and support of others. She is a resilient fighter who has found her voice. We first met in 2016 at a conference for survivors where we were presenters and I was speaking about my research. It was there I first heard her story. I found myself feeling her pain and shame as she described her abuse at the hands of her trusted youth minister. I also witnessed the hope reflected upon the faces of the attendees as she spoke of her own journey of healing. Her story you will discover is not only powerful, but will ask you to examine your own understanding of clergy abuse. Her story provides validation for survivors, hope for those recovering, and exposure to some of the very unhealthy ways the institution of the church covers, conceals, distorts, and often further harms survivors.

I am a clinician who specializes in working with women who have been sexually assaulted or abused, and who have experienced complex developmental trauma. In 2015, I surveyed 280 women who had been sexually abused by a pastor, priest, or other leader. The results of my survey can be found in the appendix.

Participants needed to be sixteen or older at the time the abuse started. I followed up with twenty-seven of these survivors and conducted in-depth interviews to better understand the nuances and complexity of their experiences. I interviewed women just like Sandy and I have been changed by my encounters.

In 2011, I wrote an article in the journal, *Pastoral Psychology* that explored how congregations are complicit in their abuse of vulnerable members. Clergy perpetuated sexual abuse is not just bad actors harming people, it is about a structural problem in which a congregation is focused more on leaders being charismatic, knowledgeable, popular, and persuasive (image) than looking deeply at the character of the leader. It is also about placing too much trust in a leader thinking they are "above reproach" and failing to hold leaders accountable. Oftentimes, members of the congregation elevate a pastor to a place they do not belong. They view the pastor as not completely human but not God either, but somewhere in between.

Society is approaching a tipping point around gender discrimination and sexual violence and churches will get caught in the wave. We now know religious communities can be just as oppressive and hurtful as they are helpful. Change is coming because victims are finding and using their voices to reclaim their lives, call out injustice and evil, and working to make our churches safer for those of all ages. Sandy Kirkham is one of those people. I hope you will allow yourself to be inspired and encouraged the same way I have been after reading her story.

PART ONE
VICTIM

"The saddest thing about betrayal is that it never comes from your enemies."

—ANONYMOUS

QUEENSGATE— NEXT EXIT

The lie had been hidden for so long I hoped it might disappear. Some people say lies grow bigger with time, small white lies spawn bigger fibs, and soon they grow to mammoth proportions, but maybe the opposite could be true. Maybe big lies could dissipate over time. I wanted to believe if a big lie was hidden and wasn't hurting anyone, it didn't matter, and its power was gone. Maybe, just maybe, there was a statute of limitations for the lies he told me.

It was a gorgeous spring day and the late afternoon sun peeked through the smoky haze covering the Tennessee mountains. My goal was to reach the Hampton Inn in Greeneville, Tennessee, a city I had never visited before, before dark. It was March of 2004 before cell phones, Google maps, and GPS were common navigational tools, and I had already made one wrong turn twenty miles back. I headed down I-75 from Cincinnati armed with my AAA Triptik and an oversized Atlas as my navigational system to reach my daughter's college golf tournament in Greeneville.

My husband and chief navigator, Bill, was unable to make the trip. I was left on my own. In spite of a carefully mapped-out route, fear of becoming lost was ever present. I had never driven this route before. Throughout our married life, in the car and in general, I always counted on him to keep me on track. Once off I-75, the route would involve many turns, and a few backroads. I was getting a little nervous not having Bill with me.

My daughter's golf season was going well, and I, too, was content with this season of my life. I was forty-nine, had a great husband, two kids in college, a suburban house, two fairly well-behaved dogs, and good friends. Bill and I were enjoying our life as empty nesters, and I could finally start focusing more on myself. For years, the joys and chaos of children had taken precedent.

My CD player was loaded with my favorite songs, but I flicked on the radio instead. Reception was still good and the oldies station played one of my favorite Beach Boys songs, "Good Vibrations." I bellowed along, until I saw the sign.

Queensgate Exit 1 mile.

Queensgate? Queensgate? I had not thought of this place in years. My hands clenched the leather wrap of the steering wheel. I held on tight trying not to wavier an inch in order to stay steady in the left lane. I focused on the semi in front of me; it was passing a maroon Buick. No matter what, I did not want to veer toward the exit lane for Queensgate.

Queensgate? Queensgate? That's where he lives. Or does he still live there? My mind spun into overdrive. How close am I to his church; to where he may live? Reminders of Queensgate flooded my head. My legs sought the grounding offered by the accelerator. Memories raced in my head. I could feel the car respond and surge forward. I told myself to stare straight ahead. Follow the semi. It held me in its wake. I kept repeating, "Keep going; just keep going."

Queensgate ¼ mile.

Every muscle in my body tightened when I saw the next sign. I felt his presence slither into the car. I felt him all around me. I felt his touch. I heard his voice. I smelled his musky aftershave. His presence smothered me. Almost as a wicked joke, The Carpenters' song, "Rainy Days and Mondays" came on the radio and took me back to 1972. I felt paralyzed, unable to turn off the radio. I felt him in the seat next to me, putting his hand on my right thigh. Tears rolled down my cheeks and onto my lap. I no longer heard the music. Or, had I turned it off? I didn't know.

Queensgate next exit.

Unable to breathe, gasping for air, I found myself in the right lane. I pulled off the expressway just prior to the exit. All I could do was sit there and sob. For the first time in almost three decades, I was consumed with pain and incredible sadness.

My heart raced; my body shuddered with sobs as I lay my forehead on the steering wheel. I wrapped my arms around it, wishing this inanimate object would steady me and hug me back. I could not stop the waves of sorrow. I wanted the sadness, the memories, and the sound and smell of him to go away. I needed air. As I opened the car door, the rushing wind and the roar of semis brought reality to the moment. I stepped out of the car and held onto the hood to keep myself steady. Still, once I made it to the passenger's side, I collapsed next to the guardrail.

Why was this happening? Over the years there had been small reminders of him, reminders which stung like a slap on the wrist, but this was no small reminder. This was a huge reminder, a hard punch in my gut. It had been twenty-nine years since I last saw Queensgate, the place which reminded me of the Sandy I left behind, the Sandy I loathed.

I looked at my watch and realized I had to get back on the road to beat the setting sun. I forced myself to think about the golf tournament and told myself for the next forty-eight hours I would somehow put on my "mom face" and be strong. What would happen then? Could I push these memories, these feelings, and this pain back into the abyss and go on like before? Whatever this was, I was sure I couldn't ignore it any longer.

Arriving just before dark, I called Bill from the room to let him know I arrived safely. His steady voice calmed me and I felt better. Grateful for a weekend full of activities and the joy at seeing my daughter, I managed not to let the events on the highway ruin the weekend.

Two days later, I was back in the driver's seat. I desperately wanted to find a different route home. But my fear of getting lost and ending up in Queensgate, possibly in front of the church, made the known route a better option. I steeled myself as I drove along the freeway, gripping the steering wheel. For seven hours I could think of nothing other than what he had done to me. Even after I was well beyond Queensgate, the memories continued to permeate my mind. I found myself quickly moving forward into my past.

For the next two weeks I was in a constant state of turmoil. I tried to keep it hidden from Bill. Whenever he left for work, I walked through the house, wringing my hands asking myself questions for which I had no answers. Why me? Why did he pick me? What did I do?

Each night Bill came home and I would pretend everything was fine. I needed to be strong, to put on my "wife face." This was the exterior I had perfected over the years. One evening as Bill sat at the kitchen table to eat dinner, I poured him a glass of iced tea, as I did every night. I was about to join him at the table. I poured another glass of tea. Then I poured another and then a fourth glass of tea. I started shaking; aware I was losing my ability to function. Quickly, I poured the tea down the drain and set the glasses into the dishwasher. I glanced at Bill as he sat at the table reading the newspaper. He had not witnessed me pouring the four glasses of tea. Relief filled me, but I knew I needed help. I had to unload the secret threatening to crush me. I had to tell someone.

Then I heard *his* words, "Don't ever tell anyone. They will think you are lying and never believe you."

Who *would* ever believe my story? Who should I tell?

A NEW HOME

My parents belonged to a water ski club in the early 1960's. They performed in ski shows and competitions across the tri-state on the Ohio River. One of my best childhood memories was five-year-old me sitting on my dad's shoulders during one of these shows. "Hold on tight," he said. I wrapped my arms around his neck and away we went!

I was a fairy princess flying across the water on my dad's shoulders. "Don't worry," he would say as he tightened his grip around my legs, "I'm not going to let go of you." I was secure enough to let go with one hand and wave to the crowds along the shore. With his strong arms holding me, we circled back past the crowds, bravely waving again. My mom, waiting on the dock to perform in the next act, always waved back.

The next day, August 8, 1960, a picture appeared in *The Cincinnati Enquirer*, with the caption, "What strong muscles you have Daddy!" The following fall in kindergarten, I asked my mom to find the picture so I could take it to Show and Tell. I wish I still had the photo of that happy day.

One of my worst childhood days came a little over a year later. Mom sat my younger brother, Mike, and me down at the kitchen table. She told us we would be moving to a new house with a big yard, and I would meet new friends at my new school. She paused, and then said, "Dad won't be coming with us to the new house."

Dad's not coming with us?

"Why not?" I wondered. I looked down and pushed my finger through the hole in the white lace tablecloth and began twisting the fabric around my index finger. Not wanting to think about what Mom was saying, I concentrated on the tablecloth wrapped around my finger. I was confused and hoped she was wrong. *Dad has to come with us!* Wrapping the tablecloth tighter and tighter, I watched the tip of my finger turn a deep red.

I wanted to say something, but being only seven, I didn't know what to say. I just sat there, staring at my finger. I worried about Dad being alone. Who would take care of him? Who would fix his dinner? How would he kiss me goodnight if he didn't live with us? Surely Mom would answer my questions, "What about Dad?" I blurted out. "He will still live here," she replied.

That wasn't what I meant! Who will take care of him?

Mom did not understand my question. All I could think to do was concentrate on my now throbbing finger. "Look at me, Sandy. I promise we will get a puppy and a guinea pig. It will be fun. Plus, you will have another dad. You will have two dads."

Two dads? How do you have two dads?

A few days after our conversation at the kitchen table I met my new dad. A man with a black crew cut came over after dinner. His name was Chuck. I'd seen him at the water ski club talking to Mom whenever my dad wasn't around. Looking at his hair, I wondered how it went straight up. He stood in the doorway and Mom scurried us upstairs to get the suitcases we packed earlier in the day. As I reached the bottom of the steps, suitcase in hand, I was afraid to say I didn't want to go. It was easier to just keep quiet. Besides, I didn't think it would make a difference anyway. We loaded up Chuck's blue Pontiac convertible and left for our new house with the big yard. The worst part, I wasn't able to say goodbye to my "real dad."

As we drove across town, I wasn't sure where we were going. I pressed my face against the backseat window, fascinated by the backdrop of the black dark sky, the glow of the neon lights, and the huge beams of lights from the car dealership along North Bend Road. When we stopped at the traffic light in front of McDonald's, I asked, "Are we almost there?"

"Almost," Mom replied.

I looked at the funny hamburger man with the walking legs as he held the sign with lots of numbers on it. The apprehension I felt dissipated for a brief moment as I thought about living this close to a McDonald's! How much fun it would be! Along with the promise of a new puppy, I felt some excitement. Then I soon realized how far we had driven and how far away I would be from Dad.

The McDonald's and the new puppy did not seem like a very good trade-off. As sad as I was, I felt even sadder for Dad. We had left him. My mother's decision to leave my dad would always be a struggle for me.

When we first moved to Chuck's house, finances were tight. The new house was bigger than Dad's house, but it had no furniture. Chuck's first wife had taken it all; her retaliation for the divorce. My brother and I found without furniture the large living room with its shiny hardwood floors made a great place to slide in our stocking feet. Eating meals at the card table was "cozy," but life without a TV was most unbearable. For the first few weeks, Mike and I slept in sleeping bags. I missed my bed at Dad's house. Eventually Mike and I shared a set of bunk beds in one of the three bedrooms. I didn't know whether to tell Dad I liked his house better. I didn't want to make him feel sad, and I didn't want to make Mom feel bad for moving us. As usual, I kept quiet.

I turned eight in March 1963, after moving in with Chuck. As my birthday present, while I was at school, Mom decorated a new room for me. When I opened the door I found a little girl's room she had created just for me; I felt like a princess! It didn't matter the room consisted of nothing more than a very old dresser painted white with drawers which stuck every time they opened, an old desk she transformed to a vanity table by sewing a white chiffon skirt around it, and a very dated lamp which I recognized from my aunt's basement. The walls were painted pretty lavender. It was a room all to myself!

Things changed quickly though. Eight weeks later, my baby sister, Vickie, was born. That "new" dresser was moved to make room for a crib. Later, another sister, Jackie was born, and then there were three of us in my birthday present room. I just accepted it. With only three bedrooms, there were no other options at Chuck's house. I knew it was easier to be happy and accept it rather than create more tension.

The next year Mom announced she was going to have another baby. I prayed for a baby brother; my birthday present room was full! Soon my new baby brother, Randy, joined my brother Mike in his room down the hall.

With five kids in our house, life was hectic and loud. While I loved being a big sister, I missed having time alone with Mom the way I did when we lived with Dad. She was always busy with the younger kids or some project around the house. Still, she always found time to look her best. Every afternoon before Chuck came home, she would take time in her small bathroom to put on makeup, tease her dark brown hair, and then spray it with Aqua Net. I loved to sit and watch her put on her makeup. I thought she was very pretty. The beauty routine always finished with a spritz of "White Shoulders" perfume.

Many of the conflicts and tensions in the home surrounded Chuck. He was a "disciplinarian" and Mom acted as a go between when she felt he was too harsh with us. Most of the time to avoid conflict, she remained silent. It was clear Chuck was in charge.

Life at home was noisy and busy with so many little ones. I looked forward to seeing Dad on the weekends. He was an active dad. He took Mike and me roller skating, hiking in the park, waterskiing, and to movies at the drive-in theater. I would help him work on his car, which simply meant sitting next to the car handing him his tools. He was a great dad. It was hard seeing him only once a week, but when we were together, we got *all* of his attention and he made it fun.

Things changed in 1966 when his new girlfriend entered the picture. I was eleven. I didn't like Sauni, and I made sure she knew it. When it was time to get in the car, I ran to get the middle seat to sit between Dad and her, leaving Mike alone in the backseat. I could tell this bothered her by the look she gave me, but I did not like seeing her with Dad or sharing my time with her. On the ride home, I'd "accidentally" give her an elbow jab in the ribs or kick her in the shins. The competition for my dad's attention was one I did not want to lose. Even worse than having Sauni around, I was expected to play with her two small children who occasionally joined us.

As hectic as my home life was, it was about to get worse.

One day, over the phone, Dad told me he and Sauni were married. I had lost. He told me they would be moving closer to where she lived. "Will Mike and I still see you?" I asked. He assured me we would. The same year, Mike and I went to Thanksgiving at my Grandma Phillips' house. Her house was a hub of activity at the holidays, always full of relatives, but I felt alone. I ached for the Thanksgivings when it was Mom, Dad and Mike, and me around the table. Instead of Mom being here, it was Sauni and her two children. After finishing dessert, Dad said they had an announcement to make. I had no idea what he was about to say, but I feared the worst; yes, a new baby was coming and I was going to have *another* brother or sister. After a round of congratulations and clinking of glasses to toast this new arrival, I went into the living room and cried. Being protective of my brother Mike, I hoped it would be a girl so he wouldn't feel replaced. Again, I didn't say anything.

My sister, Wendi, was born June of 1968 and, just two months later, Mom gave birth to my brother, Randy. Two new siblings in the same year! Not many can say or explain that. I was thirteen and now had one brother, three half-sisters, one half-brother, one step-brother and one step-sister. I didn't see them as half or step of anything. To me they were all just my brothers and sisters, but when asked how many brothers and sisters I had, my answer was, "I'm the oldest of five." I didn't include Wendi, or my step-siblings. It was embarrassing to have this mixed up family. It was all so difficult to explain.

After Dad's marriage, he spent more time with his new family. Mike and I saw less and less of him. He would miss our birthdays and school events; eventually we saw him only on holidays. I missed him terribly.

I didn't like living so far from Dad. It was hard to adjust to my new life but when I met Molly and Holly Gardner, the twins who lived up the street, life seemed brighter. We were in the same grade and became instant friends; an inseparable threesome. Their mom took me places and treated me like I was part of the family. Church attendance was not a part of my family's lives, but in the Gardner house, it was front and center. Mrs. Gardner's religion was broadcast on her Ford station wagon, a rolling sermon on four wheels, with bumper stickers proclaiming *God is not Dead* or *Christ Lives* and, my favorite, *Are **YOU** Going to Heaven*? I never knew where she found the bumper stickers, but like a pastor with new sermons, Mrs. Gardner updated them regularly.

If I wanted to know anything about the Bible or any questions about God, she had the answer straight from the Bible. Conversations with her were peppered with Bible verses. My questions usually received the same standard answer, "The Bible says..." My mother had *Good Housekeeping* and *Ladies Home Journal* on our coffee table. Mrs. Gardner had *Christianity Today* and *Guidepost*.

Being a good Christian meant, among other things, converting those who were not saved. Clearly, Mrs. Gardner included me in this category. Standing in her kitchen one day she asked, "Sandy, would you like to go to church with us on Sunday?" Since my parents did not attend church, Mrs. Gardner enthusiastically took on the task of saving me. I nodded. Thereafter, I went with the Gardners to Walnut Branch Christian Church every Sunday.

In addition to church, Mrs. Gardner took me to my first of many Billy Graham Crusades. On Saturday mornings she took us to the Bible Book Store to buy key chains, bookmarks, and various trinkets with Bible verses written on them, and coloring books about Jesus.

If the Gardners were headed to church, so was I. Hanging out of the back window of their Ford station wagon was my happy place. It meant we were on our way to church. While the twins thought my house was the greatest because we had a pool in our backyard, I preferred their house because their mom took me to church and talked about the Bible. I became not just a Sunday morning churchgoer; in those early years, I attended everything I could at Walnut Branch Christian Church—the services, Junior Choir practices, Wednesday night supper, Sunday evening Vespers service, and Vacation Bible School. I worked on paper drives and fundraisers. *I loved it all.* Church provided a place of security. I loved learning about Jesus.

In Junior Church we learned the pledge:

> *I pledge allegiance to the Bible, God's holy word.*
> *I will make it a lamp unto my feet,*
> *And a light unto my path:*
> *I will hide its words in my heart,*
> *So that I may not sin against God.*

Each of us would recite this pledge every Sunday from memory. The Bible was the final word, and the only way to know God was to read the Bible. We were taught the literal interpretation of the Bible. As Mrs. Gardner said, "The Bible said it, I believe it, and that settles it forever."

Family life was an adjustment. There were many happy times as well, but not what I would consider the typical family with a mom and dad and two kids. For those who lived in the suburbs in the mid-60's, divorce was about as strange as a mobile phone. *Leave it to Beaver* and *Father Knows Best* were the family role models on TV. I did not know anyone who had divorced parents and I made sure no one knew my parents were divorced. Even at a young age, I knew people were supposed to stay married. Divorce was wrong. I didn't like explaining why my mom, after marrying Chuck, had a last name different than mine. I was embarrassed by it, and it made me feel different from the other kids.

This embarrassment came to a humiliating head at the age of ten in Mrs. Woods' fourth grade class. When parents joined the PTA, Mrs. Woods put the parents' names on a red apple cut from construction paper. One by one, Mrs. Woods placed the apples on the corkboard with thumbtacks, calling out each parent's name, "Mr. and Mrs. Seibert, Mr. and Mrs. Graber, Mr. and Mrs. Hofmann." With that, my classmates began giggling and pointing out Mrs. Woods' mistake. "Hofmann? We don't have anybody named Hofmann in our class! Who is Hofmann?"

"That's Sandy's parents," Mrs. Woods said. I sat there humiliated as all eyes were on me. The question I tried so hard to avoid was waiting for me at recess.

My face was red as I fought to keep tears inside. Then I concocted a brilliant idea. *Why do I have to tell them?* Needing so desperately to fit in and not wanting to be different, I decided to tell them my dad was killed in a truck accident and I had a new dad. At ten years old, I saw no flaw in this plan, so it's exactly what I told them, with confidence.

It was my story, and I stuck to it until the seventh grade when a friend and I were sitting together at a basketball game. Her mother walked by. She introduced her mother, who had a different last name. "Oh, I'm sorry," I said to my friend, "Did your dad die too?" Puzzled, she looked at me. "No," she said, "my parents are divorced." Her honesty was a lesson for me. It was okay to have divorced parents. I didn't need to make things up. It was a relief to tell the truth.

Summer was the hardest part about my parents' divorce. Like every kid, I loved vacation and being off school, but I missed boating with Mom and Dad together. It was even harder because the twins were gone for a week at church camp. To me, it seemed like the week lasted forever. I had nothing to do when they were gone. Then the twins returned singing great Bible songs, showing off the crafts they made and talking about the fun times at camp. I decided, right then and there, I wouldn't miss camp the next year. For the next six years, church camp was the best week of my year. This camp was not about swimming, canoes, and campfires with ghost stories and roasting marshmallows; this was a church camp. There was no pool and the lake had a sign that said, "Keep Out." The camp program made things clear,

> *"The purpose of camp is to develop a commitment to Jesus Christ through prayer and Bible study. To develop Christian character through Christ centered activities."*

The cost my first year was $16.00 for a week at camp. Two years later, I begged my mom to let me go to camp for two weeks. "You can go if you pay for it," she said. With a pay scale of fifty cents an hour, the camp payment required lots of extra babysitting jobs and chores around the house, but it was worth every penny.

The camp was rustic. We didn't care. The dorms were old with rusty metal army barracks bunk beds and lumpy mattresses, probably leftover from the Korean War. A shower required a walk across the yard. The "chapel" was an old barn with a dirt floor and a makeshift stage. Meals were served in the long dining hall and always ended with the campers chanting and banging on the tables with our utensils, "We want to see the cooks, we want to see the cooks, bring 'em out and let us look; we want to see the cooks!"

Each night camp featured a different production put on by a "team." There was Stunt Night, Bible Drama Night, Talent Night, and the grand finale, the Friday evening Galilean Service. While there was free time and recreational sports, the focus was prayer and the study of God's Word. The Devil's idle hands would not be found here!

For kids in Junior High, camp was also a place to meet a special someone with puppy love in the air. Most of the Christian/Church of Christ churches in the greater Cincinnati area sent their kids to camp. Since it was discouraged to date outside our faith, the great thing about meeting someone at church camp was you knew they were Christian. Romance consisted mostly of holding hands; it was safe, and it only lasted a week.

My first kiss came from a boy I met at camp after the eighth grade. We were about to leave the chapel when he pulled me onto his lap and kissed me. It was exciting; then I panicked. I recalled reading in an Ann Landers' advice column, "Never sit on a boy's lap, and if you do, keep a phonebook between the two of you." With no phonebook handy, I figured the safest thing to do was to get up as quickly as possible and escape. He avoided me the rest of the week. I did the only thing I could do; I prayed to God that he would convey to the boy I was sorry and I had not meant to hurt his feelings. Years later, I wondered if he thought his first kiss was so bad the girl ran off!

On the last night of camp at the Vespers service, following the sermon, a call was given to accept Jesus as your Savior. After a week of frenzied Bible study and inspirational singing, someone *always* came forward at church camp to accept Jesus as their Savior or to rededicate their life. The call to come forward was given as everyone sang the hymn, "I Surrender All." The hymn had five stanzas with the chorus in between. There was plenty of time for the Spirit to nudge someone forward. If by the fifth stanza, no one had come forward, the camp leader would ask us to hum and then, "Just the girls sing; now the boys, and one more time, altogether."

At age thirteen, on a muggy summer night, as the campers sang, I walked forward to accept Christ as my personal savior. The following Sunday I was baptized at our church by the senior minister, Mr. Wilson. While excited to be baptized, I was reminded this was not my first baptism.

No, my first baptism occurred five years earlier in 1963 when I was eight years old. I was sitting next to my little brother and Grandma Phillips, Dad's mom, at her church. I could sense Grandma's agitation. She kept looking over her shoulder. With just a bit more than aggravation in her voice, she appeared to ask no one in particular, "Where *is* he?"

The "he" was Dad, who was never on time, even for baptisms. On days when he was supposed to pick us up for weekly visitation, my stomach would ache as I waited for him. Dad was always late and, on occasion, he would not show at all. The longer we waited for him, the more anxious I would become; not so much because he was late (I was used to that), but because my mother would become upset and Chuck would be even angrier, "God damn it. Where is he?"

Usually, after an angry phone call from Mom, Dad would show up. On those days, I spent the time waiting for Dad trying to decide who made me angrier, Dad for not being on time and creating this tension, or Mom for divorcing my dad in the first place. In the end, I sided with Dad. I felt sorry for him. He didn't want the divorce.

On this day, my "first" baptism, as we sat in church waiting for Dad, I knew not to let on I was upset. My little brother Mike impatiently kicked the back of the pew in front of us. I just sat there. I was old enough to understand it would not be in my best interest to add to Grandma Phillips' already agitated state. Although she was just 5'2" and barely 100 pounds, she was a force to be reckoned with. But really! Even for an event as important as a baptism, Dad was not on time.

Finally, Dad arrived, clearly out of breath. He slid into the pew next to Grandma, and whispered loud enough for me to hear, "Her mother is upset I didn't discuss this with her first. She does not want Sandy baptized today." There were many times Mom and Dad had disagreements regarding Dad's handling of situations. I hated the arguing between the two of them.

More whispers were exchanged between them, and then silence. I didn't know what was said, but when the minister asked those to be baptized to come forward, we didn't go. All I knew for certain Dad was in trouble; *big trouble*. Not only disappointment, but anger also engulfed Grandma as she slowly shook her head back and forth and squeezed my hand for the rest of the service. Clearly upset with Dad, but even more upset at my mom, as we left the church she declared, "You ARE going to be baptized today!"

As we entered Dad's house, Grandma took my hand and began pulling me toward the bathroom. My little legs were no match and I struggled to keep up. Once we reached the bathroom, she pulled my navy-blue dress over my head with such force my feet left the ground, leaving me dangling in the neck of the dress. I stood on the black and white tile floor wearing only my white lacey slip. Grandma opened the tub spigot full force. She whisked me up and placed me in the middle of the pink bathtub. With my slip floating around me, the water filled the tub. Kneeling on the floor, still obviously upset, Grandma bent over me, reciting the Lord's Prayer.

She held my head under the faucet with one hand, making the sign of the cross in a large swooping motion with the other, as if she were directing a symphony orchestra.

In a booming voice she pronounced, "I NOW BAPTIZE YOU IN THE NAME OF THE FATHER, SON, AND HOLY GHOST!" No holy-roller preacher could have done it better. Looking up at that moment, I saw both love and fire in Grandma Phillips' eyes. The sanctity of the moment was lost on me. Water was everywhere. My only concern was to keep from drowning.

Within a few moments, sitting on the edge of the tub, she picked me up and sat me on her lap. She tightly wrapped her sopping wet sleeves around me. Water puddled on the floor. "Now, you have been baptized!" I am certain the statement was meant for my mother as much as it was meant for me. Drenched, we both looked as if we had been on the losing end of a water balloon fight.

Despite my unusual first "home" baptism, I remained excited with the anticipation of becoming a member of the believers in Christ through my "real" baptism at church. Baptism in the Christian Church requires complete immersion. As teenagers, we jokingly referred to it as "The Dunking." No sprinkling. The scriptures were very clear on this, "Jesus went *down into* the water."

While it was a solemn moment, there was a lot to worry about. What if I drown? My experience with "baptism by Grandma" planted this fear. There were six steps to navigate to get down into the "real" baptismal pool. What if I slip on the steps? What if I come up coughing and spitting water out of my nose? How cold is the water? What if people could see my underwear through the wet, white gown? With the baptismal pool front and center of the church, all fears were legitimate.

When the time came, I walked into the water holding tightly onto Mr. Wilson's hand. We stopped at the bottom of the baptism pool with the water just past my waist. The organist softly played the hymn "Just As I Am." As the curtain was pulled back, the music stopped. Mr. Wilson raised his hand and asked, "Do you, Sandy, take the Lord Jesus Christ to be your personal Savior and promise to be faithful to his calling?"

"Yes."

With that, he put his left hand behind my neck to support me and with his right, put the handkerchief over my nose, leaned me back, and immersed me in the water. I came up from the water and wept tears of joy. I loved Jesus and my church and this public display was my declaration of that love. I felt different. That moment was, and to this day still is, special to me. I knew God had a plan for my life. My baptism gave me a purpose… to follow God. The security I felt in the church now took on even greater meaning for me after my baptism. Joining the church gave me a sense of belonging. Something every teenager needs.

"Belonging is at the core of our human experience. It is this exact human necessity abusers exploit for gain."

—SHANNON THOMAS, *HEALING FROM HIDDEN ABUSE*

YOUTH GROUP

During my high school years, if the doors of the church were open, I was there. I was active in the youth group, taught Sunday school, led the Saturday morning girls' prayer breakfast, sang in the youth choir, helped organize the Mother-Daughter Banquets, participated in church clean-up every year, and helped in the church office.

The church's main sanctuary was built in 1959 and had a modern look. It was attached to a traditionally styled, older, red brick building built in 1927. The church and the parsonage, which no longer served to house the pastor and his wife, were separated by a small graveyard. The former parsonage became a youth center and the home for Sunday school class for the junior high and high school kids.

When Mom planted flowers at our house, I used my allowance and bought flats of red geraniums. I planted them secretly on a Saturday morning in front of the church. I considered church my home. I didn't want anyone to see, following the scripture,

> *"Beware of practicing your righteousness before men to be noticed by them; otherwise you have no reward with your Father who is in heaven."* —MATTHEW 6:1 (AMERICAN STANDARD VERSION)

Three weeks later, my clandestine gardening was discovered when the congregation was made aware in the May 20, 1973, church bulletin:

> *"We have finally discovered who is responsible for the lovely flowers beautifying the entrance-way. It is none other than sweet, smiling Sandy Phillips! Thank you, Sandy. This is so like this fine young Christian, who is always seeking ways to spread joy and blessings to others; our Miss Sunshine."*

Each summer, I attended Vacation Bible School (VBS). It was my favorite week of the year, second only to church camp, but the songs at camp couldn't hold a candle to the great songs at VBS and I was the song leader. I loved the role and roused the little kids into singing, clapping, and stomping their feet. One of my trademark songs was "Stand Up and SHOUT If You Love My Jesus." The second verse goes, "Sit down and whisper if you love my Jesus." We would lead the kids singing, shouting and then whispering. No matter what, we would end up laughing. From the littlest giggles to my oversized, distinctive laugh, everyone had fun, especially me.

Our youth pastor was kind and involved with the youth in the church. Pastor Tom wasn't dynamic but he had a good heart and loved what he did. He had a three-year-old son for whom I frequently babysat. It was quite common for pastors to tap into the wealth of babysitters from our youth group, and I loved being chosen to help.

When I was in the seventh grade, a young couple from the congregation, Steve and Mary Lou, volunteered with the youth group. They had two small girls who were, in spite of their ages, always a part of whatever the youth group did, tagging along with their parents. I became quite close to the family, helping with the kids and just hanging out in their house. At age fourteen, I started babysitting for them. They had a small little house; perfect for a young married couple and two small children. One spring I helped Mary Lou plant flowers in the front yard. I loved babysitting and imagined what my family and house would look like someday. Hoping to eventually go to Milligan College, a Christian College in Tennessee, I imagined myself as a minister's wife living in a house just like the home of Steve and Mary Lou.

I idolized Steve and Mary Lou. They were my role models. As my parents were not church members, this couple generously took me under their wings and were instrumental in the development of my spiritual life. I admired their love and devotion to one another. Whatever Steve or Mary Lou asked, I did without question. I trusted them completely and was grateful they were so good to me. Babysitting one evening, after putting the girls to bed, I saw a box of pictures sitting in the corner of their living room. Curiosity took over and I began looking through the pictures. Holding a photograph of the girls sitting on Steve's lap, I closed my eyes and painfully recalled a terrible night at my house, just three months after moving in with Chuck.

That night I was awoken by laughing in the living room. I crept down the hall to discover Mom and Chuck burning all the family pictures of Dad and us. Pictures were scattered across the floor. I wanted to shriek as they grabbed handful after handful and tossed them into the fireplace. I covered my face with my flannel night gown to hold back the tears.

One picture was separated from the others, close to where I stood and I wondered how to retrieve it without being seen. I stood there frozen, watching Chuck pick up the newspaper article with the picture of me on Dad's shoulders skiing across the water and throw it into the fireplace. In shock, I watched as the picture disintegrated into ashes.

I never forgot that night. I eventually forgave mom, but I never forgot. The fact she brought the photos with her to our new house told me she had every intention of keeping them. I blamed my stepfather for destroying my memories. It was Chuck who decided the photos needed to be destroyed. I don't think Mom would have done so on her own accord, but she didn't stop him either. If not for the very few pictures Grandma Philips kept of Dad and me I would have none. When I was twelve, I visited Dad and brought home a picture of the two of us together. Fearful they would take the picture from me, I hid it under my mattress.

Youth group included numerous activities: paper drives, car washes, bake sales, and social events. I was at every one; often as the organizer. On occasion, I was asked to give the prayer at the Sunday evening service. I was emerging as one of the leaders in the youth group. The attention and encouragement I received from both Mary Lou and Steve filled the need for attention I felt I was missing at home. Their trust in me gave me confidence.

The middle of my sophomore year in high school just before I turned sixteen, Steve accepted a teaching position in another city. I was crushed. Shortly thereafter, Pastor Tom announced he too was leaving; an even bigger disappointment. He was the only youth pastor I knew. I learned from Mrs. Gardner he was asked to leave because the senior pastor, Mr. Wilson, wanted to bring in a new youth pastor named Jeff Coulier, a youth minister from Tifton, Georgia. I tried to convince the others in the youth group we had to do something, such as approach the elder board to keep Tom from leaving. However, Tom had accepted another ministry and there was nothing to be done. The three most important role models in my life were now gone. Again, I felt lost and alone, just like when we moved from Dad's house.

Mr. Wilson was excited about this new youth pastor and assured the youth group members we would like the change. I knew I had to trust the senior pastor. After all, he was in charge of the church and we all knew the lines of authority in the church. He explained how it was natural to miss Tom, but we needed to be enthusiastic and welcoming to our new youth pastor.

There was an unusual excitement among the adults with this new youth pastor's arrival. Hearing of the growth and enthusiasm Jeff Coulier had created in youth participation at his church in Tifton, the elders were eager to have this vibrant, charismatic youth pastor on staff. Sitting in the choir with my friend Cindy, I watched Mr. Wilson introduce Jeff Coulier to the congregation one Sunday morning in June 1971. The new pastor seemed nice and appeared eager to be part of our church. Just like Pastor Tom, he too had a little boy. Moreover, his wife Nancy was stylish and attractive in her light blue dress and pretty, blonde hair. Cindy and I eyed each other and smiled. Perhaps this wouldn't be so bad.

At the reception after the service, Mr. Wilson made a point to introduce me to Jeff Coulier. "Jeff, I would like you to meet Sandy. She is one of our fine young people here and one of the leaders of our youth group. We call her Miss Sunshine because of her radiant smile." I was totally flattered by the compliments. "Miss Sunshine." I knew people saw me that way and it made me feel special and appreciated. I was touched Mr. Wilson made the effort to single me out and introduce me to the new youth pastor. Reaching down, taking my hand and smiling, Jeff Coulier said to me with just a hint of a southern drawl, "You do have a very pretty smile." Waiting for him to let go of my hand, I was surprised when he continued to hold onto it as he talked. Before he walked away Mr. Wilson said to Jeff, "She will be a big help to you in your ministry." I hoped I had made a good first impression.

From the beginning it was clear Jeff Coulier was a different kind of pastor than our beloved Pastor Tom. Jeff was thirty years old, close to Tom's age, but he dressed and acted more youthful, wearing cutoff jeans and other current styles of the 70's. His blonde hair and sideburns were longer. We called him Jeff, instead of Pastor Jeff. He understood our jokes, kidded with us, knew our music, and talked sports with the guys. He drove his orange convertible VW to our high school football games. He introduced us to the poetry of Rod McKuen and the music of Neil Diamond.

A few weeks after he arrived, I was at his house babysitting. After he came home, he asked me to go to his basement to listen to the song "Brother Love's Traveling Salvation Show" by Neil Diamond. After putting the record on the stereo, and in spite of the fact there were many other places to sit, he came and sat close to me on the couch. This felt odd. I sat there wondering what he wanted me to do or say. He asked me what I thought of the music. I didn't understand the lyrics. The whole thing seemed a little weird.

Jeff's behavior was so unlike anything Pastor Tom would have ever done, taking me to his basement alone and asking me about popular song lyrics. I had not talked to any pastor about anything other than church and the Bible. This attention made me feel uneasy and unsure of myself, but it also made me feel special.

Within months of his arrival, the transformation of our youth group was evident. Gone were the boring Bible lessons; those were replaced with interactive group discussions and skits on topics relevant to teenagers in the 70's. The hymns and cute Vacation Bible School songs were replaced with meaningful new Christian songs, guitar accompaniments, and holding hands as we sang. Until then, the youth group was a revolving door of adult volunteers who taught high school Sunday school and led group activities. With Jeff Coulier at the helm, many young married couples, eager to please this new youth pastor with his persuasive ways, became involved in the youth group.

The youth group was growing and developed an electric atmosphere. A monthly "Youth Night" was added to the Sunday evening Vespers service. With a group of enthusiastic adults under the direction of Jeff Coulier, the service was conducted entirely by the youth group. We felt we were a part of something important. We were making a difference. It was all because of Jeff Coulier.

No one wanted to miss out. When Jeff asked someone to do something, they felt privileged to be invited to help. Of all the kids in the group, no one was more eager to help than me. I loved the changes we were seeing. The spiritual growth was evident throughout the church not just within the youth group. Word of what was happening at Walnut Branch was spreading. New kids continued to join our group. My grief at losing Pastor Tom was gone. I was excited to have Jeff Coulier as our pastor.

Jeff didn't come to the youth activities just to supervise; he became a part of our group. Charisma surrounded him. His dynamic personality drew people into the church. He made each person feel as if he or she was the only person in the room. He never forgot a name. Even the adults were drawn in and captivated by his manner and demeanor. His sermons were like none we had ever heard with eloquent speech, personal touches, and humor. Attendance exploded. Parents no longer had to drag their kids to church. It was the place to be. He also did something no one else had ever done at church or camp: when meeting someone, he hugged them; men and women alike. This was new for all of us.

Jeff encouraged and expected members of the youth group to follow his lead. It was contagious. We welcomed each other with hugs. It became a part of who we were. We were Christians caring about each other and expressing it physically with a hug and verbally expressing our love for one another. Jeff didn't just thank a person for helping at the church by simply saying, "Thank you." He took the person's hand and told them how much he loved them and appreciated their work. Then he would hug them and say, "You know I love you and think you are special." No pastor had ever used words as direct as "I love you."

It was not uncommon for Jeff to compliment women and girls on their appearance. A response of, "Thank You" would be followed by Jeff saying, with a smile, "don't thank me darlin'. I had nothing to do with it." He could also be critical of someone's appearance, but usually in a disarming way. Once in a sermon he remarked, "I don't expect women to dress like the cupboard, but I don't want them dressing like Mother Hubbard either." Everyone laughed. When I came to youth group wearing my hair in pigtails, Jeff looked at me and began making oinking sounds while flapping his hands about his ears, "You look a little funny in those pigtails; oink, oink." Several times after that, whenever he saw me, he made an oinking sound. It embarrassed me, but I laughed it off.

This was the 70's and the mores of the secular world were rapidly changing. Free love and drugs were a part of society. *Jesus Christ Super Star* was the new hit musical on Broadway. Jeff Coulier, in his own way, brought radical change to our church. Now we were seeing the kind of growth and enthusiasm that occurred at his previous church in Tifton.

Jeff also brought what we called YAC-Youth After Church. We met after church services on Sunday evening at one of our member's home. Most of us had already been to Sunday school and church in the morning and then came back for evening Vespers service. We had light snacks, devotions, singing, sharing, and prayer.

Early on, Jeff picked his leaders for YAC. It was no surprise to others when he zeroed in on me. He asked me to be the song leader and "unofficial host" for meetings. Just as I had been with Pastor Tom, I couldn't wait to be a part of the ministry.

Not only was my involvement growing, I was more mature in my faith. I had moved beyond the paper drives and car washes. I served on committees with adults doing things such as organizing the Easter Sunrise Service and overseeing the youth division for the North American Christian Convention when it was held in Cincinnati; a major responsibility. I felt a profound seriousness about my church life. I had a deep commitment to growing in my faith. Not only did I read my Bible every day, but I studied it and wanted to apply its teaching to my life. I wanted to *live* my faith. I had a hunger to follow God and do whatever

I could for the church. Even to school, I carried my Bible daily, hoping it would spark conversation with my friends and be a witness for Christ. Knowing and following what the Bible said was part of my faith. This was who I was, an eager sixteen year old, when Jeff Coulier said he needed me in his ministry.

Youth After Church, became a phenomenon. Jeff's main purpose for YAC was to bring new kids into the group, involve them in the youth program and hope they would join the church. The attendance at YAC skyrocketed from twenty-five to over two hundred, largely because of Jeff, the cool new minister. YAC was the place to be, where you could feel welcomed and loved; a place with a sense of belonging, a place to be inspired. Teens came from other churches to attend YAC. Jeff expected his core leaders to constantly invite new people.

I remember writing about Jeff in my letters to my camp friend, Janette. This was one of her responses:

> *"Your new youth minister sounds really neat! I hope he can do for your youth group what he did in Tifton. I will pray for God to raise you up and do great things through Jeff. Are you nervous being the song leader? That's cool he picked you to do that. Maybe he will come to camp this summer and I will get to meet him. You guys are lucky to have such a cool guy."*

Jeff could also be forceful at times; in fact, abrupt about what he wanted or expected from us, both teenagers and adults. One evening he asked the organist to play "Bridge Over Troubled Water" for the Sunday night youth service. She refused saying, it wasn't appropriate in church. He quickly found someone else to play the song. The next Youth Night, fearing she'd be replaced again, the organist played James Taylor's, "You've Got a Friend," and every other song Jeff requested.

One Sunday evening service I sat in the back with my friends, instead of up front like I usually did. He pulled me aside after the service and scolded me, telling me he did not appreciate me sitting in the back with my friends, not paying attention. In a stern voice, he demanded, "As a leader, you need to set an example." Pointing his finger at me he continued, "Next time, I expect to see you sitting up front." Being reprimanded by my pastor was new to me. I was embarrassed and ashamed. I didn't like the thought of him being mad at me and I knew I had to try harder to win his approval. He also made it clear YAC was not a social time for the leaders, but an outreach to new kids to make them feel welcomed. As always, we did as he told us. If he felt we spent too much time talking to our old friends, he let us know, usually with harsh words. He was not hesitant to reprimand leaders or tell them to leave the church if they failed to meet his expectations. He scolded people for missing YAC meetings. "If I can't count on you," he would say, "then perhaps you might want to find another church." Intimidated, we wanted to remain in good stead with Jeff to prove we were good Christians and worthy of our expanded roles.

Walnut Branch Christian Church was a non-denominational, independent congregation. The church was run by an elected board of men called deacons and elders with authority over the church. Each Christian Church/Church of Christ operates independently of others, while cooperatively working together on outside church activities, such as missions, Christian education, and youth activities. Youth Rallies were held once a month to bring kids from all the area Church of Christ/Christian Churches together for worship and fellowship.

We took pride in not being a specific denomination. We believed we were like the early Christians. We were not Baptist, Methodist, or Catholics. We were simply Christians and needed no other labels. We often participated in city-wide conferences with different denominations to exchange thoughts and ideas. We would sit in a circle and each participant would be asked to give his or her name and church affiliation.

"I'm Susan and I am Methodist."

"My name is Diane and I am Baptist."

Sitting next to me was my friend, Fred, "Hi, my name is Fred and I am a Christian."

A little taken aback by the response the moderator said, "Fred, we are all Christians."

"Well, why didn't you say so?" asked Fred.

"Hi, I am Sandy and I'm with Fred. We are both Christians."

Over the years, my happy place had moved from the back of Mrs. Gardner's station wagon to the church. School was important to me but being part of church activities was even more so. It connected my faith with serving, volunteering, and singing. Moreover, it was a place where I was loved and surrounded by adults I loved and trusted. Fortunately, my mom thought it was great I was so connected to the people at Walnut Branch, even though she did not attend. She could see how I blossomed and found a place to belong. While other teens in the early 70's were exploring drugs and sex, she knew I was safe at church. She saw Jeff's interest in me as a positive influence. What place could be safer than the church?

Eventually, she too, would join the church because of Jeff. Just as Mrs.

Gardner had brought me into the church, I had been praying for many years for my mother to be baptized and saved. Still, it was unexpected when she chose to go forward to be baptized one Sunday morning. Mr. Wilson baptized her. Afterwards, he told me how glad he was to have her as part of our church congregation. He knew how important it was to me to have her as a member of the church.

Jeff did not typically attend the service when Mr. Wilson delivered the sermon. Following the service, which included Mom's baptism, I rushed to tell Jeff the great news. Locating him in the fellowship hall, with tears in my eyes, I told him my mom had come forward and was baptized. He looked at me and simply said, "That's nice," and walked away. I was hurt. He knew how important it was to me to have Mom finally join the church. I wondered how he could be so indifferent. Even more than being hurt, I was puzzled. I expected a pastor would be thrilled when a person chose to accept Jesus.

A week later in the church newsletter, senior minister, Mr. Wilson wrote:

> *"Tears of joy were shed this past Sunday as Louise Hofmann, the mother of our own Miss Sunshine, Sandy Phillips, came forward to accept Christ as her Savior."*

This made Jeff's apathy even more confusing and mysterious to me.

Looking back, I realize why Jeff Coulier did not want my mother around, active and involved at the church; a watchful parent is never in the mind of a predator.

"Whenever power is used in a way that wounds the vulnerable or that exploits trust, abuse has occurred."

—DIANE LANGBERG PHD, DIANELANGBERG.COM

SWEET SIXTEEN

"**S**URPRISE!" In March 1971, I turned sixteen. Mom planned a surprise birthday party sleepover with ten of my girlfriends. Mom was a great party planner. The evening was full of fun for everyone, but especially for me. Turning sixteen was a milestone. It meant I would be able to get my driver's license even though Mom and Chuck made it clear I would not be driving until I could afford my own car (highly unlikely at this point). It also meant I would be permitted to date; not that there was anyone in the picture, but the possibility was exciting. I was busy at church and school with lots of friends.

It was December 1971. Jeff had been our youth pastor for six months. YAC (Youth After Church) grew larger each month. As a YAC leader, I was filled with pride. I was part of something big. Jeff told us we were helping to grow Christ's church by bringing more of our friends to YAC. More than fifty teens squeezed into my house on a cold December night for a YAC meeting. I was thrilled. Mom and Chuck left for the evening and I had successfully begged Mom to let my little brothers and sisters stay at my aunt's house.

I made sure we had plenty of chips and soda and carefully selected songs for the group to sing. I wanted the evening to go well to please Jeff. As one would expect, Jeff placed enormous responsibility for the evening on my shoulders, "I'm depending on you tonight. Be sure to make the new people feel welcome." Jeff expected all of us to deepen our involvement and time in the church and the youth group. With Pastor Tom, attendance at youth group activities, while encouraged, was voluntary. With Jeff, there was an expectation for us to be there; no excuses. A missed youth group activity in the past might be followed by a "we missed you at church on Sunday." Jeff's response was more likely to be, "why weren't you at church on Sunday?" Wanting to please God and help the church, I felt pressure to follow Jeff's direction and do what I could to please him.

More times than not, Jeff stayed for only the social part of the evening. He would leave before the start of the program. The kids flocked around him, wanting to talk to him before he left. He made each person feel special, remembering details about their classes at school, their favorite sports teams, and who their friends were. We were all drawn to him. We relished the chance to joke and talk with him.

After snacks and social time, I led the singing and Fred gave the devotional. We ended the evening by singing the song "Pass it On" as we walked the room hugging and telling one another we loved them.

I was both excited and surprised to see Jeff still at my house as the evening ended. My insecurities could have set in, worried he would find fault with something I had done, but I knew the evening went well. We had the highest attendance yet at YAC, and a spiritual atmosphere had filled the air. Jeff had stayed to see how well I had done, and I could not wait for his praise. He hugged me and told me he was proud of me, stating, "I always know I can count on you. I appreciate so much what you do for this church."

Slowly, kids found their coats and headed to the door, some stopping to talk to Jeff again. Within twenty minutes the only people remaining were my best friend, Chris, and Jeff. I met Chris our freshman year and we were inseparable. By high school, the Gardner twins weren't as active in the church. We were still friends, but we had drifted apart. We each found a different set of friends.

I thought it a bit odd Jeff had not left yet, but the three of us stood in the living room chatting. I went into the kitchen to get a drink while Chris and Jeff remained in the living room. Chris popped her head in the kitchen to say goodbye, "See you at school tomorrow!"

As I walked her to the door Jeff gave her a hug and said, "I love you Chris." And she replied, "I love you too, Jeff." As she and I stood at the door, her scarf became tangled up in her purse and she couldn't get it around her neck. We began giggling like only two teenage girls can do, finding this mundane occurrence hilarious.

Chris left and I turned to see Jeff standing in the hallway. It was now just the two of us. He walked over to me, he looked at me, and he told me again how great the evening was. I felt so special. I was on cloud nine. Then he cupped my face in the palm of his hands and moved my head upward toward his. With his thumbs behind my ears, he brushed my hair away and he told me how much he loved me. Then he bent down and kissed me.

My thoughts raced as I wondered, *"What is he doing? He just kissed me and not just on the cheek! This was a real kiss."* For a moment I was stunned. It was a soft, gentle kiss, almost innocent. It didn't seem wrong. Yet it didn't seem right either. I trusted him. I stood there for a moment, but it seemed like much more. I was afraid to move. I was trying to process what happened, unsure what to think, as he continued to compliment me and tell me how much he appreciated me.

Confused, it took me a second, but then I calmed myself with the thought, "This is my minister; this is Jeff. He wouldn't do anything he shouldn't do. He's just showing me how much he loves me and how happy he is the evening went so well." Just like that, he kissed me again, only to be interrupted by Chris bursting through the door hysterically screaming and crying, "I HIT YOUR CAR BACKING OUT OF THE DRIVEWAY! Oh Jeff. I didn't see it!"

I had never heard Chris so distraught. Jeff immediately went to her to calm her down. He put his arms around her and assured her it was all right. She was crying so hard she couldn't talk. He laughed and said, "These things happen. At least you didn't hit *me*!" Together they went outside to inspect the damage. I stood there concerned for my friend, but totally dumbfounded about that kiss.

After a few minutes Jeff came back in alone and said something about the car. He hugged me, saying what happened before was a special moment just between us. Before I could respond he turned and went out the door. After he left, I went to bed sure the kiss from him meant friendship and nothing more. My mind would not let me believe anything other than that. This was my pastor after all. I didn't question his motives.

Chris never questioned me or said anything about what she may have seen. I was pretty sure she saw him kiss me. Maybe she was too upset. After all, she had her license for only two months and her first accident was hitting the preacher's car! I never brought it up to her. It felt too private to share. I worried if I told Chris, it would make Jeff mad. He might choose someone else to help him, and I would no longer be the special one in the group. Being special to him and maintaining my place in the church was more important than worrying about a kiss and questioning his motives.

I regularly babysat at Jeff and Nancy's house, usually two to three times a week. Nancy worked evenings, and since I didn't have a car, she picked me up at about 5:30. One evening, after she had only been gone thirty minutes, Jeff came home. I assumed he would take me home right away. I was disappointed he came home so early. I had counted on being paid for an entire evening and not just for a half hour. But instead of taking me home, he asked I if would stay and help with dinner and bedtime for his boys. I was happy to help and make more money. It brought back the memories of babysitting for Steve and Mary Lou's little girls.

As time went on, this became a pattern. Nancy would leave and shortly thereafter Jeff would arrive home. After making the kids' dinner and putting them to bed, Jeff would make it a point to begin discussions on various topics. He would ask me about who I was dating and what was going on in my life. He seemed to want to know everything about me. Mostly, we talked about church and how we could get more teens involved. He gave me a book on spirituality and asked me to read it. He introduced me to the Christian writings of Frances Schaeffer and C. S. Lewis. Jeff was helping me grow spiritually and become a better Christian. I soaked up his every word.

"What did you think of my sermon last week?" he would ask. *He was asking me about his sermon last week?* I felt so grown up and flattered he was interested in my opinion. After talking an hour or so he would take me home. Just before I got to the door to go home, he stopped me and gave me a hug. It wasn't a quick hug but a lingering hug. Sometimes he would kiss me, but not always. I felt cared for and happy. For about a year, Jeff continued the pattern of kissing or hugging when he was happy with me after babysitting.

If the same situation had occurred with the thirty-year-old married neighbor down the street, I would have told mom about how weird it was this married man would want to talk to me all evening instead of bringing me home, but I felt no need to tell Mom about Jeff being there while I babysat. Somehow it all felt perfectly natural to have this time with him. He was a pastor and a friend. Still, I became a little nervous around him, wanting to please him and fearing I would embarrass myself by saying something stupid. I always looked for his approval. He often commented on what I was wearing, sometimes complimentary, but not always.

One night when I got home from babysitting, a letter from Reggie, my camp boyfriend was waiting for me.

Dear Sandy,

I miss you. I am hoping to get to the Youth Rally in Bethel next week. Could you come? I would love to see you 'cause I really like being with you. I hope I see you there and won't have to wait until camp.

Love, Reggie

I was so excited to think I might get to see Reggie again. He was my first real boyfriend. It was weird thinking about how Reggie and I kissed, and how

Jeff kissed me. I told myself they were different. I was nervous and intimidated by Jeff. He was my guide and leader. I wanted to please him and help him in his ministry, but with Reggie, I could just be myself and have fun. Reggie's kisses meant he liked me. It was a boyfriend/girlfriend relationship. I rationalized Jeff's kisses were his way of showing me how much he appreciated me as someone helping him. Jeff was my minister; a married man. Reggie was my boyfriend. I was trying to make sense of this affection. This was the only way it made sense.

I put Reggie's letter in my camp scrapbook. Looking through the scrapbook reminded me of all the things I had learned at camp and the memories. I flipped through pages and read the camp guide of 1969:

> *At camp learning is fun!!! After a few moments of free time (to make beds, etc.) the first bell sounds for the FIRST-CLASS PERIOD. It isn't often that young people consider studying as being "FUN"... but at Clermont Christian Assembly they do!*
>
> *The subjects of the lessons and the teachers are especially chosen to meet the needs of the youth today. God gave us OUR ONLY TEXT, THE BIBLE! All people can trust the message recorded on these pages as being true, lasting, and final. Each camper will find it a "MUST" as the classes unfold during the week.*

The 1971 camp schedule listed Jeff as one of the teachers. Jeff's class title was "Test Tube Religion." I remembered his lesson. I thought about my Bible and what I had been taught and if letting Jeff kiss me was wrong. *Would he have kissed me if it was wrong?* Moreover, he had taught at the camp, and as my minister, he was to help me spiritually, so it must be okay. Who knows the Bible better than my minister? I thought about all the other adults I had met at church whom I totally trusted. If anything, he was the most spiritual and trustworthy of them all.

After receiving permission from Mom to go the Youth Rally and with butterflies in my stomach at the thought of seeing Reggie again, I sat down to write Reggie to tell him I would be there. I couldn't wait! First, I needed to tell Jeff I couldn't babysit next Wednesday. I reached Nancy and told her. She told me to have fun at the Youth Rally and she would ask someone else in the youth group to babysit. I was relieved. After hanging up the phone, I couldn't wait to write Reggie and tell him I would be there. I finished the letter and put it on my dresser, to mail in the morning.

Later that evening the phone rang. It was Jeff. "Hey, I have an organizational meeting scheduled for next Wednesday with you, Tom, Fred, Mark and Cindy at the church. I want to talk about the upcoming retreat and a few other things."

I hesitated and then said, "Oh, umm."

"Is there a problem?"

"Well, no, it's just the Youth Rally is next Wednesday and I was going to go."

"Can't you go next month?"

Yeah, I thought, *but Reggie won't be there next month*. I like the Youth Rallies but my main interest was seeing Reggie. It was odd Jeff was having this last-minute meeting. As much as I wanted to, I just couldn't say no to Jeff and replied, "Sure. I'll be there; what time?"

Tearing up the letter, I was *so* disappointed, but church was more important than Reggie. I even felt a little guilty for hesitating when Jeff asked me to be at the meeting. The next week, just a few hours before the meeting, Jeff unexpectedly cancelled. I had missed both the Youth Rally and seeing Reggie. I ended up babysitting.

At age sixteen, Mom and Chuck permitted me to date on the weekends. Occasionally, I was asked out. However, I had a strict curfew of 11:30 P.M., a half hour earlier than my other friends. This made it difficult because it meant someone always had to take me home early. Chuck was very strict about dating. Probably like many dads and stepdads, he was critical of those I dated. He often took his criticism to an embarrassing level. Greeting one of my dates at the front door with a pair of scissors, he said, in a menacing voice, "You are welcome to come in after you get that long hair of yours cut. You look like a girl." The poor guy waited outside until I came to the door. Humiliated, I apologized for Chuck's behavior.

On another occasion, I invited a friend I had dated a few times to dinner at our house. Chuck had made it known from the beginning he did not like the fact I was dating an eighteen year old when I was sixteen. David was a nice guy who worked for another church's youth ministry. I was convinced if Chuck got to know him, he would like David. Over Chuck's objection, Mom invited him. My stomach was in knots. The tension in the room was palpable. Mom had prepared one of my favorite chicken casseroles and red velvet cake for dessert. Showing her usual flair for entertaining, the dining room table looked beautiful with the fine china and crystal. After rounding up my little brothers and sisters, we all took our seats. Chuck was the last to come to the table. After we had all been seated, he looked at me and then at Mom and said, "I told you I didn't like this guy and I have no intentions of having dinner with him." With that he stood up, threw his napkin on his plate and left.

I was mortified. Wanting to burst into tears, I just sat there. The awkward silence was finally broken as my Mother said, "Sandy, why don't you pass the chicken." As odd as mom's reaction may have seemed to David, I expected it. She would do her best not to let Chuck's behavior ruin the evening.

Mom was an expert at avoiding confrontation. She saw every conflict as the potential for the start of WW III. If a situation was unpleasant and she didn't know how to deal with it, she simply avoided it. Her motto was, "keep going and somehow it will work out." Difficult discussions were not simply sidestepped, they were flattened, crushed, and not to be discussed again.

When my sister Vickie was about eight, she asked mom, "Why do Mike and Sandy have a different last name than ours?"

Her response; "don't ask me that again."

My sister Jackie asked, "Who is the man who picks Mike and Sandy up every Saturday and where do they go?"

"That's nothing you need to know."

Much of Mom's coping mechanism stemmed from growing up during a time parents didn't discuss family matters. Her father suffered from paranoia/schizophrenia. His behavior was erratic and sometimes abusive. Mom's father had a very good job with the railroad. Just after my mother turned fourteen, her father lost his job, forcing my grandmother to support the family. In 1959, at age sixty-two, he committed suicide by standing in front of a train. I vividly remember the very tall policeman coming to our house telling Mom that my grandpa was dead.

Confrontation was not Mom's strong suit. I was disappointed and hurt in her failure to stand up to my stepfather that night at dinner. Still, she had so many qualities making me realize how lucky I was to call her Mom. I loved her. I learned from her a sense of style and grace. Beneath her picture in her high school yearbook from 1952 the words "Sharp dresser" were written. No one could look better on a budget than she did. She was quite the looker and an excellent seamstress. Each August we would go to the fabric store and shop for material that would eventually become my new wardrobe for the coming school year. Those trips to the fabric store were some of my favorite times with Mom. It was one of the few times it would be just the two of us. As we walked up and down aisle after aisle of brightly covered fabric, I could hardly contain myself. If a bolt of fabric was on sale, you can bet all my sisters, Mom, and I, would end up in matching outfits. Even my Barbie dolls were donned in her creations.

The day after the dinner when Chuck walked out, I called Jeff in tears. He encouraged me to come to his office. With concern in voice he said, "You can tell me all about it when you get here." I asked Chris to drive me to church. I went directly to Jeff's office. He closed the door and held me as I cried in his arms. His care and concern helped relieve some of my anger and embarrassment. I told him how much it meant to me that he would take the time to listen and help me. He responded by telling me he cared for me and would always be there for me. He then kissed me and told me he loved me. I never felt more cared for than I did at that moment.

Other than my early curfew and conflicts with Chuck, I'm sure my early high school life looked pretty normal: movies, pizza, sleepovers, going to the mall, and trying to figure out how to pass Mr. Dickens' biology class. Chris and I were inseparable at both school and church. She was my best friend.

Jeff often took a group of high school kids to lunch to talk about church. I was always included. There were times it was just Jeff and me. Our discussions revolved around church or how I was doing with school and at home. He would ask about my dates. I talked to him about everything in my life. He was most helpful when I would share my frustrations with my stepfather and not being able to see my dad as much as I wanted. By the time I was sixteen, visits with my dad had become sporadic at best. He was involved with his new family, and I was busy with church, school, and my part-time job in the mall at a store for teens' clothing. I missed Dad terribly, but I accepted the situation because it was just the way it was. Being angry at him would only mean I would lose what little time I did have with him. I knew he loved me, but it hurt because Mike and I came second to his other family. There was a tremendous void.

Being able to talk to Jeff about all of this took away some of the pain. He was willing to listen and encouraged me to share things with him. I opened up to him and told him things I didn't share with anyone else. Because he often encouraged all of the kids to come to his office to talk, I did not see his interest in me as any different. My friend, Cindy, had a steady boyfriend and she was always confiding in Jeff about her relationship with him. She would share with me how helpful Jeff was. Cindy and I agreed we were lucky to have such a caring youth pastor.

To me, this extra attention confirmed Jeff cared for me. I reciprocated by doing all I could to please him and help the church. "You know I need you in this youth group and this church needs you," he would say. I was in his inner circle of a few select leaders. The more I grew as a leader, the more attention and praise he gave me. The more he praised, the more I wanted to please him.

One evening, members of our youth group rode the church bus to Cincinnati Bible Seminary to watch a basketball game. Chris and I missed the bus home. No doubt we were goofing around and not paying attention to the time; one of our most practiced skills. As only teenage girls could do, we found it hysterically funny the bus left without us. The question became, who do we call to pick us up?

Knowing our parents would be annoyed or angry to come pick us up at 11:00 P.M., we opted to call Jeff. Surely as our youth minister, he would understand and wouldn't mind driving over to take us home. After waiting on the curb for about thirty minutes, Jeff finally arrived. I opened the back door and hopped in. Chris sat in the front. "How in the world did you miss the bus?" he asked.

Giggling, we gave the most honest answer possible, "We don't know!"

"You do know what the bus looks like don't you; the big yellow thing on four wheels?"

"I guess we lost track of time."

"For Christmas I am going to get you two girls a watch!"

A couple days later at the Wednesday night church supper I was talking with Cindy. Jeff came by, put his arm around me, and slowly walked me away.

"Are you mad at me?" he asked.

"Mad at you? No why?"

Jokingly and in a fun way he said, "Well, the other night when I picked you and Chris up, you let Chris sit in the front seat with me, and you sat in the back. I thought maybe you were mad at me."

I had not thought about it. I just got in the car with no thought as to where I should sit. Perhaps he was right. I should have sat next to him. The last thing I wanted was to hurt his feelings or make him think I was mad at him. But why would I be mad at him?

Many times that year he made subtle remarks about my behavior; sometimes critical, but more often telling me how he wanted me to behave. I became guarded around him if something funny happened. If he heard me laugh, he would say, "You sound ridiculous," or "It's embarrassing the way you laugh. It's loud and obnoxious."

Following a church event filled with lively conversation and laughter, Jeff took me to his office.

"I could hear you all the way in the back with that laugh of yours. What's wrong with you? Why do you have to draw attention to yourself like that?" I felt stupid and humiliated. He *hated* my laugh.

As time went on, Jeff prodded me to be even more involved in church activities. He asked me to accompany him on hospital visits and home visits to the new members. In the beginning, I was nervous and not sure what to say. Though he was demanding, Jeff made me feel comfortable and mentored me. I depended upon his guidance. His attention became more focused on me than the other girls in the youth group. I assumed this was because of my hard work. He began requesting my attendance at events or functions I would not have otherwise attended. I spent more time with him and less time with my friends. My world was becoming smaller, revolving only around the church.

"The ladies in the kitchen need help on Saturday afternoon. I told them you would help."

"We need help collating and stapling the elder meeting minutes Monday evening."

"I think it would be good for you to serve on the Christmas Banquet Committee."

"I am going to Virginia Beach to help facilitate a weekend youth retreat for an old college friend of mine. Fred and Mark are going, and I need you to go as well."

But I didn't mind. I was serving God in an even greater way now. By helping Jeff, I was helping to grow God's church.

My senior year began in September 1972. Chris and I were in charge of building the senior float for our school's homecoming. It would be fun, I thought, but I worried how Jeff would feel, knowing it would take time away from church during the fall. I knew I shouldn't feel guilty, as I had been working really hard at the church. Still, I had trouble saying no to him. Oddly, Jeff seemed more upset was I unable to babysit than he was when I missed the Wednesday night church potluck dinner/prayer services.

"Don't worry about missing Wednesday night, but I'll miss having you babysit." I was relieved he wasn't upset and did not try to make me feel guilty. His response did not raise any red flags. Why would it? This was my minister. Any worries I felt about our relationship were negated by the words of those around me. They all loved Jeff and his ministry. Members flocked after the service just to talk to him. He had become a cult leader, developing a loyal following. I watched as adults would follow his orders and answer his requests for help at church, wanting to please him. He saw any refusal to any of his requests as an affront to his leadership. Just like the night when the organist refused to play "Bridge Over Troubled Water," he would find someone else.

Attendance numbers at church were important to Jeff. A common "request" of his to an adult was to have two new people in church with them on Sunday. More times than not, on the following Sunday they would attend with two new visitors. One of my youth group leaders once remarked, "I'm so nervous. Jeff wants me to invite someone new to church next week, and I don't know who I can ask." Even this adult did not want to disappoint Jeff.

The senior minister, Mr. Wilson, wrote this in the Church newsletter:

> *"There is NO WAY to express my pride in our splendid young people, and Jeff Coulier, our wonderful Associate Minister for our first Youth Night here at Walnut Branch. A host of young people from Southwind Christian Church in Tifton, youth who dearly love Jeff, who led them for years in service of Christ, came to Cincinnati to add their warmth and enthusiasm.*
>
> *Have you ever seen a more radiant song leader than Sandy Phillips? Denny read the word for us, Jim lifted our hearts in prayer, faithful, dependable Mark expressed their gratefulness for the offering and support of Jeff, the communion led by Fred, and Charlie's inspiring prayer.*
>
> *What can I say in describing the moving, meaningful message preached by Jeff? It was simply wonderful. God has granted us the service of a truly remarkable young man, who has a great variety of talent and ability, and a deep resource of love and affection."*

While the senior minister's praise of Jeff continued to grow, so did the frequency of the kissing. The intensity of the kiss grew more passionate but nothing more. At one point he reassured me, "You know I would never touch you." I believed him. Whenever I babysat, we spent much of the night talking then kissing on the couch once the children were asleep. He assured me it was okay and I believed him. He was blurring the lines and slowly breaking down the boundaries.

What I didn't realize then—he was grooming me that year for what would be his ultimate control over me. His manipulation was methodical and carefully planned. This wolf was so cleverly disguised in sheep's clothing and I, a child of God, had become his prey.

"Tell me all of your secrets. I want to know you inside and out. I say this because I adore you. In reality, I am building an arsenal of weaponry to use against you, to emotionally cripple you...to rob you of your freedom...to ensure that I will always feel like god."

—THRIVEAFTERABUSE.COM

NUMBER A36D_ _

It was a cold January day in 1973; my senior year, and nothing seemed out of the ordinary. I had homework to do when I got home from babysitting at the Coulier's and I wondered if I'd be able to finish it. It probably depended on when Jeff decided he would take me home. I tucked his boys in bed, started down the stairs, and saw Jeff waiting at the bottom of the steps.

He stopped me right there, embraced me and began kissing me. I expected we would go into the family room and sit on the couch as we usually did then we might watch TV or talk about the church and the Bible. I felt special during these moments, and, secretly, I knew every girl in the youth group would love to have this kind of attention.

I turned to walk down the hallway toward the family room when he stopped me again. Taking my arm, he led me to the living room where only light from the kitchen lit the room. There was no furniture there, with the exception of an old console stereo cabinet with four legs sitting on the thick gold shag carpeting. I wondered why we were going into the living room.

He put me on the floor near the stereo, laid on top of me and began kissing me as he put his hands beneath my blouse. Then he began undressing me. He had never done this before. It was happening so fast. I figured he would stop. *Surely, he would stop*, I told myself. He felt so heavy; smothering me lying on top of me. No one had ever been on top of me like that. My heart raced with fear. Then I sensed he was **not** going to stop. His breath became heavy, almost as heavy as his body.

He repeatedly asked if I loved him and I answered yes, each time. I didn't know why he kept asking me that. Yes, I loved him, but was he asking me if I loved him a different way?

"You know I love you. You know that, don't you?"

"Yes." It was all I could think to say.

With his head pressed against my neck, with his hot breath, he whispered, "You know I would never do anything to hurt you."

He pulled off my vest and unbuttoned my blouse. As he continued to undress me, he pushed me a little bit until my head was partially under the stereo. I tried to close my eyes and think of something else to block what was happening. I didn't know how to tell him to stop and, if I did, would he get mad? I was afraid to say anything. I didn't want to hurt him or make him mad.

Just close your eyes, I thought.

Eventually my head was almost completely under the stereo. Even though it was nearly dark in the room, I could see some of the numbers printed on the bottom of the stereo. There was an A, a 3, a 6 and then more letters. Some were hard to see but I kept trying to repeat the letters. I repeated them over and over and over again as he pressed against me. A36DP, or was it an F? I repeated them again.

At one point as he touched me, I remember looking at those numbers and thinking, "I wonder why they call it a serial number with so many letters in it. It's really not a number." I just tried to think of anything else, anything except what he was doing to me. I don't remember how much time passed before he slid me from beneath the stereo and lifted me to my feet. I was still partially clothed and thankful for that. He took my hand and led me to the stairs. In a hypnotic, monotone voice, he kept repeating, "It will be okay. You know you can trust me. I love you."

I felt powerless; too scared to tell him no. Even though my body followed him up the steps, I wasn't sure how. I felt like I was in one of those horror movies where the girl stays crouched in a fetal position in the corner of a room as an attacker with a knife slowly approaches. She could jump up and run, yet all she does is stay there crying, whimpering, saying, "Please, please don't." You want to stand up and scream at the movie screen, "Run! Do something! Don't just sit there!!! Run!" but she never moves. My head was telling me to run but my body felt frozen. It was scarier to say no than to follow him.

We reached the top of the stairs. As we entered the bedroom the light was on and I hoped he would turn it off. He didn't. He put me on the bed, pulled down my pants and immediately penetrated me.

This can't be happening to me!

I bled onto the sheets. I was terrified. *Why was I bleeding?*

He panicked when he saw the blood all over the sheets. Even though Nancy was not due home for a few more hours, he was clearly worried about the sheets. He mumbled something about not knowing how to work the washer and how he had to get it cleaned up before she came home. He told me to get up immediately, get dressed, and get ready to go home. All he needed to do was put the sheets in the washer. As he headed to the door with the bloodied sheets, I sat with my head down, not wanting to look at him, with the bedspread wrapped around me, unable to move, stunned. How is it I just had sex with my minister in his bed? I felt sick.

Standing in the doorway, he turned and looked at me and pleaded, "Sandy, please hurry." I remembered some of my clothes were still in the living room and I was too embarrassed to stand up in front of him without my clothes on. I waited for him to leave the room. I felt so ashamed. I met him downstairs and he told me to wait in the garage while he pulled the car from the driveway out front so no one would see us. For the first time he didn't want anyone to know I was there.

I don't remember much about the ride home just that it was dark and I was glad he could not see my face. As I got out of the car, he took my hand and kissed it. Smiling he said, "I can trust you not tell anyone, can't I? You know I love you." I heard his words, but I was confused. I loved him as a pastor, but now I wondered if his "love" meant something else. I didn't know how to answer him. I flatly mumbled, "I love you too."

The next morning, I went to school as usual. Sitting in government class, I began to panic. Would I start to bleed again? I was seventeen and I didn't know. I wanted to cry. Holding back the tears, I couldn't let anyone know I was upset. They might ask me what was wrong, and I might tell and ruin everything. I had to be sure his secret, and mine, was safe. No one could know what we did last night. I had lost my virginity. It wasn't supposed to happen this way.

I pretended nothing was wrong, but I could not stop thinking having sex changed everything. From both church and Bible camp it was drilled into us, sex outside of marriage was wrong; a sin. I had been able to justify the kissing as just affection, but what we did last night was wrong, and I knew it. What did it mean now? Would he want to marry me? Even my friends at school said that if you had sex at seventeen you either planned to marry the guy or the guy would dump you. More worries surfaced. What if I'm pregnant? What if someone finds out? Maybe he will just dump me.

I wasn't sure what to think. The questions just kept hammering at me. This was my minister, and not just any minster. This was Jeff, the kind man who really cared about people. He was the man everyone loved and trusted. I couldn't untangle my thoughts about love and sex. I knew you shouldn't have sex with someone unless you were in love with them. He knew having sex with me was wrong, so why did he do it? Maybe he did it because he loved me. I never wanted to have sex with him, but now it happened. Did this mean because I was no longer a virgin, I had to find a way to love him back? That seemed creepy and odd to me. I had always thought of him in the same way I thought of Pastor Tom; just my minister, yet, now it had all changed.

But if it wasn't love, what was it?

Sitting in class, I was totally lost in my confusion, unsure what to think. I just had sex with my pastor! Startled by a tap on my shoulder, Karen was asking me to pass a note to Janice sitting in front of me. Almost in a catatonic state I passed the note. As the bell rang for the next class, I thought about going home sick. Hiding my feelings from my mom would prove even more difficult, so it was easier to just stay at school. I met Chris in the cafeteria for lunch period. Grateful for the familiarity of the noise and friends around, I looked at the tray of food. I could not eat. All I could think about was Jeff having sex with me. I wanted so desperately to tell Chris, but I knew I couldn't betray Jeff. The secrets had started.

He called me in the evening after school and again reassured me he loved me. "Are you okay? Last night meant something." I still didn't know what it meant, but I asked when I would see him again.

"I don't know. We are going to have to be very careful now. You understand, don't you?"

"Yes, but I will see you soon, won't I?"

"I'll call you; don't call me at home. We better hang up now. You sure you are okay? You know I love you."

"I love you too," I said; still very confused as to what love meant.

For the next three days he called me every day to see how I was and tell me how much he loved me. It became clear to me, not only because we had sex, but also because of his tone and words, he was now speaking to me as a boyfriend would speak. Now when he said he loved me, it wasn't out of appreciation for what I had done, but rather because he really loved me.

"You love me, don't you? Do you know how much I love and care for you?"

"Yes" was always my response. Of course he cared for me. He had shown it from the day Mr. Wilson introduced us when he took my hand and told me what a pretty smile I had. He showed his love for me over the past year by always being available to me and listening to my problems. Also, he'd chosen me to have an important role in the youth group and the church. He could have chosen anyone else. I was just sixteen when I met him and his encouragement and trust helped me to become confident. I would do whatever he asked me to do.

I had grown dependent upon his attention. We had developed a special friendship over the last year, but he saw this as love. Was it love? I still needed him and didn't want to lose what he had given to me over the past year. I was grateful for all he taught me.

My thoughts were a jumbled mess but I kept coming back to the notion, *"this is Jeff Coulier telling me he loves me; really loves me! How could I not love a great man like him back?"* If all the attention I had received in the past year meant something to me, this was the ultimate attention. How could I hurt him and tell him I didn't love him? Didn't I owe him for all he had done for me? Is this how love begins? Isn't this wrong? The questions really didn't matter; I had already answered them by having sex with him and giving him my virginity. I was now committed to him. It was too late to go back.

Four days later, I was babysitting again at the Coulier's house. He didn't come home until after the kids were in bed. After going upstairs to make sure they were asleep he came down the steps into the family room where I was watching TV. I hoped he would take me home; instead he sat next to me and began caressing my face. I froze. I knew what was going to happen next. As he turned off the light, he told me how beautiful I looked and began to kiss me. This time I tried to figure out how I was to respond. Sensing my nervousness, he whispered, "Just let me help you." Unlike the first time, he touched me with tenderness, without the forcefulness of before. As scared as I was, his whispers of loving me lessened some of my fear. I still didn't know what I was supposed to do, but he assured me, "I love you, it will be okay. You are a woman now." To my horror, I found my body responding. My body was betraying me, telling me his touch felt good, while my mind said it was wrong.

I went home feeling guilty *and* loved. Guilty, not only because I knew this was wrong, but also because I wanted Jeff's love and approval. I always prayed before bed, but that night I begged to God to help me understand.

We had unprotected sex for several months and Jeff never brought up the subject of birth control. I was terrified of getting pregnant, but had no way to see a doctor or go to a clinic. Once I got a car I immediately looked in the phonebook and located a doctor as far as I could on the other side of town. I needed a prescription for birth control pills. Alone, I anxiously navigated the drive across town to the doctor's office. I took the pills home. Just like earlier, when I hid the picture of my dad and me under my mattress, I hid the pills there too.

In July 1973, just after I graduated from high school, Mr. Wilson retired and Jeff was promoted to senior minister. I was proud of him. He promised me we were married in God's eyes and I was now the helpmate of the senior minister. He would remind me he was just like David in the Bible, a man God used in spite of his faults. I couldn't argue with what he said. God did seem to be doing great things at Walnut Branch and it was all because of Jeff. There was vibrancy and a spiritual movement among the members. Attendance was growing at an unprecedented rate. For the first time, a second church service needed to be added. A new educational wing with a larger office for Jeff was built. In spite of our sins, God was still using him and me. So I, too, began to accept our relationship.

During these early stages, I wanted so desperately to tell someone. It was not only my promise to Jeff to keep our relationship a secret, but the shock and disappointment I knew would come from people in church learning this *about me*. One Saturday morning, about two months after we first had sex, I received a letter in the mail. It was from a woman in the church, "Sandy, you are such a wonderful example for the rest of the youth. God has blessed your life." After reading the letter I put it in a box with other letters I had received and saved over the years. With the letterbox out, I began to read a few of them. "You are such a fine, sweet, Christian girl." Another read, "You are such a blessing to Walnut Branch. Thank you for all you do." Those words now seemed to be taunting me, mocking me. Feeling too guilty to read anymore, I put them back in the box.

Along with the letters were several church newsletters and bulletins reaping praise upon me for all I did for Walnut Branch. I was chosen to appear on the cover of the Christian magazine, *Lookout*, to represent the graduating seniors of 1973. Mr. Wilson wrote in the church newsletter, *"The editor could not have picked a finer, sweeter, nicer person to represent the high school graduating seniors, Our Miss Sunshine."* So proud, Mom sent a copy to practically every relative.

It was not only the guilt of having sex outside of marriage with my pastor, but lying to those around me haunted me. I was not who they thought I was. I was deceiving them. I was an imposter. It was one thing at ten years old to fib about my parents' divorce, the only coping mechanism I knew then to keep the pain and hurt away, but this was deceitful and wrong. I was no longer this "sweet, Christian girl." How could I tell anyone? Jeff told me no one would even believe me if I were to say he was having sex with me. I couldn't even tell my best friend, Chris, and we shared everything. I thought about my former pastor, Tom, and how disappointed he would be with me. What would my former youth group leaders, Steve and Mary Lou, think of me? The guilt and shame drowned any thought of telling anyone.

Fear of being exposed, along with the ominous words of Jeff Coulier, "Don't tell. They will think you are lying. You will be responsible for what will happen to me, if anyone finds out," kept the secret locked within me for years to come.

"Abusers hack our belief system; they know exactly what they can and cannot get away with for every individual. Christians are the easiest targets because we teach people to believe the best in others. Abusers exploit this belief system to get away with the unthinkable. And it works. Anyone who has spent time with survivors knows their abusers were incredibly brazen, and the church folk were naïve."

—JIMMYHINTON.ORG, "MORE ON #CHURCHTOO—OUR EXPANDED Q&A WITH JIMMY HINTON ON SEXUAL ABUSE IN CHURCHES" *THE CHRISTIAN CHRONICLE*

PLAYING THE FIELD

From that point on, dating presented a problem. I didn't want to date anyone and Jeff didn't want me to date. Yet, in order to eliminate suspicion about us, he needed my life to look like every other teenager. He needed it to appear as if I was interested in dating. If someone asked me for a date, I needed Jeff's permission. Most of the time he didn't care but other times, for no apparent reason, he said no. There seemed to be no rhyme or reason in his decisions and this kept me in a constant state of confusion. He seemed to almost delight in keeping me off balance and his jealous possessive side began to emerge.

Initially this dating game, albeit awkward, gave me a somewhat normal life. I went to football games, hung out with friends at Pizza Hut, and did typical teenager activities. However, if Jeff could get away and wanted to see me, my other plans didn't matter. I was to cancel and meet him. Early on, I didn't care because I wanted to see him too; being with him was more important to me than whatever plans I had. Dating felt unfaithful and by not dating I was proving my love for him.

Senior Prom was just weeks away. Other girls dropped hints and giggled about who might ask them to prom, but I had little interest. A small part of me felt sad to miss my Senior Prom but my thoughts were consumed with Jeff. However, Jeff insisted I had to go.

"I don't have anyone to ask me."

"You can go with Doug."

"Doug? He's dating Patty and I don't want to go with him."

"If he asks, you are going."

At that moment I knew I would be going to the prom with Doug. Jeff's control and influence were not just limited to me. He could get almost anyone in the youth group to do as he asked without even realizing they were being manipulated. I didn't know what exactly he said to Doug and it didn't matter. I just knew once he told Doug to invite me, Doug would do it.

"I'm going to prom with Doug," I told Mom.

"Great! We can go to the fabric store and look for the material to make your dress."

As much as I had protested not wanting to go to prom, there was still a part of me longing to be the teenager I was before Jeff had sex with me. For one night, I could pretend as if nothing had changed, when in reality my whole world had changed. I was no longer the same.

Jeff's power over the group led to disruptions in our lives as we were unable to see his manipulation over each of us. Patty, who expected to go to the prom with Doug, broke up with him over it. Doug and I were good friends but neither of us wanted to be together at the prom that night. We just did what Jeff required and once again, I behaved according to his script. When we joined a group of friends for dinner, I felt self-conscious because everyone expected him to be with Patty. I tried hard to be a good date for fear he might tell Jeff I didn't show him a good time. Jeff had warned me, "Make sure you show him some sugar." As instructed by Jeff, I kissed him goodnight but felt such guilt because Patty was at home and he had spent a lot of money on me.

Mom and Chuck chaperoned the prom. With them and all the other chaperones milling about, I was safer downtown on prom night with a cute guy than at church with my pastor. Who would think it was my youth pastor who had orchestrated with such deception my Senior Prom night?

As time went on, Jeff became more controlling as to what clothes I could wear, the time I spent with my friends, what movies I could see... He forbade me to see the movie the *Exorcist*. Afraid to defy him, I didn't. When Chris had tickets to see the Carpenters in concert, she asked me to go. I was so excited. Jeff insisted I attend a function at church the night of the concert. Chris, angry with me, took another friend. He began to isolate me from my friends, and especially Chris, by demanding more of my time. He expressed his concern I might tell Chris about us. I promised him I would never tell her. This Jeff was a completely different person than the caring Jeff Coulier I had come to know over the past year.

He became more controlling about whom I could date, when, and for how long. I would date a guy for a short time, and without warning or reason, Jeff would tell me, "You need to stop seeing him now. Break it off." I would. This happened so many times, but I didn't dare argue. I knew arguing was pointless. I feared making Jeff angry and the possibility of losing him.

I knew I wasn't truly dating. Other girls talked about dating as a way to meet the special someone they hoped to marry. I realized how uncomfortable and strange dating was for me, and I knew it was not fair to the guys. Much of the time I didn't care if I stopped going out with someone. It was hard to keep up the charade. Somehow my relationship with Jeff trumped everything; he was the center of my world.

It wasn't just prom night with Doug. Jeff would arrange dates for me. He called and told me to meet him at a local coffee shop for lunch so I could meet a guy named Scott he had met at a planning meeting for the North American Christian Convention. As Jeff and Scott walked toward the table, I thought Scott looked nice enough, but he was not someone I would choose for myself. It didn't matter if I was interested or not; *that* wasn't the point. The point was I had to go out with him. Sitting at lunch, I was supposed to fake interest in Scott while Jeff rubbed his hand on my thigh. The situation was so awkward I couldn't wait for lunch to end. Later in the day, feeling as if I purposely made a fool of him, Jeff called me, furious because I made no effort to be nicer to Scott. He ended the call by telling me, "Don't ever embarrass me like that again!" When Scott called to ask me out, I knew I had to go. Fortunately, after that date, Scott didn't call again.

Eventually, the casual dating stopped. Jeff's domineering nature continued to increase. He demanded more of my time and expected me to wait by the phone. If I was unavailable or he could not reach me, I knew he would be angry. "Do you know how hard it is for me to get away? I really wanted to see you and you weren't home. I don't know when I will see you."

"Jeff, please I'm sorry. Can't we arrange a time for tomorrow or the next day? You tell me when and I will be there. I promise."

"You had your chance. Next time, be there when I call." Without saying goodbye, he hung up.

After a call like this I would confine myself to my house waiting for days by the phone hoping he would call back. Sometimes we arranged for him to call me at the pay phone in the mall at a specific time. Many times, I stood by the pay phone for over an hour. I felt defeated and foolish when no call came.

The worst of the days occurred in March 1973; three months after the first night we had sex. It was my birthday and Jeff promised we would see each other and spend my birthday together. The thought of it thrilled me. He said he would call at 6:00 P.M. with the plans. After two hours of waiting by the pay phone at the mall, I called his house, certain he wanted to be with me. He answered.

"Jeff, I have been waiting for you to call." I began to cry. "You said you would call."

"I can't talk now."

"It's my birthday."

"I know," he said, "I'm sorry. Will you forgive me? I promise to make it up to you. Don't be mad. Okay?"

Silence. I was more hurt than mad.

"Okay? Sandy?"

My response was a numb, "Okay."

"Good. I love you." And then he hung up. That's it. End of conversation.

Before my high school graduation, a new, angrier Jeff began to emerge. He had taken me home after babysitting and as we sat in the driveway at my house he screamed, "GET OUT OF THE CAR!" I sat there crying, telling him it was okay and it didn't matter he was unable to "make love" to me earlier. Trying to please him and calm him down, I said, "I love you and just want to be with you. It doesn't matter."

"GET OUT! It's **your** fault!"

I was bewildered as he reached across the seat and opened the passenger door. Reaching for his arm, crying, and not knowing the right thing to say, I pleaded with him, "Jeff, I'm sorry; please don't be mad." He pulled away from me, put the car in reverse, and began slowly backing out of the driveway. I begged him, "Jeff, please stop!" With the car still moving, he pushed me onto the driveway, slammed the door shut and left. For eight straight days he refused to speak to me. When he had finished with his silent treatment, he called me to meet him. Ever faithful, I did, relieved he was no longer mad at me.

I could not figure out why he was so insensitive if he really loved me. I knew what he was doing was not right, but I didn't know how to fix it. I wanted to go back to when he was just my pastor, to our talks in his office. I wanted to go back to before the kissing, before the sex, before he became so possessive. I wanted to go back to my normal teenage life. Yet, I didn't want to hurt him. I felt a sense of obligation to him. I had convinced myself I loved him and he loved me. My high school graduation was just a few short months away. I thought about college life. Leaving town could give me an easy way to leave him.

Going away to a Christian college had long been my dream. I was accepted at Milligan College in Johnson City, Tennessee. Finances were tight, but I secured a student loan that gave me the chance to go. By now, I knew Jeff was not going to leave Nancy for me and college was a natural way to break it off. I could start anew. Surely, he too understood we couldn't continue this way and it would be good for me.

Excited about my college acceptance, I shared this good news with Jeff. I told him in the hall at church and he said we needed to talk in his office. "Sandy, I can't have you leave. Don't you know how much I need you and this church needs you? Don't you know how much I love you?" He held me and kept repeating his need for me to stay. I didn't want to hurt him and I certainly didn't want to let the church down. The last year at the church had been successful with attendance at an all-time high. It was an exciting time to be a member of Walnut Branch Christian Church.

"I need you to be a part of this church."

"But where else can I go to college?" I asked.

"Cincinnati Bible Seminary."

I wanted to go away, live in a dorm, and meet new friends. I wanted to start over. I didn't want to go to Cincinnati Bible Seminary.

"I already have the money to go to Milligan," I told him.

"I will get your tuition paid for you," he promised.

"Okay, I guess."

"Good, I'm glad that's settled."

He hugged me and kissed me.

Now I felt guilty for even thinking about leaving.

I had told everyone I was going to Milligan. When one of my youth group leaders asked me why the change I said, "Jeff wants me to stay here."

"Sandy, you shouldn't let Jeff influence you. If you want to go to Milligan, you should go."

Trying to convince her and myself, I replied, "No, it's okay, I don't have my heart completely set on it."

Besides, in my mind, Jeff knew what was best, and staying here would be okay. I would make it work.

I started my college career at Cincinnati Bible Seminary in September 1973; I made friends and became involved. A semester later, I was disappointed to learn Jeff began taking classes there too. I would be under his constant supervision, just as I was at church. Again, I had to worry about how I dressed, how I laughed, and who my friends were.

While Jeff's unpredictable behavior made me miserable, it was nothing compared to the guilt I felt for what we were doing. It went against everything I had been taught and believed. The words, *"Jeff I can't do this anymore,"* seemed so effortless to say as I lay in my bed at night rehearsing them over and over. I had to talk to him. I couldn't live like this any longer.

It was near Easter before I found the courage to confront to him. One evening after a church-wide meeting, I stopped him in the hall and asked to see him in his office. His office seemed like neutral ground where I thought I could get him to listen to me. Smiling, but obviously upset I had approached him in the hall at church, he said, "Not in front of everyone here." I held my ground.

"I need to see you now." Knowing he wouldn't make a scene, I insisted. He unhappily consented. Once in his office he shut the door. What little confidence I had when I walked in was left on the other side of the door. With all I had in me I weakly said, "Jeff, I can't do this anymore. The guilt is overwhelming."

"Do you really think you can leave me? Leave this church?"

Crying, I sat there. I had no response.

In reality, what I was doing wasn't *telling* him I couldn't do this anymore. I was *asking* him to stop. Finally, I said, "Please, Jeff, I just can't do this."

"You will never be able to leave. Who else would want you? You are no longer a virgin and what you don't understand is no one is going to love you like I do."

"But Jeff..."

He cut me off. "I need to know you are mature enough to handle this. I need you and this church needs you. You need to stop talking about leaving. We both know it's not going to happen."

He hugged me, and then said, "You know I love you. Go right to your car and don't talk to anyone on the way out."

And it's exactly what I did. I had no one to turn to but the very person creating the turmoil in my life.

Lying in my bed that night I realized he was right; I was never going to be able to leave him and who else would love me? And how could I leave the church?

During the months when I wasn't dating, I spent more time at home in my room. Mom often asked if something was wrong. I assured her it wasn't. By this time Mom had joined the church, and she turned to Jeff as her minister. Out of concern, Mom mentioned something to Jeff about me spending too much time alone at home. I don't know what she said, but of course, he blamed me. He insisted I go out more simply to allay Mom's concerns. He didn't want any questions, especially from her.

Mom's concern and her questions only strengthened my resolve to hide what was happening and assure her I was okay. I couldn't let her find out. Like everyone else, she trusted the pastor of her church was behaving morally and ethically. Anything else was out of the realm of anyone's thinking. Jeff Coulier could "hide" his actions in plain sight. He maintained the congregation's complete trust. He skillfully deceived those around him. He had the perfect cover. His reputation and title gave him the perfect mask, and he took me under the cover with him.

> *"Most people have no clue hidden abuse is taking place right under their noses. It is being perpetrated by individuals who would never be suspected of being abusers. The concealed nature of this harm is what leaves its targets devastated."*
>
> —SHANNON THOMAS, *HEALING FROM HIDDEN ABUSE*

STRIKE ONE

Nearing the completion of my first year of college, the charade of dating started again, with Jeff in charge. He thought he had found the perfect solution when he set me up with Kent, his close friend and a member of his former church in Tifton. Kent was a professional baseball player, had a great singing voice, and was much admired by the young women at church.

I was nineteen and Kent was twenty-three. Up until then, I had only dated high school boys. Jeff did not think the age difference mattered. After I turned eighteen, Chuck's dating rules no longer applied. More importantly, this "relationship" offered a solution to two problems for Jeff. By "dating" Kent, I didn't have to explain why I wasn't dating anyone else. Second, Kent's travel schedule meant I'd be available to spend time with Jeff. I was confident Kent had no trouble finding girls to date, and I'm sure in Jeff's eyes, I was just one more. What Jeff did not anticipate was Kent and I genuinely enjoyed being with one another. Our attraction grew beyond a casual friendship.

Kent took me to nice restaurants, bought me gifts, and sent cards and letters when he was away. The gifts included a gold cross necklace with a small diamond in the middle. For his birthday in May, I bought him a gift. The following Christmas he came to Cincinnati and we spent the holidays together. He joined our big family Christmas party and fit in well with my family. The men talked baseball as Kent shared his baseball stories with them.

After the party, we went downtown in the evening to look at the lights. It was a brisk night. We stopped in front of the landmark fountain on the city square. He bent down and kissed me and then said, "I'm cold. Keep me warm." He opened his coat and wrapped me inside. I felt such security in his arms. It was something I had never felt with Jeff. I didn't want Kent to let me go. It felt so good to have a normal date with someone who cared for me. The following Sunday at church Mom thanked Jeff for introducing me to Kent. Jeff's response,

"I think they make a nice couple."

Kent's visits to Cincinnati and letters became more frequent. When the Cincinnati Reds were in the World Series, in 1975, he took me to Game 5 against the Boston Red Sox. I sat in the stands thinking how lucky I was to be next to him and free from Jeff, even if only for the time it took to play nine innings.

All this, while Jeff went back and forth between encouraging me to keep seeing Kent and becoming angry about it, I walked a tightrope, hiding my feelings for Kent from Jeff and hiding my relationship with Jeff from Kent. Jeff grilled me about where we went, what we did, how far I let him go. He always wanted to know whether I kissed him and how long we made out. We had done nothing more than hugged and kissed, but Jeff didn't believe me.

Once, Jeff told Kent we should come back to his house after our date. After Kent and I arrived at the Coulier's house, Jeff took me aside and told me with a smile, "Nancy and I will give you and Kent time alone. Then I want you to make out with him downstairs while I am having sex with Nancy upstairs. Think about that." He always liked to tell me how great sex was between the two of them. I tried not to let what Jeff said ruin the evening with Kent but how could it not?

Even away from me, Jeff found a way to invade my life. Because Kent didn't know he was just being used by Jeff as a pawn, I was certain the two of them talked about me. Whether under the guise of being his friend or guys being guys, I worried about their conversations. I knew Jeff pumped him for information. Kent told me, "I know Jeff cares about you and he's interested in our relationship. He asks me questions about us, but I want you to know I don't tell him everything." Whether it was true or not, I was relieved.

Kent usually called on Sunday evenings. Our phone conversations lasted no more than fifteen minutes, as that was my time limit on the phone and it was long distance. Our limited phone conversations and his winter schedule of playing ball in the Dominican Republic meant letters were our main communication. His Sunday phone calls and letters were the highlight of my week. He had no idea of the reprieve he gave me from the reality of my otherwise despairing life. I knew I was leading a double life, but Kent made it all somewhat bearable.

I found myself falling for Kent. Jeff had arranged many dates for me over the last two years and no one ever captured my feelings like Kent. From his letters, I could tell the feelings were mutual. I understood from the beginning of Jeff's plans the sole purpose of my relationship with Kent was to be a charade, a cover for us, just like all the others. Yet, Kent was a lifeline for me. I kept his letters in a box by my bed to read and re-read. I secretly hoped Kent would come into town one day, and say, "Let's get married. I love you and I want to marry you. Let's elope." I would say yes and, by the time Jeff found out, it would be too late. There would be nothing he could do. A fantasy, I sadly knew would never happen.

I was never happier than the almost two years Kent and I "dated." Jeff still controlled my life, but Kent gave me hope. I knew I was being deceitful to Kent and selfish, but my life otherwise was such a nightmare and dating Kent offered an escape. My time with him, our phone calls, and reading and re-reading his letters allowed me to pretend my situation with Jeff was just a bad dream.

But then the bad dream got worse.

Jeff became more domineering. Our time together was reduced to nothing more than sex in hotel rooms. Worried about someone being suspicious, he no longer wanted me to be seen in his office. We didn't meet to talk, he never bought me a gift and no matter what I did, it was never enough to please him. No longer on a pedestal, I was now a doormat for him to step on at his whim. Moreover, Kent stood up to Jeff in subtle ways. Jeff did not have the same power over Kent he had with other people. Jeff couldn't keep control of the situation.

Jeff called me into his office one day, which was unusual because he did not want anyone to see us together. *What did I do now?* On very rare occasions, he had me into his office for sex. This, I could tell, would not be one of those times. I could see anger in his eyes. "Sit down."

I waited, nervously shifting in my seat. He sat at his desk shuffling papers.

Sitting there I couldn't help but think of all the times previously, before the fateful night in his bed, I had been happy to be called into his office to plan the Youth Night or talk about an upcoming retreat. How many times had he called me in just to see how I was doing and to let me know if I needed anything, he would always be there to help. Now, I felt more fear sitting in his office than if I were facing a firing squad.

I began recounting the previous week: *Did I not pay enough attention in church? Had he caught me in the hallway laughing too much with my friends?* Those actions always elicited a reprimand; he hated the way I laughed. Maybe I said something inadvertently to his wife I should not have said? Did he disapprove of what I was wearing one day? Was he going to tell me to go home and change? It was no use to guess.

I suppose it should have entered my mind what was coming. "You are to stop writing Kent. I don't want you to see him again." Stunned, I sat there silently. My heart felt ripped out. My head dropped and I wrapped my arms around my shoulders. All I could think was how I would tell Kent I did not want to see him anymore.

"Do you understand?" His words jolted me back.

"Jeff, I can't just stop writing without any reason. I just can't do it."

Did I just say those words? I had *never* talked back to him or questioned him in any way, but I genuinely cared about Kent. All the other times Jeff pronounced the end to a relationship were unpleasant and I felt badly, but this was much different. This hurt. This was Kent.

"He will be so hurt. I just can't all of a sudden stop talking to him. He won't understand."

"Yes you can. **No more letters; no more phone calls.**" Jeff was angry; very angry.

I can't be that cruel, I thought. It would do no good to argue. I had my orders. Crying, I got in my car and drove aimlessly. I drove until I knew it was late enough that Mom and Chuck would be asleep and ask no questions. As difficult as it was to think about never seeing Kent again, the thought of hurting him by stopping all communication with him without an explanation was beyond anything I could do.

Regardless of what Jeff told me, I decided I would write one more letter and find a way to explain the end of our relationship. But I couldn't make myself write the words, so, unlike my previous letters. I wrote one brief letter without much of a personal touch. I hoped he might see the change in my feelings without coming out and saying it was over. In the letter, instead of signing it, "Love, Sandy," I signed it, "Love in Christ." Kent noticed and his next letter asked why I did that. I didn't respond. I let a few letters pile up without responses. Of course I read them, and felt awful, but I was afraid to defy Jeff any more than I already had by writing Kent another letter.

In one letter he asked there to be a letter from me waiting for him when he returned from his road trip to Sacramento. I ignored the request. It was something I'd never done before. He wrote telling me how disappointed he was I had not written. He expressed how much he cared for me and would call me Sunday.

Dear Sandy,

I am finally going to break down and write. I haven't gotten a letter from you.

Why haven't you written? I was disappointed when I didn't get my letter when I got home. It would have meant a lot to me, but maybe I am being silly, that's in the past.

> *I have so many things I want to tell you. Please write. Maybe I can call? Will you be home Sunday evening? Here is my number. Maybe you can call me.*
>
> *I know your time is limited. I actually have more time to write than you. All I need and want is not just a letter but a feeling of caring for me and that you miss me. Know that I love you and care for you and miss you. I pray for you and ask God to have what he would in your life. He is listening. Life has been so good to both of us and my being away just isn't right. I want to be with you and I hope you feel the same way.*
>
> *I love you,*
>
> *Kent*

Looking down as I read the letter, my tears fell upon his words and the ink began to smudge. I quickly tried to dry the paper. I didn't want to lose any part of what I knew would be my last letter from him.

The phone rang and interrupted my tears. It was a Sunday evening and my heart jumped. Oh, it's going to be Kent! What will I say? I had not responded to his letter. I had not thought about what I would say if he called. A break; I could tell him I needed a break and ask *him* not to write or call. I figured telling him over the phone would be better. No, it would be worse. I could just let the phone ring. But I so desperately wanted to hear his voice and talk to him. The thought of him on the other end of the phone was more than I could bear. I reached the phone before it stopped ringing.

With hope in my voice, I said hello.

There was a pause and my heart jumped. This was long-distance connecting; the call from Kent. What would I say?

Instead, I heard Jeff's voice, "I have some free time tomorrow. Let's meet at the hotel."

What a cruel twist. I slumped into a chair.

"I have class and studying to do. I can't meet you."

"Ok. I'll call you later."

I was shocked, but relieved he didn't fight me on this and insist I see him anyway. Right then I realized he didn't have to fight. He had won.

When Kent's last letter arrived, I waited to open it. As long as it remained unopened, I still held out hope of my fantasy of escaping with him. Opening the letter would be the final good-bye. The words in this letter would not be kind. Will he hate me? He should. Whatever he said, I deserved.

> *Dearest Sandy,*
>
> *I don't understand, and if there is something I did I am sorry. I will always remember you as a wonderful person and continue to pray for your life.*
>
> *Love,*
>
> *Kent*

It was over. I was a **horrible** person. How could I hurt someone like that? I didn't even know who I was anymore. I hated myself for hurting Kent. I hated myself for not being able to say no to Jeff. I hated who I had become. Today those letters are tucked away in a dust covered shoebox in my basement; a reminder of a light in my life at a very dark time.

Three days later, knowing I scheduled a dinner with a friend downtown, Jeff told me to reserve a room and he would meet me that night. In spite of my overwhelming sadness at losing Kent, defeated, I booked a room. Sadly, things were back to normal. We watched TV and then had sex. As he was leaving the room, he casually asked, "You did stop writing Kent like I told you, didn't you?"

"Yes."

With that, the back of his hand landed across my face, knocking me to the floor.

Disoriented for a moment, I sat on the floor holding my face.

"GET UP!!"

I didn't move.

"How stupid do you think I am?" NOW GET UP! I SAID TO GET UP!"

I remained cowering on the floor. I saw fire in his eyes and his clenched jaw, as he told me again to get up. He towered over me and his size overwhelmed me. *If I get up, he's going to hit me again.* I was both terrified and yet ashamed of myself for lying to him. I hoped he would forgive me.

Instead of getting up, I grabbed him around his legs holding onto them, begging his forgiveness.

"Jeff, I'm sorry. I am so sorry." I just kept repeating it.

"Please forgive me."

He began to walk away dragging me across the floor.

"I told you no more letters!"

Finally, he reached down and pulled me up within inches of his face, squeezing both my arms so hard I momentarily forgot about the pain in my cheek and eye. My body was limp like a Raggedy Ann doll. My feet barely touched the ground as he held me up by my arms.

"Don't you *EVER* lie to me again!"

He waited.

Still crying, but petrified he might hit me again, after a few moments, with my voice quivering, I said, "I won't."

"Don't you know I know everything you do?"

He pushed me onto the bed and left. He left me alone sitting in the room, with my eye throbbing and my heart breaking.

It was a moment of complete and utter clarity. Any hope I ever had of getting away from him was lost. Any silly fantasy I had about my prince charming whisking me away to elope was forever gone. There was no one to rescue me, no one to tell, no one to ever really love me. This was to be my life and I had to accept it. Defeated, from now on, I would do whatever he told me. There was no point in fighting back.

Around 11:00 P.M. in the evening I left the hotel. I got off the elevator in the Pogue's parking garage. It was very dark with only three cars left on the upper level where I had parked my car. I was alone in the garage with only the sound of my footsteps and a few creaking pipes. Despondently, I shuffled to my car, recognizing the danger, but not afraid. I wished someone would attack me and kill me. After what I had done and who I had become, I deserved to be found dead lying on a cold, dirty garage floor. Then the pain of these last few years and losing Kent would be gone.

The next morning I awoke relieved to see my eye had only a slight cut above my upper lid. With a generous amount of makeup, the discoloration was covered well enough. Looking in the mirror as I got dressed, I kept second-guessing myself.

Why did I lie to him? Why did I think I could lie and he wouldn't find out? Why did I ever agree to go out with Kent? Why didn't I just do as he told me and not write Kent?

If I had not lied, none of this would have happened and I wouldn't be staring at a person I hated in the mirror. It was my fault. I had disobeyed and then I needed to lie. From now on, I would do as he told me. The question of how long Jeff would make me suffer for my sin of lying loomed largest in my mind.

After last night, anything was possible. I would never know what lies Jeff told Kent about why I stopped writing.

I finished dressing, got in my car and drove to church. Putting on my choir robe, I took my seat in the choir next to Cindy. She noticed something was wrong. "Are you okay?" she asked.

Lowering my head and pulling my hair over my eye, I responded, "Yeah, I just don't feel well."

I looked over as Jeff took his seat just to the right of the choir, holding his Bible and notes. No expression. As the organ began to play, he looked over at me and smiled and nodded. He then stood up and with his hands on the podium, he simply said, "Welcome to our service this morning. We are glad you are here." I then stood with the choir as we sang, "Lead on, Oh King Eternal."

Back to normal.

"We've all eaten lies when our hearts are hungry."

—COACH TIM, FACEBOOK.COM/RECOVERYCOACHTIM/

BY THEIR FRUITS YE SHALL KNOW THEM

Each week Jeff Coulier sent a newsletter to the congregation. The August 23, 1973, publication was called, *"By Their Fruits Ye Shall Know Them."* In the newsletter he wrote, *"God constantly gives vitality and love to his people. May we continue to be open to the spirit as God transforms us into his image and leads us to where we should be. Love, Jeff."*

Pastors' words always had meaning to me because I believed pastors were men of God; ordained for God's purposes, here to teach us. I had been taught they provided spiritual authority and weren't to be questioned, which I didn't. I truly believed Jeff Coulier embodied what he had written in the newsletter. God gave love and vitality to his people, just as Jeff was reviving our church in 1973.

The following January, his weekly message from the newsletter focused on the New Year, 1974:

> *"The old world is in labor. The New Year is being born. God has blessed this church here in 1973. There's something refreshing about new beginnings. A New Year comes bringing new lives, new faces, new horizons, and new hope. Resolutions for the religious should include a new priority—a new ultimacy—a new commitment to the Lord and His church.*
>
> *Therefore, if any man be in Christ, he is a new creature: old things are passed away, behold. All things are becoming new. A Happy New Year—A Happy New You!*
>
> *Love, Jeff"*

A New Year for me did not hold the same promise of a refreshing new beginning. Though he had written these words as a man of God, he had spent this past year having sex with me and telling me to keep it a secret. Yet, I still believed in Jeff and I leaned on him for understanding. He was right, God had blessed the church and I was a big part of the reason. Jeff would often explain to me God loved him and God loved me in spite of our faults, assuring me of God's mercy and approval. He pointed to Biblical examples of sins and often told me the story of David and Bathsheba. In my mind, the truth had become so twisted I saw my commitment to Jeff as evidence of my commitment to God. I realize now he had brainwashed me to believe what he was doing was the action of a righteous man.

A year and a half later in 1975, after months of continuing to have sex with me, Jeff preached a four-week sermon series on marriage and the family. He began the series by explaining, "These topics are so important, a cassette tape of each sermon will be made available to anyone who requests one." I still have the tapes.

As he often did, he began by commenting on how crowded the church was because the topic of marriage "touches a nerve of need" and people from all over need to know how God sees marriage. He admitted he had some weaknesses as a husband, namely behaving as though he was married to the church instead of keeping his young family a priority, but he quickly said, he was beneath "the canopy" of God and we all needed to know God made the plan, "Until death do us part."

He also addressed sexuality and said the church makes people feel guilty; "Don't do 'it' before marriage; 'do it' after marriage," drawing laughter from many people in the congregation. He underscored "God gave sex to produce unity, cleaving, and one flesh" and went on to preach through 1 Corinthians 7, which is Paul's advice on marriage. As a pastor counseling parishioners, he said he was "tired of picking up the pieces of extramarital affairs" and "we can't have the playboy philosophy where people are used as things." He then said, "To all you husbands out there, the greatest gift you can give to your children is to love their mother." He ended the sermon by quoting Jesus' words in Matthew 7, "Everyone who hears God's words and does them is a wise man... but those who do not act on them will be like the foolish man who built his house in the sand." He closed by saying how we all try to look better in the church than we really are.

Through those four weeks, both Jeff's wife Nancy and I heard him speak from the pulpit about being a faithful husband, loving a spouse like Christ loved the church, and raising Godly children. He preached with authority and tender expression. While he told me we were married in God's eyes, I could not make sense or reconcile his words with his actions. I didn't know how.

I wondered how Nancy felt about the series, particularly one part where he admonished wives to be "chaseable;" no curlers or bathrobes if a woman wanted to be chased by her husband. I had witnessed their home life and his treatment of Nancy was, at times, far worse. His belittling and berating of her, whether it was about her looks, her parenting skills, or her housekeeping, often left her in tears. One evening, I arrived to babysit and they were in the middle of an argument. As she turned to go up the stairs, he picked up a book and hit her in the back of the head. I quickly left the room. I felt sorry for her. As for his parenting, he never had much time for his boys. Pastors work extremely long hours, often being at church meetings in the evening when children need attention. Many evenings when there weren't church activities, he would be with me.

I had become so confused; I could not reconcile his words from the pulpit from his private words. Week after week, I was shown a man of God through his weekly newsletters and inspiring sermons. I watched as those around him praised this Godly man for doing great things in the church. Meanwhile, I was having sex with this same man during the week. I knew sex outside of marriage was considered adultery, but he continued to tell me our relationship was part of God's plan. Whenever I started to question what we were doing was wrong, he would assure me it was OK and he loved me. It was the sin of deceit as well as the sin of sex keeping the relationship going.

Unable to process the difference between his words and his actions, I tried to make sense of his distorted use of the scripture. The truth was I could not. I should have zeroed in on the title of his newsletter, *By their fruit ye shall know them*, but it's not so easy to spot a false prophet. His public persona was so far from the man I saw behind closed doors.

> "Abusers often hide behind good deeds, kind words, and a good reputation in public. They cultivate such things for the purpose of deception." —DIANE LANGBERG PHD, DIANELANGBERG.COM

Kathy, a youth group leader, was one person who could be critical of him. She and Jeff differed on some issues and he often complained about her to me. She was one of the few who saw through his charismatic charm. She wasn't afraid to question him or stand up to him.

After I had written Kent for the last time I was depressed and lost. One evening at YAC the guilt overwhelmed me. I didn't want to live this way anymore. Kathy approached me and asked me what was wrong. I couldn't tell her. She finally asked, to my utter shock, "Is something going on between you and Jeff? Is he doing anything to you?" I denied it, but I knew she did not believe me. She said she knew something was going on and that I should tell her.

Every part of me wanted to tell her. I was so close to saying something and she knew it. Instead, I kept my head down, afraid to make eye contact. I heard the words of Jeff repeat in my head, "Don't ever tell. You won't be believed." Fearful of saying anything, I assured her I was okay. She hugged me and told me she loved me. The next day on Monday, she went to Jeff's office and confronted him about her suspicions.

Just prior to the start of the Wednesday prayer/potluck dinner, he called me into his office. I could tell he was upset and angry at me, "How could you come so close to telling Kathy about us? You almost told her, didn't you? Didn't you? I need to know I can trust you. Obviously, I can't."

"Jeff, I didn't tell her anything! She asked me, but I didn't tell her anything! I promise."

"She approached you because you were crying."

Infuriated, he continued, "What were you crying about?"

"We were at YAC and after the prayer I was just feeling guilty and sad."

Jeff mockingly said, "Are you going to go crying to Kathy every time you are unhappy? If you are so unhappy why don't you leave? There's the door. Leave!"

Crying I said, "I don't want to leave."

He pushed me against the wall, my head snapped back.

"If you think you can leave, you are sadly mistaken. No one else is going to love you."

His anger intensified. I was afraid he was going to hit me again.

"I am the only one who knows how to love you!"

Never again would I ever think of telling anyone. Leaving his office, smiling as if nothing were wrong, I entered a hallway full of people, talking to each other, yet he had shown me I had no one to talk to.

In 2005, I reconnected with Kathy and her husband, Jim. I asked her if she remembered the night after YAC when she asked me if something was going on with Jeff. She said she remembered it well and had strong suspicions about Jeff but could not prove it. She then recounted to me Jeff's response when she confronted him. His reaction was hostile. "How dare you accuse me of something like that!"

"I don't believe you," she told him.

"If you have no more trust in me than that, perhaps you should find another church."

She and her husband, Jim, eventually left Walnut Branch.

"Spiritual abuse means taking the sacred things of our God, the things of the Spirit in order to harm or deceive another human being. ...Such a pairing is diabolical. We're talking about the words of God, himself being used to do evil to others."

—DIANE LANGBERG, DIANELANGBERG.COM,
"SPIRITUAL ABUSE AND TOXIC SYSTEMS"

TRAPPED

Now I realized the decision not to go away to college I had made two years earlier kept me trapped. I was suspended in time. I couldn't go back and I couldn't move forward. I had nowhere to go.

After I saw his anger in the hotel room when he hit me and again later when Kathy confronted him, I knew I was never going to be able to leave Jeff Coulier. Yet, he still had moments when he made me feel loved and special by telling me how much he needed me. At age twenty, I had no one else. My best friend was gone, all of my other friends were away at college or involved in their own lives. I had outgrown YAC and Kent was long gone.

Teri was a member of the youth group and even though she was five years younger than me we developed a friendship. Yes, I had been her Sunday school teacher, but we started meeting for lunch and had fun together. She reminded me of who I once was. She looked up to me as a mentor and friend to her. Occasionally she told me how much she admired me, and often she would seek my spiritual advice, although I felt like the last person on earth who should be advising anyone on spiritual matters. My own spiritual life was such a mess. Over time we became close. She was my only friend and without knowing it, she filled the void of loneliness created by Jeff. Her friendship kept me sane, in spite of the insanity of my life. I enjoyed knowing I had a positive influence on her.

My relationship with Jeff evolved into nothing more than sex. It was only sex in hotel rooms; hotel rooms paid for by me. Oftentimes, I worked two jobs to keep up with the expense. I was still living at home so my expenses were minimal, but it wasn't always easy. Initially, he would arrive early enough to have dinner in the room with me or spend time talking. He no longer kept up the charade of a relationship; now it was only about sex and exerting his power over me.

One Christmas, I bought him a nice wool dress coat. I was so excited to give it to him.

I asked Jeff, "When can I see you? I have your Christmas present I want to give you."

"I don't have anything for you. Why don't we wait so I can give you something too?" he replied.

"Oh, I don't want to wait. You can give me your gift later."

"I don't feel right taking the gift from you when I don't have anything for you."

I gave him the coat and he wore it to the Christmas Eve Service. Of course, he never did buy me a Christmas gift. The pattern of my giving and his taking without ever reciprocating never changed. Seeing no alternative, I accepted this behavior. It was easier knowing he wasn't going to change.

Very early on, Jeff showed his unpredictable side. As the years went on, the unpredictability became more evident and more frequent. It started with the little things. He would become angry about a missed phone call, or angry about someone I was dating even though he arranged the date. His anger escalated to hitting me after he discovered I had written to Kent.

Living with the anxiety and worry of his unpredictability became my norm. I never knew what might set him off or why. One day he would be in a good mood, I could do no wrong, and he loved and needed me. The next day he would berate me. He made me feel as though I would never be good enough for him. If he was unhappy, he was sure to point out it was *my failure* in not knowing how to love him. "You don't love me enough," was his favorite accusation.

His unpredictability carried over into how careful he was about our meetings. He would insist our cars not be in the same hotel parking lot. He would tell me never to call him at the office. Other times, those things didn't matter. Once he took me to a public park and had sex with me. I was as petrified of being seen, as was he, but for Jeff it was worth the risk.

We would make arrangements to meet by phone or during quick conversations at church, such as when I would go through the receiving line after the service. He would tell me what day and time he could meet and I would find the hotel and call him with the location and room number. He always wanted me to book a different hotel so there would be less chance of us being caught. I would leave the room number on a hallway table in the lobby or on the windshield of my car.

He would become angry if the hotel room I picked wasn't far enough from the lobby or if I picked a hotel not far enough from the road. Once I had a room at a hotel off Sharon Road in the northern part of the city. He knocked on the door and I let him in.

"What were you thinking picking this place?"

I didn't have an answer and it didn't matter anyway. He wasn't looking for an answer.

"I can't be seen here. I'm not staying."

I began to cry, to apologize, to beg.

He left.

Later I saw him at church and he approached me. Still hurt and upset, I fled to the bathroom. He stood outside and begged me to come out, telling me how sorry he was. Crying, I told him I wasn't coming out but he continued to plead with me. I finally told him if he left, I would come out, but I wanted him gone when I came out. Ten minutes later, I felt safe enough to come out of the bathroom. He was gone.

Later the same day we had a group meeting at church. I was still upset. Knowing I couldn't refuse to see him and make a scene in front of everyone he said, "Sandy, I need to see you for a minute in my office after the meeting."

Once in his office he began apologizing and begging me to forgive him. "I'm sorry; I know I shouldn't hurt you like that."

He seemed sincere and sorry. I wanted to believe him.

Confused I responded, "Jeff, I don't know what you want from me."

"You know I love you and I need you. You know, don't you?"

"Yes, but I never seem to be able to make you happy."

"I know, but you know I love you and I am sorry."

He hugged me and then smiled, "You know you can't stay mad at me. Forgive me? Now let me see your pretty smile."

Still upset, but giving in, I looked at him and smiled. He kissed me and I left.

Jeff's unpredictability continued to keep me off balance not only through his actions but his words as well. When he was angry with me, often for no apparent reason, he would call to tell me something like, "I will have Patty lead the singing at Youth Night instead of you," or "I am having a meeting with a few of the kids in the youth group but I won't need you there."

One Sunday morning he said to me, "I've changed my mind about having you serve on the committee for the church picnic. I chose someone else." Feeling hurt and disappointed, I would ask why. His response was, "I think you know." Of course, I didn't know. He always kept me in a constant state of turmoil. Of all the things he did, excluding me from church involvement was the most frightening and hurtful for me. He demonstrated more than once he had the power to take away from me the one thing *meaning more* to me than anything in the world, *my church*.

Sex continued in his home, car, or hotel rooms. Occasionally, we had sex in his office at church. Most of the time, I felt safe at church because he was very careful not to draw attention to us. One evening, during choir practice I saw him standing in the darkened hall in the back of the church watching me. He lingered for a few minutes and then walked up the center aisle of the church. He approached the choir director and said, "Excuse me Jan, I need to see Sandy in my office for a minute." I walked back to his office with him. He shut the door and began kissing me. Rubbing up against me, he bent me over his desk and had sex with me. He then sent me back to choir practice where I sat next to his wife. I felt ashamed and uncomfortable. This was not a romance. There was nothing romantic about it. He had power over me both physically and emotionally. I was powerless. If there was a way out, I could not see it. I was blinded by his control. I was trapped.

When talking to me at church, he would appear to be talking to me as just another member. Our conversations were not like other members' conversations. They were about where we would meet next. Going through the receiving line one Sunday after church, he shook my hand, smiling, and said, "Get a room at Quality Inn on Thursday. We can enjoy the view."

"Okay. Should I call you when I get there?"

"No, I will be making hospital visits. Leave the room number on one of those hall tables on the 5th floor. I'll be there around 7:00 P.M."

Thursday evening, I pulled my car into the garage beneath the hotel and backed the car into a tight space. As I wandered aimlessly looking for the elevator, I passed a young man who looked as lost as I did. I noticed he found the steps and I continued to look for the elevator. I was completely turned around but finally found the elevator, wondering if I would ever find my car when I returned. Once I found the lobby, there were a few people in front of me, including the young man I'd seen in the garage.

The desk clerk asked to help the next person; she gave me my room key and announced I was in Room 6022. First, though, I had to stop on the fifth floor to leave the room number on the table for Jeff. After leaving the note, I boarded the elevator for the sixth floor. As the doors opened, I stepped off the elevator. The doors closed behind me. I recognized the man I saw in the garage standing in front of me. With the full weight of his body he lunged at me with a knife, pressing it against my throat. He pushed me up against the wall and demanded, "Keep walking and don't scream." He reeked of smoke. I stumbled as he shoved me forward with the weight of my overnight bag pulling at my arm. The knife dug deeper into my neck. I felt faint. *"Am I going to die? Will anyone know where I am?"* We were about two rooms away from Room 6022.

Frozen with fear, I tried to scream, but nothing came out. Trying to keep my balance as he continued to push me, I finally begged in a whisper, "Please, don't." I could hardly breathe.

"Keep walking and don't scream," he ordered as he pressed the knife deeper against my skin.

At that moment, down the hall, we could hear the elevator bell ring and the doors open. We both looked in the direction of the elevator and as he looked back at me with panic in his eyes, he relaxed his hold ever so slightly. It was my only chance, I pushed him away. He ran toward the steps away from the elevator. I ran toward the elevator but there was no one there. The doors shut. Too afraid to wait in the hall for the elevator to return and fearing he might come back, I ran back toward the room. With my hands shaking, I put the key in, opened the door and locked it behind me.

Trembling, I sat on the bed realizing how close I had just come to being raped or killed. I burrowed under the covers. I pulled my knees to my chest and curled up into a little ball crying. It was only then I saw the blood on the pillow. I felt my neck and to my relief it was just a small cut. It must have happened when I pushed him to run away.

It was almost as if time had stopped. I just laid there, thinking of nothing else. I lost all sense of my surroundings. I kept replaying the moment in the hallway. There was a knock at the door. I jumped! My heart was pounding! I took in a quick gasp of air. It was almost as if I forgot Jeff was coming.

Terrified, I ran to the door and looked through the peephole to find him standing there.

Opening the door, I began sobbing and told him what happened.

"Calm down. Are you okay? Did he do anything?"

"No, but Jeff, I was so scared. I thought he was going to kill me! He had a knife to my throat!"

"But you're okay?"

"Well, yes, but he could have killed me!"

He hugged me and I said, "I can't stop thinking about it! I'm so afraid."

"There is nothing to be afraid of. He's probably long gone by now."

I was still shaking.

"Let's just sit on the bed until you can calm down and then we can order some dinner and you'll feel better."

"I don't know."

"Come on, in a little bit, after you have had some time to calm down, you'll feel better."

I did feel better; Jeff was there with me.

"What would you like from room service?"

Then he began to kiss my neck.

"Feel better?"

Not wanting to ruin Jeff's evening, I lied.

"Yes."

I jumped; another knock at the door. Even though I was still shaken and afraid, I knew he expected me to answer the door. I always had to answer the door.

"I don't want to answer it."

"Sandy, it's room service! You have got to calm down. Now answer the door."

I began to cry again, I just looked at him and shook my head.

"I can't."

Clearly frustrated with my reaction, he finally answered the door.

After dinner I was still shaken, but feeling better. I was hoping he would understand I wouldn't want to have sex with him. I just wanted him to sit and hold me. My needs didn't matter. We had sex. I had to pretend I was okay.

It was 11:00 P.M. Time to leave. Jeff left first which meant I had to walk through the garage and to my car, alone. In the dark basement parking lot, I kept telling myself, *"It will be okay, just keep walking. Get in your car as fast as you can."* I was terrified my attacker would be waiting for me behind my car. Instead, I found a note left on my windshield, "You're a lucky bitch." Trembling, I jumped in my car, locked the doors, and drove home. Years later someone asked whether I thought Jeff actually cared for me in some way. I thought of my terror walking to my car the night I was attacked and his selfish, uncaring attitude, and knew he didn't.

Jeff, consistently worried the two of us would be caught, put forth a new routine. First, he found a small, low-budget motel about forty minutes north of Cincinnati which became our designated meeting place. Second, we only met during the day. This new routine minimized our need to communicate. When I went through the receiving line after the Sunday services at church, he would simply say, "Tuesday four o'clock." To anyone watching, it was a smile and a handshake. I was no different than any other parishioner.

I may have been a parishioner but by now I was primarily his prostitute.

He was no longer my minister, but my molester. He would only be in the room for an hour and was certain to criticize me; primarily my looks. He thought I was too fat, even at 118 pounds. I tried harder and harder to please him, dieting constantly and trying to look nice. Heaven forbid if I ever laughed too hard in front of him. He also made me feel intellectually inferior. He told me every week I was to learn a new vocabulary word. He expected me to show it to him and my understanding of the definition, which of course, I did. It was just another way to control me, to make me feel inadequate, and to convince me this act was all to "help" me. I had given up everything for him and all I wanted was his approval.

It had been four years since the first kiss after the YAC meeting. I lost all faith there could ever be anyone else in my life besides Jeff Coulier. I felt obligated to stay with him. I had become totally submissive to him. He was all I had and all I had really known. If this was going be my life, and I could see no other way then I needed to accept my fate for what it was. My shame and guilt were gone. I had now given up.

I never again made any attempt to leave him. Now I didn't know how. My world became darker and darker. I was in a deep black hole with no way to get out. I had finally bought into his lies and his lies became my reality. His biggest lie: he was the only one who could love me and because I was no longer a virgin, no one else would want me.

He needed me in his ministry and was always reminding me in God's eyes we were married. To convince him I believed this, and I did, I bought him a gold wedding band. To my surprise he wore it, telling Nancy it symbolized his commitment to *their marriage*. He was wearing it the day he preached the sermon on marriage.

> *"When the amount of pain associated with a situation is too much to bear, we numb-out emotionally. Delusion is one of the main components in the learned powerlessness of the victim...it is a warp in the thinking process that filters out or twists information coming in from the outside. It is probably the most significant factor in keeping a victim trapped in an abusive situation."* —DAVID JOHNSON AND JEFF VAN VONDEREN, *THE SUBTLE POWER OF SPIRITUAL ABUSE*

I had very little social life outside of church, and even my church life began to fall away. Eventually, I stopped singing in the choir. I stopped teaching Sunday school. I stopped reading my Bible. Between work and school, my days were busy, but my slow withdrawal from church had begun.

Looking back, one might wonder where my parents were through all of this. He first kissed me at sixteen and another year passed before he began using me for sex. When the abuse first started, there was no reason for anyone to suspect anything was askew in my life. I was dating a little bit, hanging out with my friends and active at school. I was happy at church. The most abusive time occurred after I turned eighteen and was going to college, a time when parents, especially mine, let go of the apron strings. Terms like "helicopter parents" did not exist. Many parents at that time mostly worried about drug use or their daughters becoming pregnant. My involvement in the church and not having a steady boyfriend alleviated those fears for my parents.

It may have appeared Mom and Chuck weren't aware to what was going on in my life. Actually, they were very much aware of where I was and what I was doing. *I was in church*. There would be no reason for them to be worried or concerned. Most mornings Mom could find me in my room doing my morning devotions. My time was spent at church or school, and when Mom did become concerned about my change of behavior, who did she turn to—her pastor, the very person sexually abusing her daughter.

Perhaps I should have gone to my mom for help, but in my confusion, loyalty to Jeff, fear of being exposed, and fear of being judged, I kept silent. Even still, would she believe me? As Jeff was always quick to remind me, no one would. It was easier to pretend everything was okay, and I had so convinced my parents I was fine. Sexual abuse wasn't discussed. Sure, there was the stranger lurking in the shadows, but no one discussed sexual abuse within the family and certainly no one would ever suspect the pastor of the church.

I had submitted to Jeff and accepted my fate. By doing so, there was less arguing. We had fallen into a comfortable pattern of daytime sex in a motel room. As the relationship continued, the sexual behavior became more deviant. Although I was blind to this, what little affection there had been in the beginning was now nearly nonexistent. I was convinced he loved me and I needed to love him back by obeying him. I led him to believe I was happy because it allowed for less stress with him. I had resigned myself to this life. I still understood leaving him meant leaving my church. I could not risk that. The ability to think clearly and trust my own judgment was all but gone.

Victims of sexual abuse say pornography is often a part of the abuse. Jeff never showed an interest in pornography, but he grew obsessed with the idea of watching me have sex with someone else or participating in group sex. He would mention it and talk about it, but that's all it was for a while; just talk.

The one area he showed complete trust in me was as a confidante about church members who had come to him for counseling, breaching the trust they too had given to him. More often than not, the counseling was about marital problems involving their sex lives. Jeff broke their confidences and told me what they had told him. He would also confide in me about other activities which happened in his office. He bragged about the women in the church whom he had kissed and touched and how easy it was. He then would tell me these moments in his office didn't mean anything and how he loved only me. Always looking to please Jeff, my response was, "As long as you love me and I am the only one you love, it's okay. I don't care."

There were several women whom he seduced. Some I knew at the time because he told me. Others I learned about later. It was also during this time, I first learned I was not his first teenage victim. He told me about the accusations made by a young woman in his first church in Tifton, Georgia. He delighted in telling me, to show me what power he had and how he had escaped punishment. She exposed him, and he suffered no consequences.

Just after he arrived in Cincinnati in June of 1971, the girl went to the senior minister of his first church in Tifton where Jeff was the youth pastor; a man named Ron Williams. She accused Jeff of sexual misconduct. Jeff did not give me details, but Ron Williams believed her and flew to Cincinnati. He, along with the elders from Walnut Branch and our senior minister at the time, Ben Wilson, confronted him.

Jeff told me he asked for their forgiveness. He said it was a mistake and promised never to do anything like that again. I remember Jeff said he was angry with Ron Williams because Ron wasn't so willing to forgive him. Smiling, Jeff told me, "Finally, Ron agreed to let the matter drop if I told Nancy." Surprised, I asked, "What did Nancy say?" He responded with a smirk, "I never told her."

"Did anything ever happen?"

"No."

He had created a safety net by skillfully manipulating and lying to those around him.

The elders at Walnut Branch decided to keep this information quiet. The congregation was not informed and Jeff was permitted to continue as our youth pastor. Less than six months later, in my hallway, he seduced me. I suspected there may have been others and not only because he was so cavalier with his actions with the women at Walnut Branch. There was one teenager from his first church youth group in Tifton he talked about frequently and often compared me to her. She made several visits to Cincinnati, along with other kids from Tifton. I noticed how he paid more attention to her. She was obviously special to him. I asked him once if there was ever anything between them. He said, "No."

"Not even a kiss?"

"No."

I didn't believe him.

His confessions and ideas sickened me. One day he told me, "You are never going to believe who is having an affair and divorcing his wife." It was a deacon from a nearby church. He and Jeff had worked together on a city-wide project for the homeless. This deacon had also been one of my camp counselors. While the information shocked me, little did I know how this turn of events would shake up my life. He and this deacon now had something in common and Jeff felt safe enough to boast of his conquest with me. The two of them became best friends. Jeff now had someone to talk to about us. Still, I was to remain silent.

Soon Jeff and I would meet at the deacon's apartment with him and his girlfriend. I was twenty and they were all in their mid-thirties. One evening the talk of group sex was no longer just talk. The ordeal sickened me and much like the first time Jeff Coulier had sex with me, I blocked out what was happening. Keeping my eyes closed, I could at least avoid watching what was happening to me. Then I felt Jeff leave the bed. Unable to perform, he got dressed, and sat in a chair from across the room to watch. I hated myself even more as I allowed myself to be pulled into Jeff's sexual fantasy. It was so abhorrent to me; every scrap of self-worth was now gone. He had dominated me, dehumanized me, and finally exhausted me. I had no fight left. I was sick to my stomach and even now I am sickened by the thought.

His next request paled in comparison so I didn't flinch when he asked to take pictures of me nude. I assumed we would be alone and the photos would be just for him. When I went to the ex-deacon's apartment, I was surprised to see Jeff was not there. He had asked this friend to take the pictures. Undressing and posing barely bothered me; it didn't matter, I had become a robot to Jeff's demands. Afterwards, Jeff gave the pictures to the ex-deacon, for safe keeping. I believed I was worthless and I could sink no lower. I deserved to be treated this way. I was unable to see a way out.

I was trapped.

Trapped by the perception of the reality he had created.

Trapped by his lies.

Trapped by my hopelessness and lack of power.
Trapped.

"Trapped—A confining or undesirable circumstance from which escape or relief is difficult or appears to be impossible."

—MERRIAM-WEBSTER DICTIONARY

LEXINGTON

Jeff told me he had a conference in Lexington, Kentucky on December 8, 1975, and he would be spending the night there. I could meet him there and we could spend a full night together at the Holiday Inn. It was such a rare opportunity. Trained to be cautious, I was pretty sure he would not want our cars in the same lot. I asked him, "Where should I park my car?" To my surprise, he figured since we were not in Cincinnati, it didn't matter.

I arrived about 7:30 P.M. We ordered room service and spent the evening talking and watching TV, eventually having sex. He apologized for not being able to take me out to dinner. He had considered it since we were not in Cincinnati but couldn't risk it. I told him I understood. I was just happy to be there. He was relaxed and in a good mood. At around 6:30 in the morning, I was startled by the ringing phone.

He answered and I heard him say, "Okay." "No. Don't do that." He listened. "Okay. I'll be right down."

I knew before he said the words,

"Two people from the church are here."

"They know I'm with you?" I asked, already knowing the answer.

"Yes, they saw your car in the parking lot. Wait here."

He got dressed to go to the lobby where they were waiting.

Every possible scenario went through my mind. What would they do? Would they want to come up to the room to confront me? Could I go out the window? After all, we were only on the second floor. In agony and fear, I just waited. My heart was pounding. I got dressed and waited and waited. After what seemed like hours, he came back to the room. "I am going back with them."

"What's going to happen?"

"I don't know. Don't do anything or say anything to anybody."

He left and I waited to give them enough time to get on the road. Two long days passed and I heard nothing from him. I was going crazy and realized I was powerless. All I could do was wait until I was told what to do. We were about to be exposed.

The elders, the governing body of Walnut Branch, were informed about the parishioner's discovery in Lexington and they would decide what would happen next. Jeff's wife, Nancy, and a few of the people at the church had suspicions about us. It was obvious to me the goal of the elders was to protect Jeff and Nancy, his job, and the reputation of the church. Even though he was caught, his behavior was to remain a secret. No one else would be told.

I was instructed by the elders, through two women in the church, what I was to do. Donna was a Sunday school teacher in her mid-thirties and was married with two small children. She and Jeff worked together on Sunday school curriculum and various church programs. Mrs. Graves was an older woman who had been widowed a few years earlier and since then she had taken it upon herself to be the designated "church lady." She seemed to be everywhere making sure things were done with proper decorum. With her silver-grey hair pulled tightly in a bun, and stern mannerism, one look from Mrs. Graves told you to straighten up. Gum chewing or whispering in church by any of us could almost guarantee an admonishment after the service. I was always a little afraid of her. These two women were now in charge of me. I was told where to sit in church and how I was to act. I was told not to tell anyone, including my parents. All this was an effort to keep as few people as possible from learning the truth.

The All-Youth Christmas Banquet was scheduled for December 13 at the church, just five days after the night in Lexington. I was part of the planning committee and in charge of special guests. We had a couple people coming in from out of town to speak and provide the music. One guest was from Jeff's former church in Tifton, and I needed to pick her up from the airport. I knew some of the conversation with her would eventually center around talking about Jeff and what wonderful things Jeff had done for the church. I went to Mrs. Graves and told her I didn't think I could continue to help with the Christmas Banquet, much less pick Diane up at the airport and pretend as if nothing was wrong. It was just too much to ask. Couldn't she please find someone else?

"Sandy!" Clapping her hands quickly together as if I were a trained animal to get my attention, she looked at me and with her all too familiar stern voice and said, "There can be no change of plans to raise any questions. We must protect Jeff and Nancy."

Oddly, as she took my hand, she was both warning me and encouraging me at the same time. "You must do this! You can do this!" So, I did as I was told, in a near catatonic state, pretending nothing was wrong. Over the next few weeks I heard the same phrase over and over again, "We must protect Jeff and Nancy." And it's exactly what everyone did.

In spite of the intended cover up by the elders, word spread. I can only assume the elders told their wives and they told someone and so on. Church gossip was filled with land mines as the rumors began flying. Who would find out next? Phone calls and letters filled my life. My phone rang, "Sandy, I heard something I can hardly believe is true." "Is it true what I heard?" Letters came to the house, a few forgiving me, others asking what they could do to help, but the majority were hateful, blaming me.

As soon as I learned someone new had discovered the truth, I was instructed to let the elders know and they would handle it. I was to talk to no one, and remain silent. While Jeff and Nancy met with the elders, I was never called to talk to them or tell my side of the story. No one asked me any questions and I had no idea what Jeff had told them other than one thing: he told them he never forced me to do anything and it was all voluntary.

Unexpectedly, Jeff called. Surprisingly calm, he asked me, "How are you doing?"

"I'm worried Jeff, what's going to happen?"

"I don't know, it's really out of my hands. But I do need you to do one thing. If anyone asks, tell them we have only been seeing each other for a year." I didn't question this, even though it had been four years. I had been trained to follow his instructions.

There were a couple reasons for his request. One, he didn't want my true age to be revealed. If he told everyone it has been just a year, my age would be closer to twenty when it started, not sixteen. But more than that, he knew he had a better chance of being forgiven if he could say his indiscretion was a lapse in judgment. The argument would be more difficult if it had continued over *four years*. I also knew he did not want them to know that virtually his entire ministry while at Walnut Branch was a lie. He had fooled them all for four years. For four years he stood at the pulpit preaching God's word, preaching about the sanctity of marriage, counseling them on their own broken marriages, all the while committing adultery.

Putting out the fires of gossip and rumors was as futile as putting out a wildfire with a garden hose. Just about the time it seemed contained, someone new heard. In an attempt to quell the rumors, only the elders were to respond to questions. They did not want me to talk to anyone, fearful of what I might say, perhaps fearful I might contradict Jeff's version of the situation. By keeping me silent, they controlled the narrative.

Three weeks went by. I began to worry someone would tell my mom. I had to tell Mom and Chuck before anyone else would. As difficult as it would be to tell them, I didn't want them to hear it from someone else. The elders would not support my request to tell them; their main concern was to protect Jeff and keep as many people in the congregation as possible from learning the truth. Telling Mom and Chuck did not fit into their plan. Even if the elders had given their permission to tell Mom and Chuck, I did what I had for the past four years; I asked Jeff for his permission. Whatever I did, I didn't want to hurt him. I was told not to contact him, but I *had* to talk to him. It wasn't right to keep what was going on from Mom. I needed her to know.

As scared as I was to tell her, I needed her. I was beginning to crack under the pressure of keeping up the façade everything was okay. I couldn't call Jeff at his office so I called him at home. Fortunately, he answered the phone. Through my tears I babbled, "Jeff, don't be mad I called. I had to call. I know I am not supposed to tell anyone, but somebody is going to say something to my mom. I need to tell her. Too many people know already. I don't know what to do." I was distraught. "I don't know what is going to happen next. Are the elders going to ask me questions? What should I say?"

His response shocked me but comforted me. "Oh hell, come on over. The three of us can talk about this."

And so there the three of us sat: Jeff, Nancy, and me. I think Nancy was in as much of a state of confusion as me. Jeff had manipulated her and controlled her as he had done with me. Jeff was the calmest of the three. I think I told her I was sorry. I then asked again, "Jeff, is it okay if I tell my mom and Chuck? Please tell me it is okay to tell them."

"Could you just tell your mom? Does Chuck have to know?"

He had fooled my mother. She, like everyone else, in the church, adored him and therefore her response might not be as harsh. Chuck, as he might have guessed, would want to kill him.

"If I tell her, even if I ask her not to, she will tell him. It would be better to tell them both at the same time."

Resigned, he said, "At this point what does it matter?"

I didn't stay long and as awkward as it was, I felt there was this bond between us. We were all at the mercy of the elders in some way. What would they do? How can we all get out of this without it all blowing up in our faces? I was worried about how embarrassing this would be. How would people feel about me? Nancy was trying to save her marriage and Jeff was trying to save his job or find a new one. No decision had been made by the elders on the status of his ministry. The elders were divided as to whether he should stay or move to a church in Queensgate, Tennessee. Some still hoped they could find a way for him to remain at Walnut Branch.

I went home that night and confessed to Mom and Chuck. "Jeff may be leaving the church and part of the reason is that he and I have been having an affair."

Then I waited. Chuck was enraged; angry at me and Jeff. Mom and I both tried to calm him down. "How long has this been going on?"

Just as I had been instructed by Jeff, I replied, "A year."

"Are you pregnant?" asked Chuck.

"No."

"I am going over there and talk to him!" he said.

"Please don't! I am as much to blame as he is!"

He stood up and said, "He should be shot for what he has done."

I looked at Mom, begging her not to do anything while trying to calm Chuck down. I could see the struggle in Mom's face. What should she do? Dealing with a crisis, and this was a big one, was not in her makeup. Chuck's face showed anger and rage. Mom remained silent as he ranted on about losing trust in me and how could I let this happen. "You had an affair with a married man! I have no respect for him and I am disappointed in you."

Hoping Mom would come to my rescue, but knowing she probably wouldn't, after all, her goal was always maintaining peace, I sat there feeling judged, not loved. I couldn't help but think, here was this man judging me for something to which he too had been guilty. I shot back with the words and only defense I knew, "You two did the same thing!" I wish I could take back the hurt those words caused Mom. It was the first time we both acknowledged what she had hoped I never knew, and now I had shifted the shame to her.

Silence.

Chuck got up and left the room.

Mom asked what would happen next.

I responded the only way I knew how, "I don't know. I'm sorry. Please don't do anything or say anything to anybody." Mom wanted to let it end and move on. She did not know of the previous accusation of sexual misconduct in Jeff's former church, or that his sexual advances really began when I was just sixteen. She did not grasp the gravity of the entire situation. She saw it as I described it, an affair. His charisma had reached her as well. She joined the church and she liked him. In her mind, he would be moved to the next church and that would end it, sparing me more embarrassment.

I called Jeff to tell him I didn't think Chuck or my mom would do anything. Jeff called Mom the next day. He apologized and told her how much he cared for me and he never intended to hurt me, and how wonderful I was. He said all the right things. He was going to work on his marriage; he knows he was wrong. He asked for her forgiveness. It was all a lie.

A week after telling Mom and Chuck, and a month after Lexington, the elders voted to move Jeff to Queensgate, although the vote was not unanimous. It was decided he would move in March of 1976, three months after the night in Lexington. The next few months were a blur.

In spite of the effort by church leadership to conceal and cover up his actions, the rumor mill was in overdrive.

Almost as difficult as telling Mom and Chuck, was telling my friend, Teri. I didn't want her to hear it from someone else. I knew she looked up to me, and now I was going to reveal who I really was. I cherished her and depended upon her friendship. This revelation could very well destroy all of that. I wanted to tell her when there would be no one around. We met at the park. Sitting at one of the picnic tables, I looked at her and wished I could spare her the pain and shock. Just like most everyone else, she loved and idolized Jeff. She was upset he was leaving and now she would learn the reason—because of me. How angry would she be at me? Her response could be anything from sadness to rage. I couldn't predict.

I wanted to look away when I told her, but I steeled myself and forced myself to look at her. As much as I wanted to fall apart and sob into her arms as my friend, I wanted to be strong for her. I needed to be able to support her after hearing what I was about to tell her. With tears beginning to well up in my eyes I said, "Part of the reason Jeff is leaving the church is because he and I have been having an affair."

Her eyes widened; her mouth dropped open. Almost in a whisper, in disbelief she said, "You and Jeff?"

I waited. "I'm so sorry Teri," was all I could think to say. Asking me how long it had been going on, I once again lied and followed Jeff's instructions, "A year." Still wanting to protect him I said, "Please don't blame Jeff."

I told her I was being told by the elders what I was to do or say and the important thing was to move Jeff and his family to the next church as quickly as possible. I explained those who knew were very angry at me.

"Are you okay? What's going to happen to you?" There it was. My friend was showing concern for me. She didn't blame me or hate me. Relief filled me as I felt only love and concern in her words. Words I didn't deserve, but words I was ever so grateful to hear. In the following weeks and even months, I leaned on Teri for support.

Unlike the first accusation made against Jeff Coulier by the young woman in Tifton, this one could not remain hidden. Finally, it was decided by the elders Jeff would have to address the congregation. Coached by Donna and Mrs. Graves, I was told not to react and to sit quietly as Jeff made his confession. I had no idea what he would say. On a Sunday morning, without giving any details he stood before the congregation and said, "I have sinned against God. I have sinned against my wife. I am just a man with faults and I ask your forgiveness." That was it. That was his confession.

Two days later he called me to meet him in a hotel room and I did. I was in a complete state of confusion, unable to think clearly or function. Jeff tried to reassure me everything would be okay. He said he still loved me and when things settled down, nothing would change.

"But you won't be here anymore! You will be in Queensgate, Tennessee."

I was emotionally chained to him. I could not envision my life without him. He had been my world for four years and now I was consumed with shame. He could leave and start over. What would I do? I would stay in Cincinnati and face the consequences. I had to face the judgement, the embarrassment, and the humiliation. He could leave and start over. He would be welcomed by a new congregation leaving his past behind.

Jeff Coulier continued in his role as the pastor of the church for the next three months until he departed in March of 1976, preaching every Sunday and performing his duties as our church pastor. In spite of the fact this was now a second act of sexual misconduct committed by Jeff Coulier of which the elders were aware, there was still a discussion among the elders about trying to keep him. I learned later one elder pounded his fist on the table and said, "NO! He has to go." Years later, at the funeral of a mutual friend in 2010, I happened to see the elder. He took my hand and said "I want you to know we didn't do right by you." His words touched me far more than he would ever know.

Throughout this ordeal many in the congregation took sides, mostly Jeff's. Many were angry and upset he was leaving. Many saw me as this young, sexy, girl who had chased him and blamed me for what happened. It was easy to see why he was "tempted." Jeff had been right all along. "If anyone ever finds out, you will be responsible for what will happen." It was easy to tell who knew, who didn't know, and whose side they were on. Even more shocking to me was several men in the church sought sex with me after learning what he had done. They saw me as an easy target. Their actions reinforced my shattered self-image of being worthless except for sex. I was damaged goods, beyond repair.

I wasn't the only victim of Jeff's predatory ways. The congregation suffered as well. It divided the church. The pain and hurt caused by his actions took years to heal. Good, honest people trusted this man and believed in him and they too were forced to reconcile the man they thought they knew with the knowledge he had sinned and "fallen." The majority, if not all, saw it as an affair, not sexual abuse, sexual misconduct, or a violation of his position. As expressed to me, "I can understand how it could happen. You are pretty, with this outgoing personality, and he is this dynamic pastor and the opportunity presented itself and the two of you fell in love."

Many were willing to forgive him, especially if his wife could do so. He confessed his sin before the congregation and the Bible teaches forgiveness; he who is without sin, cast the first stone, we have all sinned and fallen short of the glory of God. In spite of this egregious sin, they still loved him. He was the pastor who held their hand at their mother's bedside when she was dying. He was there when their son overdosed. He performed their wedding ceremonies, counseled them when those same marriages were falling apart, he baptized their children and lifted them up spiritually every Sunday morning. They did not want to lose him. Being the master manipulator, he was a wolf easily disguised in sheep's clothing.

In the minds of the congregation, this one error in judgment should not negate all the good he had done. Walnut Branch Church was growing and vibrant and it was because of what Jeff had accomplished. He had created an atmosphere in the church no one wanted to lose. Now they would lose this dynamic leader which meant the church would lose members and income. Whether it was my age at sixteen when he first kissed me, his history of abusing a teen in Tifton, or the nature of his abuse, the church did not have all the facts. Their response was based on erroneous information. Later, I would come to learn and understand more often than not, churches will support and defend the offending pastor. They are too embarrassed to publicly acknowledge sexual sin for fear of harming the church.

It is often said, the cover-up is worse than the crime. Certainly more harm is done by the cover-up, not only to the church and the victim, but also to the pastor and his family. Parishioners don't want to believe their pastor is capable of such sinful behavior. I wish I could say church response has dramatically changed since those horrible days in the 1970's. Sadly, in my experience and the experience of many others, it has not.

"Perpetrators of abuse do not just groom a victim. They groom the entire family and church community. They make sure they are well trusted, well liked, charming, appreciated, and indispensable. As a result, anyone who accuses or alleges any kind of inappropriate behavior is the person who looks like they're the crazy one, because everybody loves the perpetrator."

—SARAH MCDUGAL

WHO SAID IT WAS OVER?

The following letter was sent to every member of Walnut Branch Christian Church, including me:

Dear Members and Friends of Walnut Branch,

Jeff and Nancy's decision to accept a ministry in Tennessee has caused us to look at the past, to plan for the present, and to build for the future.

Looking at the past for just a moment, we see a young minister coming to Walnut Branch in June 1971. A countless number of young people were brought into the church program. Many responded and the Lord added them to His church. Many parents will always be grateful for Jeff's influence on their children. We see a youth minister stepping into the senior ministry in July 1973. Jeff's inspiring and challenging sermons will long be remembered because of the impact they have made in our lives. His tender pastoral care has endeared him to many. We see Nancy singing in the choir and frequently blessing us through a solo such as "He touched Me." We also see Nancy as a supportive wife and busy mother, tending three small boys.

The past causes us to plan for the present—NOW. Next Wednesday, March 3, 1976, our regular evening supper program will be dismissed. You are invited to a reception and program for the Couliers in the Fellowship Hall at 7:00 P.M. If you wish to contribute a farewell gift, please send a check immediately or give to Ed Hahn or Milton Crane by Sunday February 29.

While the present closes one door in Walnut Branch's history, it opens another for us to step through as a congregation. Tomorrow and the day after, we still see Jesus adding to His church those who respond to the Gospel we preach and live.

It was signed by Ed Hahn, Chairman of the Elders, and Milton Crane, Chairman of the Board.

After almost five years in my life, Jeff was gone. He was sent on his way with a going away party, on his way to his next church, and his next victim, in Queensgate, Tennessee.

There were a few people in the church who supported me once they learned about his relationship with me. I will be forever grateful to them. Two couples in particular were my youth group leaders, Dick and Linda and Carol and Vince. Not only did they not blame me, as so many in the congregation did, they had a genuine anger for what he had done. With good intentions, some told me they "forgave me." Kind ones would ask how I felt and if I was okay since the relationship was over. The first time someone asked the question I was genuinely puzzled.

Over?

It wasn't over. "Who said it was over?" It wouldn't be over until Jeff Coulier said it was over. As far as Jeff was concerned, the only thing that changed between us was distance. He continued to call and write. He instructed me to get a P.O. Box so he could mail letters to me. Like the slave I had become, I continued to do what he said and waited for any word from him. When he demanded I make a trip to see him, not wanting me to be seen in Queensgate, he told me to book a room in Knoxville, just outside of Queensgate and wait for him to come to the room. Paying for the hotel room was one thing, but having enough money for the airfare was a hardship, even when I was working two jobs. I tried to explain I just didn't have the money. "If you cared enough, you would find a way." Not only was I not surprised by his response, I accepted it. I didn't know how to live without him. I clung to his authority over me, needing his control, and believing he needed me and loved me.

Susan Forward, PhD, uses the acronym "FOG" (fear, obligation and guilt) to help explain why victims are unable to think clearly and process what is happening to them and why they continue to stay in an abusive relationship.

"Fear" to cross their abuser for fear of the consequences.

"Obligation" to comply with his requests.

"Guilt" not to do so.

Jeff had been gone six months, and I had made two trips to visit him during those six months. To afford the second trip I used money given to me as a gift from my grandmother. She would have been horrified. It was after this trip, I got a call from Milton Crane, the head of Walnut Branch elders.

"Sandy, Mr. Hahn and I would like to meet with you."

"Okay."

"We want you to meet us in the Fellowship Hall tonight at 7:00 P.M."

"Okay, I will be there."

He gave no indication as to why they wanted to meet me, or suggest I might want to bring my parents or someone with me. I trusted them like I trusted any official in the church. I asked no questions. Mr. Crane was an older gentleman; old enough to be my grandfather. He was very well respected, not only at Walnut Branch, but throughout the Christian community. He had served on the board at Cincinnati Christian University, had published many articles in various Christian publications, and was an ordained minister. His daughter was one of my Sunday school teachers. Mr. Hahn was the father of one of my friends in the youth group. He was Chairman of the Elders. Mr. Crane was Chairman of the Board.

On the evening I was asked to meet at church, I pulled into the church parking lot to find only their two cars. Usually the church was a hub of activity, yet, this Tuesday evening it was strangely quiet and dark. Walking down the dimly lit hallway, approaching the Fellowship Hall, I couldn't help but think of the number of times I had been in the room over the years.

As I entered the hall, both men were seated in two chairs with a third chair pulled over facing them, which obviously was meant for me. I remember Mr. Crane had his Bible in his lap. Mr. Hahn stood up and asked me to have a seat. It wasn't until that moment I felt nervous and a bit concerned I was in this room alone with these two men. I wondered what they wanted to discuss.

Nothing could have prepared me for the words I was about to hear. Without hesitation and with the voice of a scolding father, Mr. Hahn looked at me and said, "We know you have been to see Jeff and you are to leave this church."

Stunned, I just sat there for a moment until the words sunk in.

You are to leave this church.

I put my hand over my mouth to stifle my crying.

You are to leave this church. You are to leave this church. You are to leave this church.

Those words are all I kept hearing over and over in my mind.

This church was not just any church; it was MY church and now I was being told I had to leave?

How did they know I had been to see him?

You are to leave this church.

Where would I go? What would I do?

You are to leave this church.

I loved this church. It was my whole life.

You are to leave this church.

It was the only church I knew and now I was being told to leave.

You are to leave this church.

I was sick to my stomach. I was scared.

They continued to talk but all I could hear were their words repeating over and over in my head.

You are to leave this church.

I sat there alone in this room with these two men who now decided I was no longer fit to worship in MY church. These were not just any men. They were the elders.

They had talked to Jeff. He told them I came without his knowledge and he refused to see me. They believed him and never asked for my side of the story. They offered me no support or counsel; they just told me to leave. Without another word said between us, I got up and walked out of the room into the darkened hallway.

I wanted to run as fast as I could out of the church. I was evil and I wanted to flee the evil in me and all that happened in this church. Feeling lost and alone, I went home and cried myself to sleep. I had deserted God and this was my punishment. I wanted to pray, but God was not there.

The next morning, I called Jeff at his office, "Hello?"

Sobbing I responded, "Oh Jeff! They have kicked me out of the church! What am I going to do? Mr. Hahn and Mr. Crane told me I had to leave! They know I came to visit you and now they told me I can never go back to the church again!"

"Sandy, someone from the church saw you get off the Knoxville flight. You understand when the elders called me and questioned me, I had to tell them you visited me without my knowledge and I refused to see you. You understand, don't you? I had to tell them."

He talked to them? He talked to them and he didn't warn me? I wondered why, after lying to them about the visit to him, he did not call me. I was too upset to ask him and nearly hysterical by now. I said, "But Jeff, I can **never** go back. I don't have a church!"

I will never forget his response, and the cold unfeeling way in which he said it. "Sandy, you don't need those people."

"But Jeff..."

"You will be okay. You don't need them or Walnut Branch Church."

"But Jeff, Walnut Branch was my whole life."

"I need to know you will be okay."

I didn't know how to respond.

He repeated, "Tell me you will be okay."

Despondently, I responded, "I will be okay."

The following Sunday, for the first time since attending with the Gardner twins, I had no church to attend. I told my mom I didn't feel well and eventually told her, without much of an explanation, I had decided not to go back to Walnut Branch. It would only make sense with what had happened over the last several months I would choose not to return. I suppose there were many who were shocked and surprised I didn't leave sooner.

Not only was the church the center of my life, I believed I could be forgiven. After all, he had been forgiven. While there were some who treated me with disdain and wished me nothing but pain for what I had done to Walnut Branch, there were those who loved me and supported me. They gave me hope. They gave me a reason to stay, but now I was forbidden to return.

I did return once shortly after being told to leave. It was for the funeral of a friend's dad. I was nervous and planned to quietly sneak in and sit in the back. Just before entering the sanctuary, I lost my nerve and turned to leave. I felt I was wearing "The Scarlet Letter." I then felt someone pull on my arm. It was Mr. Eger, a kind, wonderful, man known as Mr. Walnut Branch, a pillar of the church and community. He looked right at me and asked where I was going. Shamefully and looking down, I said, "I don't belong here."

"Oh yes, you do." He tucked my arm around his and together we walked up the aisle and sat in the second row. Everyone saw his actions. If there were going to be whispers, no one would dare now.

Maybe a new church would be better. A few weeks went by and I started attending Green Forest Presbyterian Church. It was a large, vibrant church and well known in the city. But it wasn't Walnut Branch. I struggled to make it feel like home. I inquired about the choir and attended Sunday school a couple times. I decided maybe I could talk to the pastor of this new church. Maybe in confidence I could tell him about the shame and hurt I lived with.

I hoped this new church might be able to help me. One day after the service, I found the courage to ask for help. I was a bit shaky and introduced myself to the pastor. I said I needed help and asked if he had time to meet with me.

"I know who you are and I am aware of your situation. Call the church office and if you want, set up an appointment." His response left me cold. I felt shut down, and felt he wanted to avoid involvement in my "affair" with my former pastor. I lost my nerve and never went back.

Later the same evening in a phone call to Jeff, I told him I tried to attend another church.

"Why would you do that?" He began mocking me and making fun of the fact I could somehow think I could ever join another church. He once again reminded me I didn't need a church. Maybe he was right. Church had lost its meaning and significance for me. After the shame, I felt I didn't deserve to be there. To cope, I shut down spiritually. God and church were no longer a part of my life. They had failed me and the security and joy I once felt were gone.

Looking back, I realize Jeff's statement regarding I didn't need a church was for his sake, not mine. From his perspective, it was better to keep me away from anyone who might help me unravel the web of his deception and reveal his secret. He not only wanted me away from Walnut Branch, but away from any church. Even from a distance he made every effort to keep me isolated.

Many nights I had nightmares of feeling abandoned, lost, and ashamed. Often, I was too scared to sleep and face the possibility of another nightmare. I would drive my Dodge Coronet around downtown in the middle of the night. Some nights I would stop at the Serpentine Wall along the Ohio River banks. I would sit alone, cry and stare into the dark murky waters of the Ohio River. When I was exhausted, I would return home and hope to sleep. I was in a spiral of deep depression. On a phone call, I mentioned to Jeff I had been to the Serpentine Wall the night before at 2:00 A.M. feeling worthless and lost. He responded by telling me not to do it again because if something were to happen to me, people would look to him to blame. How would he explain it? In a frustrated voice and losing patience with me, he said, "You *need to tell me* you will be okay."

I told him what he wanted to hear. "I'm okay."

He hung up.

The irony was I was beginning to be more okay without him. Now at age twenty-one, without him in my daily life, I could wear the clothes I wanted and style my hair the way I liked without his criticism. There were moments when I started to feel like me again, without his constant supervision and demands. As time went on, we talked on the phone less. I was surprised when I found myself relieved on the days he did not call. When he did call, like a trained animal, I again returned to being under his control.

"Traumatic events, by definition, overwhelm our ability to cope. When the mind becomes flooded with emotion, a circuit breaker is thrown that allows us to survive the experience fairly intact, that is without becoming psychotic or frying out one of the brain centers. The cost of this blown circuit is emotion frozen within the body. In other words, we often unconsciously stop feeling our trauma partway into it, like a movie that is going after the sound has been turned off. We cannot heal until we move fully through that trauma, including all the feelings of the events."

—SUSAN PEASE BANITT,
THE TRAUMA TOOL KIT: HEALING PSTD FROM THE INSIDE OUT

NUMBER 40

Nineteen seventy-seven was beginning. I no longer had a church home since being told almost six months earlier to leave Walnut Branch. Jeff was still in Tennessee, continuing to call and write letters admonishing me for not writing or visiting enough. However, day-to-day life was becoming easier with him three hundred miles away. At age twenty-two, I moved out of the house and had my own apartment. I could do as I liked, and I was living my life the way I wanted without facing his criticism. I started making new friends and having a social life. I learned to laugh again. I decided to pursue a degree in nursing. Slowly, I was beginning to find the real me again and peel away the layers of abuse which had buried my soul.

I dated a bit, but no one seemed right. I didn't think I was picky. One guy swore all the time, using four-letter words to describe just about every person, place, or thing. One guy was nice enough, but he was *too* nice. He bored me. Did he bore me or was it because I had been treated so poorly by Jeff Coulier maybe I didn't know how to allow myself to be treated with kindness and respect? From the time I was sixteen, when most girls were discovering who they were and growing into the person they were meant to be, I was being shaped and molded by what Jeff Coulier wanted me to be. Maybe he was right, no one else could love me the way he did. I would never want anyone else and no one would want me.

I started a new job in January 1977; a receptionist for a law firm in downtown Cincinnati. I hoped to save enough money to attend nursing school. This job was perfect for me. It allowed me to use the skills I felt natural doing: being friendly, helping others, and multi-tasking. My days consisted of greeting clients, running copies, taking coffee to the senior partner, and answering the phones. After work I would go out with some of the office assistants. For the first time, I was finding a life outside of Jeff Coulier.

Each attorney was assigned a number on the switchboard, 1 through 40. In the beginning, when I first started, learning the phone system and the name of each attorney, along with the other duties of the office, kept me busy. I can't say when I first remember meeting Number 40, but he caught my attention, and I took an immediate liking to him. He was tall and his thin build made him seem even taller. I thought he was attractive; not in a handsome way, but in a good-looking boyish way. He had a great smile. He was always friendly to me and was easy to talk to. Something about him made me want to get to know him better. I made every effort to find a reason to talk to him. I realized he often came to work around 8:00 A.M. I started to come in early hoping to catch him in the coffee breakroom. We often talked about what we had done the day before. We both liked baseball, so the Cincinnati Reds were a topic often shared. I learned a lot about him in the next few months; he had grown up in a small town in Indiana, loved golf and was close to his family. He didn't mention he was dating anyone, which I considered good news. It was even better news when one of the office assistants said she thought Number 40 liked me.

Whenever the senior partner, Mr. Lindhorst, requested I bring him coffee, I would ring Number 40 and ask if he would like some coffee too. His office was on my way and it was a great excuse to stop by and chat. Thankfully, Mr. Lindhorst liked to drink coffee! I hated the days when he was out of the office. No coffee runs.

In August, I gave my two-week resignation to the firm so I could attend nursing school. The only issue was leaving Number 40. I hoped he might ask me out before I left. So far there was no indication he would. Three days before I left, he asked me to have dinner the following Saturday at a small restaurant near my apartment. It was the first time in a long time I had a real date; not one orchestrated or dictated by Jeff. I had no idea if this one date would lead to anything; maybe not, but I was ecstatic about going out on Saturday.

And then on the Thursday before, the phone rang. As soon as I heard his voice, my heart sank. I was back to my reality with Jeff telling me what he wanted. "I want you to come down this weekend."

"I can't," I said.

"What do you mean you can't?" He asked almost incredulous.

"I just can't. I have plans."

"Break them."

In the past this is exactly what I would have done. In a weakened voice, barely audible, I said, "I just can't." *Oh, please don't make me come down this weekend.*

I really wanted to keep my date on Saturday, but I knew, just as I had done in the past, I would not be able to stand up to Jeff. His control remained. I had lost the power to think for myself.

Now he was clearly angry with me. His voice rose. "You can't or you WON'T?"

"Please Jeff. Don't ask me to come this weekend. I can come next weekend. I promise."

I was glad he was far away, so he couldn't glare at me or shove me like he often did. For a moment, I thought, nothing has changed. I will do what I have always done, do as he says and this chance of happiness too will be gone. Once again, any chance of my prince charming whisking me away would be taken from me.

He then said something to me he had never said before. "If you don't come down here this weekend, I will NEVER speak to you again."

For a moment I had to think, did he just say what I heard him say? Maybe he means it. If so, my nightmare would be over. NEVER?

As I sat there crying, I thought to myself, *"This is your out. If you don't say no to him now, you deserve whatever unhappiness comes. You don't deserve better. This is your last chance."* I took a deep breath, closed my eyes, and with all the strength I could muster said, almost in a whisper, "I can't."

He hung up the phone.

NOW it was over. I was relieved, yet still not sure. Could this really be the end? He did call me a week later and a few times after that, but it was over. On one call he informed me he had replaced me and, on another call, bragged about another sexual conquest at his church. Her name was Tara. As he put it, "I found my new Sandy" and even boasted about how much she looked like me. To convince me, he sent me her picture. I later learned from a friend who had contact with someone who was a member at his church in Queensgate, Tara became pregnant. Jeff's wife, Nancy, left him.

I didn't care. Number 40 and I had our date.

Two years later, in 1979, Number 40 and I were married. I was the luckiest woman in the world!

PART TWO
SURVIVOR

"Words left unsaid will sit inside your mind screaming."

—UNKNOWN

AFTERMATH

Marrying Bill was a dream come true. It may sound trite, but I knew firsthand what a bad relationship felt like. Bill was a great guy who I loved deeply and we had a bright future together. Our wedding took place at a large Methodist Church filled with family and friends. Vickie, Jackie, and Wendi served as my bridesmaid and junior bridesmaids. Tensions among Mom, Chuck, and Dad had lessened over the years. My fear of open animosity was unfounded. Dad beamed as he walked me down the aisle. The evening was all I had hoped it would be.

Shortly after we were married, Bill suggested we look for a house on the other side of town. I was elated because it was far from where I grew up. I would be unlikely to bump into someone from Walnut Branch, or see familiar landmarks which reminded me of my past. Taking Bill's surname, I had a new last name and we began our life in our bi-level suburban house.

To the outside world I lived a charmed life with a loving husband and eventually two great kids. That life was true, except for the shame and secret of my past which lived beneath the surface. I thought I should be free of Jeff Coulier, but I was not. Oftentimes, memories of him came into my life, an unwelcome intrusion. Something unexpected would remind me of those years, either a song on the radio or someone talking about their high school years. I learned to brace myself for the other memories I knew might be coming, such as when I would pass the downtown hotel where the knife attack occurred.

My response always had a tinge of panic. I would breathe deeply and push him out of my thoughts. Other times, I wanted to break down and cry. My main goal was to keep control during the moments when his sickening presence crept into my new life. I did not know how to stop the intrusions. I just allowed myself to be caught in the past until the nauseating feeling left me; until the next time I was forced to think about him. During these moments, it was as if he was controlling me once again.

As the years went on, this coping mechanism became my norm and a bit easier at times. I didn't know how to face this demon of intrusion, so I accepted it. It was my life and it was working; no one would have any idea of my hidden abuse. Most importantly, I believed I had to hide this from Bill. My irrational thinking led me to believe my secret past might alter my relationship with Bill and the joy of my current life. I continued to fear the consequences of telling anyone; even my loving husband, my secret.

Victims of abuse learn early on how to become Academy-Award winning actresses when it comes to hiding the abuse. I became the Miss Sunshine people once loved at Walnut Branch. I had always been outgoing and upbeat, so it wasn't hard to be positive and make friends. I'd learned to wear my "I'm OK" façade, displaying a person who was absolutely normal. I wore my façade years earlier when classmates learned Mom's last name was different from mine. Just as I hid the shame about my parent's divorce, I could hide the shame about Jeff Coulier and being rejected from church. None of my neighbors or new friends knew anything about the past life of Sandy Kirkham. I was now living the life I had always hoped to live.

My only worry in life was someone might learn of my past.

When we were first married, Bill worked with the law firm downtown and I was a nurse at Children's Hospital. Until we had children of our own, I would bring patients who didn't have parents or family home to celebrate Christmas and other special holidays. Bill would roll his eyes and tease me about my compassion, but I knew he didn't mind.

Within two years, I was pregnant. Tragically, Mom was diagnosed with cancer. She was only forty-seven and it was only a few months later when she died. I was twenty-six and six months pregnant with our first child. Grief overwhelmed me knowing she would miss so much of my life. I not only grieved for my loss, but for the loss my younger brother and sisters faced at such young ages. On all levels, I ached.

As we entered the church for Mom's funeral service, it felt like a double blow. In addition to the wrenching pain of losing her, was the fear and hurt of attending her funeral service at Walnut Branch. I couldn't imagine anyone would mention my removal from the church but I feared the whispers. While my focus was on the loss of my beautiful mom, I felt such shame because the memory of Jeff Coulier came alive when I entered the sanctuary. I clung to Bill's arm, looking at no one as we headed to the front pew.

Through the years, my life grew to contain a lot of wonderful possessions and joys: a son and daughter and all their activities, sports, PTA, a part-time job as a nurse, working on the house and spending time with Bill. I seemed drawn to organizational challenges and leadership positions, perhaps reflecting what I'd learned at YAC and youth group years earlier. I was PTA president and President of the Junior Women's Club. After moving into our second home, I helped organize the Homeowner's Association and served on its various committees. I recognized leadership often meant standing up for what was right. Sometimes this took considerable courage and determination. Bill often teased me about my bulldog ability to get things done and fight for the underdog; whether it was writing letters to the editor on a topic about which I felt passionate, addressing the school board on policy matters, arguing with a resident at the hospital about a patient's medication, or approaching a young man at McDonald's talking on his phone and using the F-word where children were present. I didn't shy away from confrontation when I believed it to be the right thing to do.

Spiritual reminders would always guarantee a reminder of Jeff Coulier, but an incident in my everyday life could also evoke a memory. At my son's 8th grade basketball game, I heard someone call my name, "Sandy?"

Mary? I had not seen her in years. Oh, please don't let it be Mary.

Mary had been my Sunday school teacher in 7th and 8th grade. Her family was involved at Walnut Branch. Even though she left for college just after Jeff Coulier arrived, I knew she had to know. Shame and fear consumed me. Would she reveal my secret? I wanted to hide. Gaining my composure, we exchanged pleasantries, and then I took a deep breath as if nothing had happened. I'd dodged another bullet.

One of my worst memories and the most difficult test was New Year's Eve 1985. Friends, all with kids under the age of seven, thought it might be fun to do something different to bring in the New Year. Busy with a one year old and a three year old, I wasn't involved in the planning to find an indoor pool and play area, which at the time were not very common. A friend, Sally, found a place about an hour and half from Cincinnati.

Pulling into the parking lot I felt horror. Why didn't I even think to ask where we were going? Bill slowly drove to the front door of the Holiday Inn in Lexington to unload the car. I wanted to grab his arm before he opened his door and tell him we had to go home.

I sat there for a moment. What do I do? I *can't* stay here.

"Mommy, can we go in now?"

With my hands shaking, I unbuckled my son's car seat and followed Bill into the lobby. I summoned every bit of my acting ability to conceal my horror. My usual coping mechanisms were failing me.

Don't think about that night.

Think of something else.

Tend to my kids.

Don't look around.

The lobby had been updated, but the front desk was still in the same place the night I met Jeff Coulier.

I told Bill to take the kids for a minute. I went straight to the ladies' room. I couldn't get there fast enough. I was about to explode in tears. Once inside, I grabbed the sink for support and leaned over it sobbing, watching my tears drip into the sink. I was sick with guilt for what I had done in this place. I had been caught having sex with the pastor here; the night "our" affair was exposed. Every memory of the night returned and I was living it all over again. Anger shot through me as I wanted to scream, *"WILL I NEVER BE FREE OF THIS MAN?"*

As much as I wanted to remain hidden, I didn't have the luxury. I had two little kids waiting for me, and a husband, who probably would have preferred New Year's Eve at home watching football games. Suck it up. Taking a wet paper towel, I wiped away my tears. I so wished I could also easily wipe away the memories too. Instead, I opened the door and walked back to the lobby.

Sally greeted me just outside the door. "Isn't this new Holidome great?" she said. "The kids are going to have so much fun."

"We all are," I said, trying to convince myself.

Later, sitting by the pool, we heard over the radio singer Rick Nelson had been killed in a plane crash. I will always remember the date of his death. I will never forget where I was when I heard it. During his lighthearted and humorous times, Jeff Coulier would often serenade parts of different songs to me. One of them was Rick Nelson's "When Fools Rush In."

With some warning, I learned to live with most reminders of my shame. Over the years we took many trips on I-75 through Lexington, passing the dreaded Holiday Inn, whether we were going to Florida or taking visits to Keeneland Race Track. These trips did not cause much anguish. I could once again brace myself, allow the memories to intrude remembering the terrible night from so long ago and successfully push them away. Anytime I went to downtown Cincinnati and saw The Quality Inn I'd recall the knife attack. Usually, I weathered the memories without breaking into a panic.

Unfortunately, some reminders remain inescapable. My 1972 high school year book falls into this category. Jeff Coulier was asked to give the baccalaureate address that year. His picture appears on page 142.

Years later, I still hadn't stopped loathing the person I had been when I with Jeff Coulier. I wanted no one else to know *the Sandy Kirkham I was then;* a woman who chose to have an affair with her pastor, where there was affection for one another. At least it is what I had believed for twenty-seven years. What I thought then was I had some say, some power in the situation. I did not recognize his behavior as an abuse of his position as a trusted minister, which meant I didn't have to face what he did to me; I did not realize I was used. Instead, I felt guilty for what I had done. I felt guilty for the secrets I told; first to protect Jeff Coulier and now to protect myself. *His* secret was now *my* secret. To reveal my secret about how I had an affair and was eventually kicked out of my church would reveal an ugliness I wanted no one to know, especially Bill. Even though I believed Bill would understand if he found out, I remained trapped by the fear of Jeff Coulier's words, "Don't ever tell." An abuser's words forever cripple logic and clear thinking until they are able to move forward.

Ironically, the secrets did not help me hide or forget my past. The secrets served as a reminder. Instead of forgetting Jeff Coulier, living with and keeping the secret forced me to store all the memories and recall them over and over each time they surfaced. With each reminder and each trigger, I had to control my response. The stress and the emotional breakdown were the result of these memories as well having to hide them. I was allowing my past, i.e. Jeff Coulier, to remain in my present. The act of keeping the secret itself became as much of a burden as the memories themselves. I wasn't controlling the secret; the secret was controlling me.

When my daughter turned sixteen, I looked at her and had a split-second thought: I was her age when he first kissed me. I was shocked at her innocence, her inexperience, and her young age. I thought about being sixteen and who I was at that age; a teen thrilled to have a church home where people loved me. Were an adult to kiss Beth at sixteen, I would never blame her for the situation. Yet somehow, I'd blamed myself for what he did to me.

Two years later, Beth was accepted to a college in North Carolina and was accepted to play on the school's varsity golf team. I was thrilled she was able to go to college in a new part of the country; a dream I once had for myself. Her departure meant Bill and I were now empty nesters, a time when the hectic pace of home life might slow down enough for me to concentrate on my own needs and the next chapter of my life. With trips to see Beth play golf and time for myself, I looked forward to the future. Little did I know then, my future would be interrupted on one of those trips and force me to face the truth about my past. That day on the side of the road in Queensgate, Tennessee, I was no longer able to control the memories.

"That which you choose to bury, you will always carry."

—UNKNOWN

SPIRITUAL WOUNDS

My life looked a lot like other suburban mothers in the 80's, with one exception. I struggled going to church, a place I once loved, but a place which now haunted me. I grew up with complete trust in pastors as the people who love and teach us and foster our connection to God. Ever since attending church with the Gardner twins, I believed church was a safe place, the home of a caring God. I made Walnut Branch my home. With my childhood homelife a bit chaotic and the absence of my father during my teenage years, the people there became my second family.

Jeff Coulier's abuse stripped away those beliefs. His abuse contaminated every part of my spiritual existence; a betrayal by the very person ordained to be my spiritual guide. This betrayal created disconnect between God and me. Even more, Walnut Branch's failure to protect me left me with a lifelong mistrust of any church. My soul had become an open wound; a deep sore which could never heal. It ached and kept me from trusting God and His church.

Once Bill and I were married, I foolishly believed I could go back to church and be the person I was before, as if nothing had happened. Of course, I could not return to the Christian/Church of Christ Church. As Bill was Methodist, we joined the Methodist Church. We attended regularly, but an uneasy feeling and sadness nagged at me when I was in church. Feeling comfortable would just take time, I thought. Years passed, but the comfortable, easy feeling never happened. The church had been contaminated for me by both Jeff Coulier and the church leaders. It wasn't just *what* they did, but *who* they were: my pastor and the leaders of the church; supposed protectors.

My own spiritual life was nonexistent. The Bible I once read daily in high school now sat on my bookshelf, never opened. Though I had no spiritual connection to the church, I took my kids almost every Sunday, even the times Bill did not attend. I made sure they were involved in confirmation class, bell choir, church retreats, and Vacation Bible School.

At four years old, my son proudly showed me a picture of David and Goliath he colored in Sunday school. "Mom, do you know about David and Goliath?"

I held his hand and together we headed away from his Sunday school class. I changed the topic, hoping to avoid any discussion. I didn't dare risk tears. Just discussing a simple story with my little boy was too much for my fragile soul.

Walking past a minister's office tied my stomach in knots. The trauma had nothing to do with that particular minister; it was just a harsh reminder. When I saw a closed office door at a church, the horrors of unwanted sex flashed through my mind. I never felt comfortable around pastors, and I knew I would never again allow myself to be alone with a pastor. On a rational level, I knew most pastors sincerely served God and were faithful to their calling, but I guarded myself from having any connection with them. Not surprisingly, I did not have this same reaction to female pastors.

The hardest aspect of being around church was hearing the words, "Let us pray." They are words spoken in every church, every Sunday. The scene is the same, with the pastor asking us to bow our heads and join in prayer. I'd bow my head though I would never close my eyes, and as he began to speak my "prayer" would begin. *"I need milk and not sure about bread but if I am going to Kroger anyway, I might as well get it while I am there. I can always freeze it. Do I have enough hamburger to make meatloaf?"*

Has he finished praying? No.

"So, what else do I need at the store? I don't want to spend too much time shopping. It will be a zoo on a Sunday. So, I'll just pick up the essentials and get home; done with my grocery list."

Talking; I still hear talking. He is still praying. Looking down at the shoes of the woman sitting next to me I'd notice how cute they are. *I wonder where she bought them.*

"Amen." He's done.

This was my desperate attempt to shut out the reminder of Jeff Coulier's prayers at Walnut Branch. I'd look up and the service would continue. For twenty-seven years this was how I prayed in church or anywhere else the words "Let us pray" were spoken. I could not pray to God.

Perhaps Jeff Coulier and other abusers may know of many of the physical sins they commit. I doubt Jeff realized his abuse left me unable to pray, in public, silently or even in the safety of my own home. The Book of Psalms says prayer is calling out to God. I wanted to call to God, but every time I tried, I felt numb.

My love for prayer as a teenager was in stark contrast to the absolute void of prayer in my adult years. At age fifteen, shortly before Jeff Coulier came to Walnut Branch in 1971, I learned about Conversational Prayer from a book written by Rosalind Rinker. It changed the way I considered prayer. Prayer was a daily conversation and I could just talk with God whenever I felt like it, about anything, anytime, all through my high school years. And talk I did. I no longer felt guilty for not finding enough time to sit and pray. I could pray walking down the halls at school. I didn't have to start my prayers with Dear God or Heavenly Father. I just started talking about anything. If I was interrupted, I could put God on hold. *"I'll get back to you in a minute God."* I wasn't interrupting a prayer; instead I had paused a conversation for a brief moment. Thessalonians 5:17 says, *"pray without ceasing."* How true this was in my life. Never in a million years would I have conceived then there would be a time I would ever be without prayer in my life. Jeff Coulier changed that. At this time, my prayers ceased.

My children never had a bedtime prayer with their mother. I just couldn't do it. After reading them a story, I tucked them into bed feeling guilty for not praying with them, saddened I was missing a special moment between a mother and her children.

Serving and giving back were incredibly important to me; after Jeff Coulier, as long as it was not for the church, I was always eager to volunteer. A friend of mine who was active at both church and school once asked with frustration, "Why don't you ever do anything for the church, you are always so active in everything else? The church needs your help too!"

"I guess because there are only so many hours in the day," I replied.

If she only knew.

How could something I used to love become so impossible now? Walking away, my eyes welled with tears, mourning the loss of my church life, knowing at the end of my life, I would not hear the words, "Well done, thy good and faithful servant."

After multiple requests, I finally agreed to teach Sunday school. It was 1986; my youngest was now two and I felt guilty for not doing more in the church. I missed being a part of the church and maybe it was time to try. Sadly, I found teaching the class to be a constant struggle and I couldn't wait to for the session to end. It only reminded me of the years at Walnut Branch. Just leading the kids in songs with the second graders reminded me of how he used to watch me in the back of the church as I led songs at Walnut Branch. Every Sunday brought a sense of nausea and renewed shame.

I returned to attending church services instead of teaching. One morning as we finished singing a hymn, the woman in the pew in front of me turned around and said, "You have a beautiful voice. Why aren't you singing in the choir?" Her comment took me back to the years when I sat next to my friend Cindy in the choir at Walnut Branch. It seemed like a lifetime ago. Sadness came over me knowing I could never get back what he had taken from me.

Even outside of the church, situations brought a massive spiritual ache. One of my favorite hobbies was scrapbooking. I made books about everything from my dachshunds to family history. Shopping was a favorite pastime. Shopping and scrapbooking can be a dangerous combination. There are thousands of stickers, colored papers and accessories for the diehard scrapbooker.

On this occasion I had a cartful of supplies at Hobby Lobby when the hymn "It is Well with My Soul" came through the loud speaker. I heard less than one stanza and tears filled my eyes. I gripped the shopping cart but knew this was more than just tears; the floodgates were opening and I was likely to sob out loud. I raced to the front door, head down. The car provided a welcome refuge for a soul who had been violated by a trusted clergyman. Despite the song's lyrics, it was *not* well with my soul. I left the cart in the store and went home empty handed.

For most people, church is a place of renewal, healing, and a place to be uplifted. It provides a sense of belonging, trust, and rituals connecting us to God and to each other. We cherish what those rituals represent. Communion, reciting the Lord's Prayer, and singing of the hymns were all tainted for me. Where do victims of clergy abuse turn? How do we seek help from the church when our pain is a direct result of the church, what it represents, and the horrible reminders of what happened there and the inability to trust again?

My soul had been ravaged by this wolf in sheep's clothing.

"Remembering a past situation can provoke a person to feel the exact emotion that was attached to that specific memory."

—THEPSYCHMIND.COM

REVELATIONS

For three months after my life-altering drive through Queensgate, Tennessee, I suffered alone and agonized over what to do. One day, I decided to go to the Christian bookstore in search of books on the topic of clergy abuse. Approaching the door, waves of memories washed over me, recalling the Saturday morning trips to the Bible bookstore with the twins and Mrs. Gardner. Would my emotions and memories once again cripple me as they had so many times in the past? "Give me Strength," I whispered. I was startled for just a moment. Wait, did I just ask for strength from God? Did I just pray to God? It didn't feel like a prayer, but maybe it was. It had been so long since I actually prayed.

Gaining in confidence, I pushed open the door and walked in. "I'm looking for books on clergy sexual abuse."

The clerk looked at me as if I had asked if they sold books on Pole Dancing or How to Become a Stripper. "You mean books about *pastors* abusing???"

"Yes."

"Oh no, but we do have one book about abuse in the Christian home."

"No, I am specifically looking for clergy abuse."

Clearly uncomfortable, she responded, "I've never seen a book on the topic or even if one exists since it is such a rare occurrence."

The clerk's response underscored the minimal awareness about clergy abuse in 2004. I began reading everything I could find on spiritual sexual abuse. I scoured the internet for websites, articles, blogs, and stories of clergy abuse. Thankfully, some information existed and it helped me understand what he did to me. *The Hope of Survivors* website was very helpful, enabling me to understand the dynamics of pastoral abuse. They are dedicated to helping victims of clergy abuse. Books on the other hand were not as easy to find. As I learned about clergy abuse, Jeff Coulier's actions seemed almost textbook. On one hand, I was relieved to realize I was not alone. On the other, I was sickened to realize he deliberately and with careful planning, targeted me, and used me for his own selfish interests.

In my studies I found the following information from Dr. Lisa Oakley, Research Associate at the Churches' Child Protection Advisory Services. She wrote:

> *"Spiritual abuse is a form of emotional and psychological abuse. It is characterized by a systematic pattern of coercive and controlling behavior in a 'religious context.' This abuse may include manipulation and exploitation, enforced accountability, censorship of decision-making, the requirement of secrecy and silence, coercion to conform, control through use of sacred text or teachings, the requirement of obedience to the abuser, the suggestion that the abuser has a 'divine' position, isolation as a means of punishment, and superiority and elitism."*

Dr. Oakley's research in this area suggests the following actions all have an enormous and powerful effect on someone's faith:
- *Scripture misuse to control behavior*
- *Suggesting God is complicit*
- *Threats of negative spiritual consequence*
- *Spiritual Leader is "called" by God to a position and therefore cannot be questioned.*

The actions described by Dr. Oakley were evident in Jeff Coulier's relationship with me and key to keeping me tied to him:
- **Scripture misuse to control behavior.** Misusing scripture is especially confusing for the victim of clergy abuse. My faith in Jeff as a church leader and teacher enabled him to distort scripture and caused me to believe what he said to be true. He often compared himself to Israel's King David, who you may recall, committed adultery with Bathsheba, Uriah's wife, while his army was at war. When Bathsheba discovered she was pregnant, David attempted to conceal his sin, first by recalling Uriah from the battle and inducing him to sleep with his wife. When that failed, King David arranged to have Uriah killed in battle. While this resulted in life-long judgement for David and his family, David repented and retained his kingdom until his death. "I am just like King David," Jeff would say. "God uses me just like he used King David, in spite of his moral failure."

I've learned comparing oneself to King David is a common ploy among abusive clergy.
- **God is complicit.** This was Jeff Coulier's explanation when I struggled with what we were doing. The few times I went to him with overwhelming guilt, his responses were, "God works through me, in spite of my faults" or "We are married in God's eyes." He even wore the wedding band I had given him. He would say, "God brought us together for you to help me in my ministry" and assured me God's approval was demonstrated by the increasing attendance at church.
- **Threats of negative spiritual consequences.** Because of his influence, Jeff Coulier had the power to take away my involvement in the church. He never hesitated to demonstrate this by refusing to include me in a pivotal role in the youth group activities or ignoring me by refusing to speak to me.
- **Spiritual Leader "called" by God.** Dr. Oakley refers to as elitism. It occurs when clergy use their position and the sense of a divine calling as rationalization for amoral behavior. I didn't question his motives as I might have if he had been a thirty-year-old neighbor. He used his position as my minister to slowly pull me into his twisted way of thinking, which I didn't see at the time. Spiritually, I looked up to him. His rationalization to me was our relationship was ordained by God. All the good he, Jeff, was doing outweighed any sins he committed.

While the use and misuse of scripture and one's position as a spiritual leader are tools for abuse by clergy, all abusers, whether clergy or not, employ basic tactics which allows them to continue their abusive behavior:
- **Manipulation.** The art of manipulation occurs when the actor influences another human being for his own advantage. Often, this manipulation involves creating a sense of emotional insecurity in the abused with direct threats from the abuser to create a sense of fear. Jeff Coulier was a master manipulator.

Deception is the key to any manipulative relationship. In order for the perpetrator to worm his way into the relationship, he must disguise his motives and actions. After all, mean, rude, unkind, malicious people are easy to spot. We tend to avoid them. There is a reason the analogy of the wolf in sheep's clothing paints such an accurate picture.

The manipulator:
- Makes fun of you in front of others.
- Tells you how to dress, how to wear your hair.

- Keeps you from spending time with your friends or family; thus, driving a wedge between friends and taking control of activities in order to isolate the victim.
- Criticizes mannerisms such as the way you walk, talk, or laugh.
- Discourages your future plans or derails your goals.
- Makes you question your own decisions.
- Alternates between criticizing and complimenting you to keep you off balance.
- Blames you for his own insecurities. It's your fault, never his.
- Uses intimidation or guilt to secure your obedience.
- Reminds you, you will never be able to leave the abusive relationship. No one else will want you. No one will be able to love you like he does. He tells you, you are nothing without him.
- Physically threatens and actually physically abuses you. This fear of violence is always present in the abused.

Employing these tactics, the abuser remains in control, keeping the victim emotionally crippled, unable to function outside of the toxic relationship.
- **Exploitation.** The abuser uses the victim for his own selfish purposes. Professionals, teachers, coaches, youth pastors, and others in charge of our young are expected to respect boundaries and help the pupil grow. An abuser takes advantage of his power and position of authority. Jeff Coulier used my innocence, my need for a father figure and my faith in the church to make me his pawn.
- **Censorship of decision making.** Censorship of decision making is a critical component of all abuse. Censorship arises when the abuser ensures decisions are made to his advantage and uses his power and influence to cause the victim to be unable to think for herself. I would never trust my own judgment or make my own decisions. Whether he was telling me how to spend my time, or who to date or where to go to college, my ability to think and decide were taken from me. I felt inadequate. I became trained to believe only he knew what was best for me.

Those who have not been abused cannot understand why a woman does not stand up to her abuser. Why would anyone accept abuse? Simply put: intimidation. The abuser undermines the ability of the abused to question anything. Being systematically and methodically manipulated, the abused loses the ability to think for herself. Without thought, one cannot defend or fight back.

- **Silence and secrecy.** Silence and secrecy are required in all abusive relationships. It starts with small secrets and grows to be a significant web of dishonesty. Jeff Coulier told me not to tell anyone what *we* were doing. This progressed to him telling me even if I told, no one would believe me. This made it difficult, even years later, to tell anyone.
- **Coercion and threats of violence to conform.** These become weapons of the abuser. Jeff physically abused me when he felt I disobeyed, but simply knowing he was *capable* of violence kept me under his control. He knew I was afraid I would lose my church home or role in the church if I did not do what he wanted.

Abusers and those who manipulate know exactly what they are doing. Their victim of choice is not by accident. They target people they know they can control. Victims are not chosen based on education or intelligence. Abuse revolves around vulnerability. What is it about her the abuser can exploit in such a way she doesn't realize the trap is being set? Jeff Coulier knew me. He knew my vulnerabilities. He used them to trap me. I was easy prey.

Psychology Today describes a spiritual trap this way:

> *"First, a good trap makes it easy for the prey to get in, but hard to get out. If it didn't have this quality, it would not be a trap. (This is why fish hooks have barbs, for instance.) Second, there needs to be an attractive bait. Really good bait will occupy the attention of the prey so thoroughly that the danger will go unnoticed. Third, once in the trap, the more the prey struggles, the more tired and trapped it becomes. Wolf traps have teeth, the more the wolf struggles, the deeper the bite. The more it hurts, the more the wolf struggles, and the vicious cycle keeps repeating itself, until the wolf struggles to death.*
>
> *Finally, the trap has to 'fit' the prey it is being used to catch. You can't trap minnows with a wolf trap, or wolves with a minnow trap. Not only this, but the more you know about the prey, the more effective trap you can devise."* –DAVID JOHNSON AND JEFF VAN VONDEREN, SPIRITUAL ABUSE QUOTING JEFFREY Z. RUBIN, "PSYCHOLOGICAL TRAPS," PSYCHOLOGY TODAY (MARCH 1981).

What I was discovering and learning about abuse was helpful for me to gain a greater understanding of what had been done to me. Only a few months had passed since I drove through Queensgate. My need to learn was insatiable. Even though I was learning so much about clergy abuse, old thinking continued to creep into my thoughts. There were times I didn't trust myself to admit I had been abused. Doubts continued to haunt me. Why didn't I stop him the night he took me up the stairs? Why did I stay so long in this abusive relationship? Was it abuse if he in some ways cared about me? Reconciling Jeff Coulier, my minister who at times showed he cared, and the Jeff Coulier who hit me, humiliated me, degraded me, and left me alone to walk to my car in a hotel garage late at night kept me in a state of turmoil.

Accepting the truth how he selfishly used me was more hurtful than my long-held belief about how I chose to be involved. I desperately wanted to believe some part of him cared about me rather than wanting to face the fact I was simply a pawn caught in his perverted world of self-gratification. The lie was easier to accept. Confusion and self-doubt continued. It was going to take time to unravel the web of lies, but with a greater understanding of what he did to me, I could slowly begin the process.

DON'T TELL! TELL?

In spite of my continuing confusion, I knew I needed to confront him. If I were to have any hope to find my way back spiritually, I needed to free myself of Jeff Coulier. The only way I knew to do this was to confront him. I wanted him to know I finally understood what he did to me. I could not move on until I held him accountable. But how? I had lost all contact with him. I had heard from a former church member, after Queensgate, he lost his standing in the Christian Church and operated a Shell gas station for a while. I could not even begin to know where he might be now, or even if he were still alive. He would be in his mid-sixties by now and even if he were alive, would I have the courage to face him? I could not do this alone. I had to tell someone.

At age forty-nine, I was still afraid of him, what he might do, and what he would say and the power he held. I could not stop the words from repeating in my mind, "Don't ever tell."

Unlike so many victims whose abusers deny the abuse or encounters, Jeff Coulier couldn't say I was lying; however, he was skillful enough to twist the truth and manipulate the situation to his benefit. I held these fears within. If he were dead, it didn't matter. He was alive in my mind.

I could not rid myself of his control; whether I was in a church, listening to 70's music, or passing a location which triggered a memory. He continued to insert himself in my life, over and over. At any time, my past could hijack the present and conjure up the dreaded memories.

Those flashbacks just became a part of my life. I functioned this way for twenty-seven years. It became my norm. While these trigger factors often bring anxiety and panic attacks to a victim, I incorporated them into my everyday life by shutting myself off from them, by holding tight to the secret. What was always present, and which needed no reminders, was my guilt for what *I* had done; having had sex with my pastor. I knew if people learned this, they would think less of me. How bad do you have to be to be thrown out of a church? My past had to remain hidden.

It was only on that day, when I saw the Queensgate exit sign I realized the depth of my wounds. My encounter with his ghost, the sense of him sitting in the car made me realize the full measure of what he took from me. He had come into my life, posing as a trusted minister and then stole my innocence, my love for the church, and my plans for college/my future. He used me until I was almost irreparably broken.

The girl I was when I met him, vulnerable, yet full of life and laughter, was no more. Slowly and surely, I became a person who believed the lies he told me. Sobbing on the side of the road the day I passed the Queensgate exit was the first inkling I realized *it was not my fault*. I had been his puppet. He didn't love me; he used me. Perhaps with this new understanding, I now could begin to forgive myself and allow God back into my life.

DON'T EVER TELL.

I was safe from him all those years because the secret was safe. By protecting the secret, I protected him. The secret kept me safe from him. Now I was going to expose the secret; expose him, and expose me.

> *"And when at last you find someone to whom you can pour out your soul, you stop in shock at the words you utter—they are so rusty, so ugly, so meaningless and feeble from being kept in the small cramped dark inside you so long."* —SYLVIA PLATH, THE UNABRIDGED JOURNALS OF SYLVIA PLATH

On a hot summer day in June 2004, I called my friend Su and asked if I could come over to talk to her. Su was a counselor, and I had seen how she dealt with difficult situations, and I knew I could trust her advice. Moreover, I didn't feel ready to tell Bill. I needed to process it all before I confided in him. I thought she might be able to understand. As we sat on her screened-in porch, she offered me iced tea.

Feeling ashamed, I tried to speak. I stared at my lap as if somehow it held the answer and would give me the words to say. Again, I tried to speak. I cried. Nothing came out. Deep breaths, I thought. Just say it. Just say it. But I couldn't. Each time I began to say the words, "I was sexually abused by my youth pastor," it was if his hands were around my throat forcing the words back. My heart so wanted to be relieved of the burden of this secret, but my mind kept telling me, *"Don't tell."*

For fifteen minutes, with my head down and eyes closed, I cried. Then after twenty-seven years of silence, in the midst of my sobs I said, "I was sexually abused by my youth minister as a teenager." Without stopping, I told her my story, digging deep into my vault of horrid memories, pulling each one out in between my sobs.

She listened patiently, allowing me to ramble. Taking my hand, she finally said to me, "Oh, Sandy, how incredibly sad for you." After consoling me, she continued with certainty. "This just makes me so mad. I cannot tell you how angry I am at this guy for what he did to you. He should be shot." As comforting as her words of support were, her anger validated for me he had no right to do what he did.

I was so relieved to finally tell the truth, not just to this compassionate friend, but to myself as well. I too needed to hear the truth; it was *not* an affair with my minister. He committed sexual misconduct and abuse using the church to accomplish his evil deed. And, for the first time, the sixteen-year-old Sandy within me heard it was not her fault.

Having Su as a confidante allowed me to once again function somewhat normally. Feeling a bit more secure with Su at my side, two weeks later I told two more friends, Sue and Beth. There were many girlfriend sessions on Su's screened-in porch as the three of them helped me navigate and process my feelings and emotions. I was still guarded, but the secret was out and I slowly began to feel free of it. Each time I revealed a bit more of my story, but I was not ready to tell it all. Parts remained a secret.

Still, I was not ready to tell Bill. In my mind, maybe I would never need to tell him. Maybe, just maybe, I could find Jeff Coulier, confront him and Bill would not need to know. I was not thinking rationally.

It was baby steps for now.

"But there is nothing covered up that will not be revealed, and hidden that will not be known. Accordingly, whatever you have said in the dark will be heard in the light, and what you have whispered in the inner rooms will be proclaimed upon the housetops."

—LUKE 12:2–3, THE NEW AMERICAN STANDARD BIBLE

NOW WHAT?

Now what? I continued to read and study everything I could about clergy abuse. There was plenty to be found about abuse within the Catholic Church but so little within the Protestant Church. Ultimately, I found two extremely helpful books, *Is Nothing Sacred?* by Marie Fortune, and *Spiritual Abuse,* by David Johnson and Jeff Vonderen. Each day I became a little stronger. Understanding brought clarity. The possibility of being able to hold him accountable gave me a sense of taking my life back and freeing myself of him. At the same time, confronting him terrified me.

By telling my closest friends of my past, I was finally able to let go of the secret I held for twenty-seven years. For the first time, I felt I had control over my past. My spiritual life began to re-emerge and I started to re-awaken from the coma-like spiritual state I had been in for the past twenty-seven years. I still wasn't able to pray or open my Bible, but I felt the presence of God in ways I had not felt in years. My spirit seemed stronger. I was a bit freer from the shame. The shame was replaced with understanding of what he had done to me. Deep within, I began to realize both Jeff Coulier and the elders at Walnut Branch were terribly wrong in their treatment of me years ago. I wasn't ready to forgive the elders or Jeff Coulier for what they had done, but I considered doing so might need to be part of the process.

Oddly enough, as my spiritual life re-awakened, attending church became more difficult and nearly impossible. For the last twenty-seven years, I attended church with my emotions intact and the memories controlled. Now, when I attended church, I found myself sick to my stomach. Every reminder of him was intensified. Just as I felt him sitting next to me in the car on my drive through Queensgate, Tennessee, on my way to my daughter's golf match, in church it was if he was now sitting next to me in the pew. In spite of the angst and sickness, for weeks I forced myself to attend. I was looking to have God back in my life. After all, it was church where I first found God and began my spiritual life. Doesn't it then make sense I should begin the journey back the same way, in church? However, being inside the church only seemed to make it worse.

One Sunday morning, I pulled into the church parking lot with an overwhelming sense of depression. Within seconds of leaving my car my sadness moved to anger; I stood there, refusing to move. I am *not* going in. I told myself, "God, if this is what I am supposed to do, why is this so hard? If this is how I am to rediscover my spiritual life, you had better help me! And I mean now!" It was my "aha" moment, a slap on the forehead; the now I get it moment. My spiritual life, my relationship with God, did not have to be tied to church. Jeff Coulier poisoned the church, but I would no longer let him poison my relationship with God.

I wasn't sure where this would lead, but I sensed God pushing me to move forward. Perhaps it was also my inner sense of newly found determination not to be silent any longer. I must confront Jeff Coulier. Determined to confront him, I first needed to find him. Google was a new concept to me. I had never used it before, but with "Jeff Coulier" in the search box and with a tap of the enter button, there he was, a minister in another denominational church, in an Alabama suburb. "Meet our Staff," the website said. And there he was.

His face filled the screen, staring back at me.

I pushed myself back from the computer. He was in the room with me! I immediately shut down the computer. After giving myself time to breathe, I turned it back on, bracing myself.

It was odd to stare at the screen of this older version of a man I once knew. I read through the June 2004 Faith Christian Church newsletter and found this:

> "With the help of Rev. Sam Fitzgerald and the Region [sic] we were able to call a full-time minister. Reverend Jeff Coulier from Maxwell, Tennessee joined our 'journey of faith' in May 1998."

I knew where he was, but little else. How would I contact him? What would I say? When would I feel strong enough to contact him? The question of when was answered, in part, after reading the church newsletter from their website, June 7, 2004.

> "Wishing Jeff Coulier rest and renewal as our thoughts and prayers go with him as he takes a much-deserved rest this summer."

He would be on sabbatical until September. This gave me time to figure out what to do.

As I read the newsletters, I waffled between a mature woman and the sixteen-year-old girl he had controlled and manipulated. Experts describe this as a common occurrence. Even though the brainwashing and mind controlling from the abuser occurs years earlier, victims have trouble, even years later, trying to deprogram their thoughts.

Su and I learned from the church newsletters Jeff Coulier's sermons were available on tape. We decided Su would contact the church, say she was moving to the area, possibly interested in joining the church, and would like a copy of one of his sermons. A week later with tape in hand, I heard his voice for the first time in twenty-seven years. I cried and felt physically sick. Hearing his voice made him real. Now I wasn't so sure I could confront him.

Crying, I called my friend Beth. She and my other two friends had been my sounding board when I needed to talk. I confided in her about my conflicts with church. I expressed my fears and doubts about confronting him. I started to question if it was the right thing to do. She suggested I speak with her husband, Zeke. He was an elder in their church. Over the years I had admired their faith. Perhaps he could offer some clarity and help me spiritually.

I didn't want to confront Jeff out of revenge or spite, or even hatred. I wanted to do this for my own healing. While I knew my anger was justified, I didn't want my anger to cloud my judgment in doing the right thing. Hours at Zeke and Beth's kitchen table helped me process my feelings and grow spiritually.

Again, I expressed my fear and doubts to Zeke and Beth about confronting Jeff. Crying, I said, "I'm not sure I can face him."

Zeke looked at me and said, "This is not a choice. God tells us to confront the one who has offended us."

He then read from Matthew 18:15–17:

> *"If your brother or sister[a] sins,[b] go and point out their fault, just between the two of you. If they listen to you, you have won them over. **16** But if they will not listen, take one or two others along, so that 'every matter may be established by the testimony of two or three witnesses.'[c] **17** If they still refuse to listen, tell it to the church; and if they refuse to listen even to the church, treat them as you would a pagan or a tax collector."*

This was the first Bible verse I had allowed myself to consider in twenty-seven years. This verse gave me courage and resolution. I kept going back to Matthew 18 and what Zeke explained and back to my friends as my sounding board. Though I was afraid, it was more important to hold him accountable, to finally face him. I feared if I never held him accountable, I would never be free of him.

The next obvious question was how and where to confront him. Su and I played with many scenarios, including just showing up in his church one Sunday morning. We would sit in the front row and corner him after the service. Yes, a part of me would delight in watching him squirm. I did not want to give him time to prepare. I wanted to catch him off guard.

I decided to hire an investigator to learn more about him and his history. Not only did I hope an investigator would provide me insight into Jeff Coulier, but the investigator could also be my go between. I had no clue about hiring anyone, so I called an investigator Su had heard of from a friend. We called the number of the investigator. I was too nervous to talk.

"Hello, my name is Su and I am calling for a friend. She is looking to locate a minister in Alabama who sexually abused her as a teenager over thirty years ago. Is this something you do and how much would it cost?" After getting the information, she ended the conversation. The investigator probably thought, "Sure, you have a *friend*."

Taking the step to call the investigator made the possibility of confronting him more real. Now I wasn't just thinking about confronting him, I was taking concrete steps to make it happen. I needed a couple days to think about it. Again, indecision. I had enough money in my checking account; money wasn't the issue. I didn't want Bill to know, and that's what bothered me. Should I do this without telling him? I didn't feel right keeping it from him, but I wasn't ready to tell him. My other worry was could I change my mind once the investigator began?

Two days later, on August 1, I called the investigator from Su's home. "Hello, Business Intelligence, may I help you?"

I froze for a moment. Looking up at Su, she slowly nodded, waving her hand at me to continue. "Go ahead. Tell him."

With my voice shaking, "Yes, my name is Sandy Kirkham. A friend of mine talked to you a couple days ago about locating my former pastor. We think he might be in…Alabama."

His first words sent me reeling. "Are you related to Bill Kirkham?"

"Yes. He is my husband."

"Does he know you have contacted me?"

"No. Would that make a difference?"

Explaining he and Bill had done some work together he replied, "I would be happy to help you but I would feel better if he were aware of the situation."

"Okay. Would it be alright if I set up an appointment?"

One week later Su and I walked into his office. I still had not told Bill.

With my stomach in knots and barely able to breathe, I sat at the receptionist desk as she picked up pen and paper and began to write. She needed my name, address, phone, etc.

Then she asked, "And what is the name of the person we are trying to locate?"

Then I heard his voice, "Don't tell! Don't ever tell!"

She wants me to say his name! I can't do this. I **cannot** do this. At that moment I was terrified. My heart was racing. Even as I write this, I can feel the fear I felt that day. If Su had not been with me, I would have left. Fumbling, I opened a file with a current picture I had taken from the church website. I handed her the photo.

She took one look and said, "What's up with his hair?"

Her comment calmed me and made me laugh. Jeff Coulier was always worried about his appearance, especially his hair. He was forever combing it and worried if it was out of place. Now here was this stranger laughing about his hair.

"His name is Jeff Coulier."

There I said it. My heart was pounding. Every part of me wanted to take back those words. The fear he had planted in my mind over the years began to control me once again. The fear of the consequences, of exposing him, what would he do? The fear of letting go of my secret. My mind kept telling me to stop, but my heart begged for healing, and this time I would finally listen to my heart. Within a few minutes the investigator came out. "Hello, I'm Jim Simon. Let's go into my office and talk."

With Su at my side, I began to tell my story, sobbing as if I were talking to a psychiatrist instead of a private detective. I wasn't looking just to give facts; I wanted validation for my story and pain. He was the first person I had told who did not know me. His kind and calming manner put me at ease and assured me, he would be able to help.

Sensing my angst and fragile state, Mr. Simon gently said, "Now you understand, whatever information I find, you are the one in control. It's your choice to do what you want with any information I find. So, if at any time you don't feel you are ready to confront him, you don't have to."

Me in control? I didn't feel in control, but his words helped to remind me, this was my journey, my choice, and my decision. Fear alone should not dictate what I would do. Of course, I was afraid, but I could not let fear paralyze me.

The only way to let go of my fear was to face him.

Before having Mr. Simon contact Jeff Coulier, I wanted to confirm and possibly learn more about the first young woman from Tifton who came forward and accused Jeff Coulier of sexual misconduct. Over thirty years ago, Jeff Coulier had bragged about his past to me and mentioned a pastor named Ron Williams who had come to Cincinnati and confronted him. I never forgot his name.

Mr. Simon's first task would be to locate Ron Williams.

FOR BETTER OR WORSE

Before I could go any further, I needed to find the courage to tell Bill. I could no longer keep this from him. Each step of disclosing my past brought a wave of anxiety. Sometimes it was nightmares. Sometimes I was unable to eat. Every time shame haunted me for what I'd done.

I didn't need to be reminded of what happens when someone discovered what I had done. The memory consumed me for years.

I was judged for "what I had done."

I was thrown out of my church for "what I had done."

I was blamed for "what I had done."

I was told to confess my sins for "what I had done."

The guilt I carried for "what I had done" only reinforced the sin I had committed. I learned firsthand what happened when someone knew "what I had done." Even though I was now beginning to understand Jeff Coulier had abused me, there was little understanding about victims of clergy sexual abuse. We not only suffer emotionally and physically but also the loss of our spiritual life. Our souls are raped. The abuse takes our faith, a sacred part of who we are, and distorts it. I was beginning to understand the dynamics of pastoral sexual abuse, the grooming and the manipulation, but I wondered if Bill would understand. My heart told me he would.

Bill loved me; I **KNEW** that. I knew Bill would always love me, but I worried how telling him might change things. Even though my heart told me he loved me and nothing would change, my mind told me otherwise. I couldn't trust myself and there were too many "what ifs." What if he too wondered why it happened? How could it have gone on for so long? Why had I not told him sooner? Would he see my secret as a betrayal? Would he feel duped? Knowing this about me, would it change how he saw me sexually?

My fear was not only based upon the reactions of those from my past, but

Jeff Coulier's words, "DON'T EVER TELL. NO ONE WILL BELIEVE YOU." My mind was an echo chamber, and I would awaken in the middle of the night hearing those words; over and over those words looped in mind, leaving no room for silence, for clear thought, or for clarity to take hold. Jeff Coulier was right about the consequences of the past. When my church found out, I was rejected. I could not bear the same rejection from Bill. I did not want my revelation to change anything between us. Our marriage was far and away the most important part of my life.

Even with the reassurance from my friends telling me Bill would understand, nausea swept through me at the thought of revealing my story to him. My friend Su later told me she understood how difficult it was to let go of this secret when she witnessed me agonize over telling Bill, the one person she knew would be nothing but loving and supportive.

Just before Bill left for work on August 20, 2004, I told him I would be downtown in the afternoon. If he was free, I would meet him at his office and we could go out for dinner. This was it. Today I would tell him.

At 5:30 P.M., I walked into his office, my heart pounding. "I have a few more things to finish up and I will be ready to go," he said. I sat down. Don't make me wait too long I thought, or I will change my mind. I still have time.

Then panic.

RUN, just Run!

Fight or flight mode set in.

Flight was winning.

Grabbing his suit jacket and heading for the door, he said "Okay, ready. Where do you want to go?" I thought, I want to go home and forget the whole thing. I sucked in some air and mumbled, "Before we go, I want to talk to you about something."

He closed the door and stood there waiting.

"I want you to sit down." His demeanor changed as he could see something was wrong.

As he sat in his chair behind his desk, I said, "No, I want you over here next to me, and I pulled his chair over to mine in the middle of the office, facing me, as our knees touched. It looked like a Dr. Phil moment.

Staring into my lap, I began to cry. Each time I caught my breath and tried to say the words, I began to cry. Leaning forward, he took my hand and waited patiently, never saying a word. I can't say how long it was before I finally managed to say, "I'm okay and the kids are okay." Then I cried more, as I sat twisting the tear-stained tissue into tiny pieces. Slowly reaching into his pocket, without speaking, he handed me his handkerchief; waiting patiently. Finally, after fifteen minutes, with my head lowered, I said in a whisper barely audible between sobs, "I was sexually abused by my minister when I was a teenager."

His hands tightened around mine. I looked up; his eyes fixed upon me.

"I was their babysitter."

His face just dropped. The color drained from his face. All the pain I had felt for years, I now saw in his face, reflected back at me. Cradled in his arms, I sobbed.

He loved me.

I gave him the basic facts. The minister was married with two kids; he was thirteen years older; his actions were discovered and I was told to leave the church. I admitted I kept it secret for twenty-seven years because I just wanted to move on with my life. I didn't want to think about him or what he did to me. Then I told Bill after I met and married him, my life was so wonderful I just wanted to forget my painful history. Still, I always carried my past with me and driving past the Queensgate exit brought it all back.

I then told him how scared I was to tell him. I didn't want to keep this from him I just never knew how to tell him. "I didn't want to hurt what we have," I whispered, almost afraid to look at him for fear I would start to cry again.

"Why in the world would you ever think this would change anything between us? I married you for who you are and nothing is going to change that. The only way it affects us is for the hurt this has caused you."

"I just didn't want this to change us," I admitted.

"I'm in for the long haul with you and the two of us have faced a lot of things together and there will be other things we will have to face, and we will, just like we will with this."

I looked at him and told him meeting him saved my life and provided a life with everything I ever hoped for. I was on a destructive path and he saved me. I then confessed how I tried to tell him when we were dating. I looked at him and said, "You may not remember your response, but you said, if it happened before you met me, it doesn't matter." He said, "I meant it then and I mean it now."

"You saved my life," I repeated.

"And you made mine," he said.

I told him, in spite of how I appeared at the moment, I was okay. I had a plan. I could still see he was worried. "I'm okay. Really," I said. I wasn't sure he was totally convinced, but he finally said, "If you tell me you're okay then I believe you." The truth is I thought I was okay, but I was far from it.

Being an attorney, Bill wanted to know the details about my plan and how to proceed. When I told him, I had hired a private investigator, Jim Simon, he grinned. "I know Jim," he said. Smiling I said, "Yeah I know. I was trying to do this without telling you and the first thing Jim asked me was, "Are you Bill Kirkham's wife?"

I explained to Bill in spite of my pain and confused state, the only thing I knew for sure was my need to confront Jeff Coulier.

"Let me say something about that," he said. "Do not do this out of guilt. You have nothing to feel guilty about. Don't do this because you think you should. Don't do this for your friends or for me. Do this for you because *you* need to, and not because of what anyone else thinks."

He continued, "I also want you to be prepared for his reaction. The bottom line is he is not going to care what you have to say. His only concern will be how this affects him. I don't want you to be disappointed by the results. Because even after confronting him you may not get the satisfaction you had hoped for."

I told him I understood, but I needed, for me, to face him and tell him what he did was wrong and how he had no right to do it. I wanted him to know after all these years I finally understood he abused me and it changed my life. I also need him to know I survived. A big part of me wanted to say to Jeff Coulier, look at my wonderful life. You almost destroyed me, but you failed.

Bill jumped in "You have nothing to prove to this guy. You have lived a life you can be proud of and he hasn't."

"I know that, but I need to confront him. My greatest fear is not the thought of facing him, although it is terrifying, but what if he refuses to see me?"

Bill responded, "Oh, he will see you alright. You walk right into his office and tell him you want to talk and if he refuses, you tell him you came to talk and if he won't talk to you, you will talk to the church secretary, the custodian or anybody else who will listen. And if necessary, he will see you at his service on Sunday morning. Sandy, he will see you. He has no choice. You tell Jim Simon to arrange a time and I promise you he will be there."

Thinking Jeff Coulier may call Bill to get control of the situation or try to lie or twist what happened I asked, "What if he tries to call you?"

"He won't call. So, what if he does?" Bill asked. "I'll talk to him. I don't think he will want to hear what I have to say to him." He knew a phone call from Jeff Coulier worried me.

My insecurities and fear were taking hold. Consequences. This would be the consequence of telling Bill and I began to second guess myself. "Sandy there is *nothing* he can say or do that is going to have any impact on us. We are in this together. Now let's go have dinner."

I listened to Bill as he talked like an attorney, but all I could think about was how lucky I was to be his wife. I felt such security with his understanding about the situation. No longer did I feel alone and, regardless of the outcome, Bill was in my corner.

I went to the lady's room to fix my makeup and when I returned, he said, "I want you to understand something. Just because I say it is your decision on how to proceed, and all of this doesn't matter to me, I do not mean I don't care. I don't want you to mistake my saying it for indifference on my part. You are the only one who can decide what you need to do."

I took his hand. "Thank you."

"Personally, I don't know why you don't want to go down there and shoot the guy! But of course, you know you can't do that."

REPEAT OFFENDER

Now that Bill knew and the investigator had located Ron Williams, I was ready to start uncovering the truth about Jeff Coulier's past. Ron was Jeff's senior minister and boss from his first church in Tifton where Jeff's first known incident of sexual misconduct occurred. It was time to have a conversation with Ron. While my purpose was to confirm the first incident of sexual misconduct as relayed to me by Jeff, my conversation with him would reveal so much more. The investigator recommended I tape the conversation and carefully explained how to use the recorder. It took all my resolve to dial his number and push the button to start the recording.

I introduced myself with the following words, "I am calling because over thirty years ago, when I was a teenager, a pastor sexually abused me and I am now, as an adult, trying to deal with it. During this time, Jeff Coulier told me you came to Cincinnati in the early 70's to confront him about an allegation of misconduct from a young woman in your church."

Ron Williams immediately confirmed he not only had confronted Jeff Coulier about his misconduct, but he had done so numerous times. He asked about my motivation for confronting Jeff Coulier, which seemed rooted in his desire for me to heal and move on. I reiterated, "I only want to confront him and hold him accountable. The fact it had happened before and it happened again after he left Walnut Branch shows a pattern."

He sighed with a quiet, "Yes."

He then asked for my name again and wanted to know more about me. He commented Jeff Coulier was an "enigmatic character; mixed up in a lot of ways." He then volunteered to find him for me. I quickly responded, "I know where he is. I have hired an investigator who found him ministering in a church in Alabama."

"*He's preaching again*?" Shock was in his voice.

"Oh, yes, and my plan is to confront him."

Our conversation continued. He counseled me to move on and not be a victim. His words were, "You need to forgive and forget by the grace of God. I know it is an easy thing for me to say, but I've been through this with people."

"How many times has he done this?" I asked.

"Hun, I don't know, we lost contact with him. I am seventy-six years old, retired from the ministry, but still a member at Southwind." Ron seemed eager to want to talk about Jeff. He recalled the last time he had seen Jeff Coulier.

"About five years ago, I saw a car late one night in the church parking lot with someone sitting in it. Naturally, I went over to see who it was and to say 'hey.' It was Jeff Coulier."

I said, "Son, what are you doing here?"

He replied, "Oh, I just come here every now and then to sit, look, and think. Some of my best memories of my life are here at this church."

Ron's response to Jeff, "You did some good things, while you were here, and you had a great ministry, but you also brought chaos to a number of people I loved very much. You need not to be preaching anywhere, anytime. You need to be doing something else. I don't see any opportunity for you to be a minister or preacher because you do more harm than good."

As we continued talking, Ron shared how he had come to Cincinnati to alert people to Jeff's past and then mentioned he almost drove himself crazy trying to chase down Jeff. In a reflective voice, he said, "I don't know what I can do to help you. He's a pied piper. You are not at fault. He's a pied piper. You have been swindled by a person who is a professional at it, I suppose. I think there are times when he doesn't want to have bad things in his life, but it always comes back. It's overwhelming."

To repeat my intentions I said, "Again, my reason in calling is I just wanted to confirm from you he had done this before."

"Lots of times; I wouldn't want to exaggerate to say a lot of times if it wasn't, but it was a lot of times. It was almost an inevitable thing, anytime he met anybody who was in any way unsettled or uncertain he was going to take advantage. He's a sick man. A very sick man, and I am not sure what you can do."

Quickly glancing at the recorder to be sure it was still running, I continued. "I want to be sure his church knows about who he is. The church should be safe and it wasn't, because of him. If they chose to ignore his past..." I began to cry. I told him I felt guilty for not speaking up sooner.

"It's not your fault honey; it was a blow to your life keeping you from being able to do what you normally would do, and it's what's made you unable to speak until now. You have the right to speak now. The thing is, I told him then and I told the people offering him jobs, he's done it over and over. I have no confidence when he says, 'I've changed. I'm a new man.'"

I agreed, "Obviously it was true after you confronted him in Cincinnati; he said he would not do anything like that again and within six months he was doing the same thing to me. He had not changed in spite of his words. Then after getting caught again, he made a confession he did not mean."

Ron offered compassion for both the abuse and the aftermath I'd lived with for years. He also continued talking about his disdain for Jeff, "He should not have peace until he makes right with the people he has hurt. To have a man who bears the Gospel of Jesus Christ and using it as a tool to hurt people, is perverse. He's made me resent him so much. I've had two churches; one for about four years and the last one for forty years. I never had a hurt like that. I was his boss. We had five preachers while I was there. I was in charge of him and it was the first time this kind of behavior was shown. Since then it's almost like this type of train keeps coming back from different places, and I would do anything if I could stop him that was right and Godly. I think he is the sickest of sick. He brings in God and the church and the Bible, and it makes a dirty mark on everything good."

It was time to wrap up the conversation. I clearly told him I planned to confront Jeff Coulier and asked him not tell Jeff Coulier of my plans.

I was relieved he didn't try to defend Jeff or make excuses. While I didn't learn specific details on the first incident of misconduct, I now had the confidence it had occurred, and the few facts Jeff had bragged about to me all those years ago were accurate.

Three days later the phone rang and it was Ron Williams. My heart dropped to my stomach with his first words. "Sandy, I want you to know I located Jeff Coulier and I have talked to him."

Ron did exactly what I asked him NOT to do, which was to contact Jeff Coulier. The element of surprise and catching Jeff off guard was taken from me. Jeff now knew I wanted to confront him and had time to spin his story. I had no idea how much of our conversation Ron relayed to Jeff or what he said to him, but Jeff said plenty in his response and asked Ron to convey his message.

"First he says he is sorry and he knows he has caused you hurt and pain."

What Ron reported next left me speechless.

"He told me to tell you, 'I think she would feel sorry for me, if she knew the agonies on my list.'"

"He says he has changed. I can't say for certain it is true, but I am relaying what he told me, and he wants to know what you want him to do. Do you want him to resign?"

I could feel Jeff Coulier's manipulation anew, making me responsible for what would happen to him. Again, he was not taking responsibility. Were he to lose his ministry, it wouldn't be because he felt he should leave, or by his *own actions*, but because I forced him out. He would be a victim again and escape without owning his sins. What he said next sent chills down my spine and sent me back over thirty years ago. "He wants to call and talk to you. He knows if he could just talk to you, he could make you understand."

I knew exactly what it meant. Understand what? Understand what *he* wants me to understand. He would take control and again use any weakness to get me to do what he wanted.

Gripping the phone, I suddenly realized Ron Williams had my phone number and probably gave it to Jeff. What if he calls me? I had caller ID. If I got his number and he did try to call, I would recognize the number and there might even be a way to block it, if I had it.

"I don't want him to call me, but I would consider calling him. Can you give me his number?"

"He says he is sorry and if you would be willing to talk to him, a meeting might not be necessary. Hon, you need to move on with this wonderful life of yours. You need to forget him. I don't think any good can come from confronting him. I think it will only bring you more heartache and pain. You need to forget it. I understand your pain; I can't really, but you need to let go of this and not let it ruin your life. He is not worth it. Meeting him would only make it worse and I'm not talking about him, but for you. He knows he hurt you. Let it go."

Jeff Coulier couldn't possibly begin to understand the hurt he inflicted.

My Plan A to confront him without much warning was gone. It was on to Plan B. Jeff Coulier now knows I have found him and I want to confront him. He's given Ron his side of the story. Both are now hoping I will, as in Ron William's words, "Let it go." Why not let them both believe they succeeded?

"Ron, I do want to let it go and perhaps meeting him would not be good. Please convey to him after talking with you, and thinking about it, I am okay and I do not want to meet with him."

"I think that is best. I will tell him. If there is anything else, I can do, you have my number."

Thanks, you've done enough.

Now Plan B unfolded for me. I would let some time pass to give Jeff Coulier a false sense of security. He could relax and think he'd dodged the bullet. Six weeks passed and there was no contact.

And, then the phone call was made.

"Hello. Is this Jeff Coulier?"

"Speaking."

"My name is Jim Simon. I am a private investigator looking into a matter for Sandy Phillips Kirkham."

THE WOLF EXPOSED

Six weeks had passed since Ron Williams called Jeff Coulier alerting him I was back in the picture. Perhaps by now, Jeff assumed I had retreated and would not want to confront him. It was not the case; I had my investigator call Jeff Coulier to set up a meeting between us. Mr. Simon began the taped conversation by asking Jeff if he remembered me and then said,

"She contacted me to address an issue of a relationship initiated by you when you were her youth pastor. She is requesting a meeting with you."

Jim described Jeff Coulier as "clearly rattled." Jeff responded by saying on the tape, "I don't deny the accusations. I am guilty and I know I have hurt her. I just didn't know how to make it right with her. I had therapy thirteen years ago and since then I have not had to look over my shoulder. I was a tragedy waiting to happen. My wife knows everything as well as my regional minister, Sam Fitzgerald. In general, he knows about my past and has a folder with my counseling and stuff. I know I had a problem and I owe her a lot. I have no excuses. What does she want?"

"I think she is looking to heal. She is not coming out of vengeance."

"This meeting could make the whole church vulnerable. I want to be sure the church is safe. Does she want me to resign? I would resign before I would let this hurt the church. I don't want my church involved. Bringing this up again will hurt my church."

"She has not expressed to me about wanting you to resign, and I don't think having you resign is her intention. I think she needs to face you for the pain you have caused in her life."

With worry in his voice, Jeff continued, "I just don't want to hurt this church with this meeting."

He said he was concerned with "her husband" being present and his possible emotions and anger. He continued, "I do not want to expose the church to any harm. With his voice trailing off, "I've been a good steward, or least I think I've done some good here."

Jeff continued by saying, "She was one of the finest young people I ever knew. She truly was." He claimed he thought I was eighteen at the time. He said he had not known how to make things right and asked if there might be a way to resolve things without a meeting; again, claiming he was afraid of what this might do to his church. His question, "Couldn't this be resolved without involving the church?" was obviously for himself, and not for the church. When Mr. Simon said a meeting was necessary, Jeff Coulier suggested his willingness to come to Cincinnati. He also asked if he could bring his second wife. (Nancy, his first wife, divorced him shortly after moving to Queensgate.) The conversation ended with Jeff praising Jim saying he sounded wonderful and was so kind and thanked him for being so discreet. "I appreciate you, Jim."

As an investigator, Mr. Simon was sensitive to nuances in people's voices, particularly their response when they are first discovered. Mr. Simon was not fooled by his words. Mr. Simon said Jeff Coulier was clearly upset. Apparently, he was driving in the car when Mr. Simon phoned him and had a two-hour drive back home. In Mr. Simon's words, "He may not make it, he was so upset. He was undoubtedly over the edge having been contacted about this." I cannot say I wasn't a bit pleased to know he was rattled. For all the pain and hurt he caused me, he deserved the anxiety.

His responses were ingenious at best; more likely blatant lies. "I owe her a lot." Or, "I just didn't know how to make it right with her. What does she want?"

When given the answers as to how he could make it right by meeting me, instead of just agreeing to meet me he wanted me to know he had changed, to talk about his therapy, and keep his past hidden from the church so as to not hurt the church. The truth was, if people knew about his past, it would hurt him. He didn't care about the church. He cared about Jeff Coulier. I thought about how he told me, "The people at Walnut Branch didn't matter" when I was told to leave the church.

During his conversation with Ron Williams and again when he spoke with Mr. Simon, he asked if there was any way to avoid meeting me face to face. He said he wanted to make it right, as long it did not require meeting with him. As nervous as I was, I now understood, this meeting and seeing me in person was causing him even more angst than it was causing me.

Wanting to resolve this as quickly as possible, not only for my own sanity, but for fear he would change his mind, I gave Mr. Simon a date for the meeting; Sunday, October 24, 2004. Only by coincidence, October 24th was "Minister

Appreciation Day." Such irony! It brought me a small smile to my face, and I certainly deserved a smile.

I also had Mr. Simon request Sam Fitzgerald's presence at the meeting; he was Jeff Coulier's supervisor/boss. There are thirty-three regions in the Disciples of Christ and Sam Fitzgerald had oversight for the churches in the Northwest Florida and Alabama area. I wanted someone with some authority in the church in attendance. In a taped conversation with my investigator, Sam Fitzgerald's first response was, "I was aware of some things in his past and there is information about his past on file in Tennessee. I have not seen the file, but I do know he had been disciplined in the past.

Mr. Simon then informed Sam about our meeting and he suggested Sam should be there. Fitzgerald said, "Knowing Jeff, as I do, I am sure he will understand after the initial surprise of it. I will talk to Jeff and let him know of the situation."

"I have already spoken to Jeff Coulier," Mr. Simon responded.

Sam Fitzgerald seemed perplexed. Jeff Coulier had not informed him of his conversation with the investigator three days earlier. Not surprisingly, Jeff Coulier was not going to inform his boss of this meeting, hoping to avoid anyone else knowing the situation. Obviously, not happy to be caught off guard, Sam Fitzgerald continued, "I would prefer not to meet on the church grounds and involve the church. I don't see a need to involve the church since the matter occurred so long ago."

Now, both he and Jeff Coulier were afraid of the church finding out.

Sam Fitzgerald went on to explain, "If she is going to take any legal action, I think it is important to know this occurred in the independent church and not in the Disciples of Christ, where we have oversight." He then asked, "Do you know if Jeff was the youth minister or the senior minister at the time?" The investigator indicated Jeff's abuse began when he was the youth minister and continued after he was promoted to the senior minister.

Mr. Simon informed Sam Fitzgerald the meeting was scheduled for Sunday, October 24th at 1:00 P.M. Sam Fitzgerald said he had a conflict on the 24th as he would be traveling to different churches for Minister Appreciation Day, but would send one of the church's disciplinary ministers. Before hanging up, Mr. Simon told Mr. Fitzgerald in no uncertain terms the date and time of the meeting was not negotiable.

Over the next few days there were several phone calls (all recorded) back and forth between Mr. Simon and Jeff Coulier. Mr. Simon made it clear, "It would be in your best interest to meet with her and if there are any changes, you are to call me immediately. She needs to face you."

Jeff's response echoed his old talent for being solicitous, "I appreciate the way you and Sandy have handled this. I am leaving any decision about what I am to do in God's hands, Sam Fitzgerald's, and most of all in Sandy's hands. I know and trust she will do the right thing."

Vintage Jeff. Once again, he was reminding me I would be responsible for what happened to him. It wouldn't be because of his actions.

Mr. Simon relayed to me Sam Fitzgerald, at the request of Jeff Coulier, would now be attending the meeting and wanted to meet at the Holiday Inn near the airport which was about thirty minutes from the church. From their conversation, Mr. Simon felt demanding the meeting take place at the church, "could be a deal breaker." Sam Fitzgerald and Jeff Coulier were concerned about who might see them and ask questions.

When I thought about these discussions, I was bothered by the fact Jeff Coulier and his boss refused to meet at the church. They were concerned our meeting might raise questions. Once again, he was keeping secrets from his current leadership. By agreeing not to meet at the church, I was participating in his secret. Even his offer to come to Cincinnati was to keep me as far away from his church as possible and not a true attempt to be helpful.

By agreeing not to meet them at the church, I was once again allowing Jeff to dictate and control the situation. My friends Zeke and Beth, who had been guiding me spiritually, were adamant we should meet at the church. "This is a church matter and should be dealt with as such. This meeting should take place at the church," they said.

Finally, asking me to meet him at a Holiday Inn Hotel seemed like a cruel joke. "Why not just meet at the Holiday Inn in Lexington," I thought!

Having a meeting with Jeff Coulier was vital for me to be released from the hold he held over me. Without this meeting, I feared I would never find the healing I so desperately wanted and needed. I had found the courage to come this far and it was not easy. Should I risk losing this opportunity by demanding we meet at the church? Mr. Simon's concern the location "could be a deal breaker" was a factor in my decision.

But this time, I would walk into the Holiday Inn with self-respect and with people who truly loved me.

PREPARATION

The meeting was set. Now questions haunted me. What did I hope to accomplish? Would I walk into the room and be my sixteen-year-old self again? How should I respond if he said he was sorry? Would I believe him? Should I?

From the taped conversations with both Ron Williams and Jim Simon, I knew a little bit of how Jeff Coulier might react and respond. He had admitted he knew he hurt me and wanted them to convey to me how sorry he was. But he had no idea *how* he hurt me. Words are easy, particularly for a narcissist like him. Still, I wanted him to know exactly what he had done. It wasn't enough for me to say to him, "You hurt me," and it certainly wasn't enough for him to say, "I am sorry."

At the suggestion of my friend, Zeke, I prepared a list of what I needed, in order to forgive him. I would attempt to articulate twenty-seven years of pain in a bullet-point list of his abuses.

I needed Jeff Coulier to read the list to me as a confession and then have him ask for my forgiveness. I started the list. I would make him read the list and require him to begin each confession by saying, "I was *wrong* when I..." And not just, "I am sorry for..." By changing those few words from "I am sorry," to "I was wrong," allowed me to remind myself what he did was indeed wrong. Simply by saying he was sorry did not acknowledge his wrongdoing.

There were so many things I could have put on the list, but the one I agonized over most was when he expected me to participate in group sex. Once again, my friends became my sounding board and Su's screened-in porch became my psychiatrist office. My admission of this act, to my friends, as painful and embarrassing as it was, was one more step to letting go.

To put the group sex encounter on the list would certainly be embarrassing for him. I wasn't looking to embarrass him in front of his wife and boss even though he deserved whatever shame and discomfort he might feel. It wasn't my purpose. I was looking to heal, and while I recoil at the thought of having participated in such a twisted act, it in and of itself didn't impact my life the way some of his other actions had.

So back and forth, we discussed the list. Did I want to include that? Finally, Su asked me, "How important is it he acknowledge the encounter?"

Thinking for a moment, "As odd as it may sound, it really isn't."

"Then leave it off the list," she said.

A major area of concern was photos taken of me. I'd always felt ashamed of them and now worried if he still had them. He might use them as a way of punishing me via blackmail.

Su asked, "What if he puts those pictures on the internet. Think what would happen if your kids saw them." This, of course, stopped me in my tracks. I had not told my kids yet. I didn't think he would still have the pictures, but I didn't know. If he were to lose his job because of my actions would he retaliate with the pictures?

Again, I was gripped by fear, and I wondered about cancelling the meeting and finding another way to heal. I knew I could not cancel; not at this point. If the pictures still existed and he used them, I would face it. I would not allow this possibility, or anything else, to keep me from this meeting. Still, the possibility of the exposure of those pictures terrified me.

Having finished my list, although not including the photos or group sex, gave me a sense of control. I felt good. Looking back, the only additional point I would have added was the night he left me to walk back to my car alone after I had been held at knifepoint. The list was important to me because, in addition to the list, I prepared what I wanted to say to him. I wasn't sure I would be able to say it all. If I fell apart during the meeting, at least the list would be read.

Knowing Jeff Coulier's need for control, I wondered whether he might refuse to read the list. Bill said there was no question he would read it. "Trust me Sandy, this creep will do whatever you ask him to do."

When I mentioned my fear to Zeke, he said, "Then you read it to him." In thinking about what I would say, I planned to memorize it. I didn't want to ramble and I didn't want to walk out of the room wishing I had said something I had forgotten. I would be sure, if the words would come out, I would say exactly what I wanted him to hear. The transference of pain written for so long on my heart, now written on paper, gave me strength. I was beginning to let go and the long journey of healing was already underway. In a distant kind of way, I began to sense God's presence.

Until the meeting, I spent all my time either rehearsing what I would say or trying to calm my nerves. Su listened hours upon hours as I rehearsed my speech over and over. My thoughts were like a teeter-totter. When I was up, I was ready, and when I was down, I questioned everything I was doing. Did I really want to do this? Could I do this? Remarkably, there were still moments when I worried about hurting him. I was still fighting an internal war between who I was now and who I was twenty-seven years ago. The battle of being my sixteen-year-old self controlled by him versus taking control now, was a constant conflict. The sixteen- to twenty-one-year-old child controlled by Jeff Coulier for those five years was not letting go. She was now fighting this forty-nine-year-old woman every step of the way.

One day, in a panic, I called Su, feeling sorry for him, "What if he loses his job because of what I do?"

"He deserves to be fired. There is no way Jeff Coulier should be a minister. Anywhere."

If I wasn't vigilant about reminding myself why I was doing this, I could easily have found myself listening to the part of my brain from twenty-seven years ago. I was not only confronting Jeff Coulier, but also the practice of the church to keep these matters secret. Just as Walnut Branch kept Jeff's sexual misconduct hidden, his current boss, Sam Fitzgerald, was doing the same thing. Neither his congregation nor his elders knew of his past. Jeff Coulier had a long history of misconduct championed by the devil. He had served in at least three churches and in all three at least one known act of sexual abuse occurred. Any teen or vulnerable woman in his current church might well be his next victim.

It was abundantly clear from both Jeff Coulier and Sam Fitzgerald they did not want the church to be aware of the meeting. I would not remain silent on this. I now understood my failure to speak up earlier helped contribute to Jeff Coulier's ability to move from church to church and continue his predatory ways. The first brave young woman came forward from his first church in Tifton; she had the courage to speak up. She trusted the church to do the right thing. They didn't.

I planned to meet with Sam Fitzgerald the following day after the meeting with Jeff Coulier and express my concerns about Jeff remaining in ministry. I would also inform his elders. I would draft a letter I intended to send after the meeting. Past experience told me elders usually don't do the right things in these situations, and with Jeff Coulier's pattern of manipulation, the elders may well not take any action, let alone inform the congregation.

While Jeff Coulier's current denomination was similar to Walnut Branch, there were differences. This branch of the Christian Church/Church of Christ had a loosely structured hierarchy. There was a president, whose office was located at the church's headquarters in Indianapolis. My letter would go to him as well as the eleven elders at Jeff Coulier's current church.

Bill, Su, and my friend Teri, would attend the meeting. Teri had stuck with me and saw me through the dark days after being told to leave Walnut Branch. She loved me when I couldn't love myself. She was my lifesaver. We remained close all these years later. Teri, Su, and I arrived in Alabama on Friday. I did not want to feel rushed. I wanted to desensitize myself. I wanted a couple days before the meeting to get a feel for the city in which he lived. Bill would join us late on Saturday afternoon.

We spent much of the two days rehearsing what I would say, talking out my fears, and thankfully laughing a bit. As I practiced what I was going to say, Su would remind me, "You keep looking down at your lap. Look up! You need to look right at him when you say these things to him."

Teary eyed and shaking my head, I whispered, "I don't think I can look at him."

Teri snatched my notebook, took a current picture of him from the church's newsletter, grabbed some tape, and taped his picture to the lampshade directly across from me, "Here! Now start over and look at him!"

We all laughed. This time Jeff Coulier could not tell me to stop laughing.

Saturday evening, Bill treated us to a wonderful dinner at Ruth's Chris Steakhouse. Our conversation was not centered on Jeff Coulier or the meeting. My best friends encouraged me and reminded me they were there for me. I went to bed that evening hoping for sleep. Lately nightmares had become a common occurrence and I had every reason to believe I would face a sleepless night.

I slept like a baby.

CONFRONTATION

For the last seven months, all I could think about was today's meeting. The day had come. In a little less than an hour I would see him for the first time in twenty-seven years.

It was a Sunday morning. We stopped at a crowded, noisy Cracker Barrel for breakfast. I couldn't decide whether to eat and risk throwing up or not eat and risk becoming weak and light-headed. It seemed as if every decision I made could have an impact on the outcome of today's meeting.

The four of us sat at the table without talking. At this point there was little left unsaid. I was nervous. I wanted to get it over. I was prepared and I knew it. My greatest fear now was walking into the room, seeing him, and being sixteen years old all over again. Would he try to make this meeting about him? Would I let him? Would this master of manipulation snare me again?

Because of the taped conversations my investigator had with Jeff Coulier prior to the meeting, these were not unfounded concerns. Jeff asked the investigator to make sure I knew things about him and said, "Tell her I have changed. If she knew the agonies on my list, she would feel sorry for me. I've had therapy thirteen years ago and I no longer have to look over my shoulder. I'm cured. I've been a good servant of this church." As always, it was about him.

He also had admitted he could not meet at his church because they did not know about his past. Listening to his taped comment, I could see this was just another way he thought he could manipulate me. "I am leaving any decision about what she should do in God's hands, Sam Fitzgerald's, and most of it's in Sandy's hands. I know she will do what is right. I am trusting her."

Arriving early, we pulled into the parking lot of the Holiday Inn at the Birmingham Airport; the irony of him choosing a Holiday Inn didn't escape me. It reminded me of the night in Lexington. Getting out of the car, nervousness blasted through my body. My hands felt cold, almost clammy, and I reached for

Bill's arm as we walked towards the hotel lobby. I couldn't let the location or my anxiety weaken me at this showdown. I took a few deep breaths. Sam Fitzgerald waited in the lobby. Pleasant introductions were made after which we went into a small conference room. I wanted to be in the room before Jeff Coulier, so we arrived early. We sat around the table, making small talk as we waited for him.

Breaking the silence, I asked Sam Fitzgerald "How long have you been a pastor at this church Mr. Fitzgerald?"

"I am a regional minister for several churches in the area. I grew up in the Baptist Church."

Su interjected, "I grew up Baptist as well. I now attend the Presbyterian Church. Too much guilt in the Baptist Church," with a little chuckle.

Sam Fitzgerald then asked, "When did you all get in?"

"Friday," I said.

Sam Fitzgerald sounded surprised, "Oh, you've been here since Friday?"

Being early only added to the tension. I could tell Bill was thinking and ready to stand up and scream, "Who the hell cares how long he has been the pastor here and when we arrived. This is not social hour. I have no desire to sit here and carry on small talk with a buddy of Jeff Coulier's!" To his credit, he maintained his composure.

Fifteen minutes later Jeff Coulier walked in the door.

Sam Fitzgerald got up, shook his hand and directed him and his wife to the seats across the table from me. Jeff's eyes were downcast and he did not make eye contact with me or anyone else in the room. Sam Fitzgerald sat at the head of the table. I was to Sam Fitzgerald's right; Bill was next to me, then Su, then Teri. The four of us were lined up on one side.

How did I feel when he walked in? I felt nothing. I didn't feel scared, angry or even nervous. I actually felt calm. He was obviously older, but in many ways, he looked the same. Of course, I had the advantage of having seen his pictures on the church website prior to the meeting. I knew what to expect. My first reaction was about his wife's appearance. I was taken aback a little bit. She was quite plain; the type Jeff had always made fun of in years past. His first wife, Nancy, was striking.

Sam Fitzgerald asked if I would like to introduce everyone, which I did. When I got to Teri, I said to Jeff Coulier, "You remember Teri, don't you?" For a moment he looked puzzled, and then I could see he finally remembered her. He sat back in his chair and looked as if he knew there would be no changing any of the facts. She was at Walnut Branch at the time.

Hesitating, waiting for him to introduce his wife, I finally said, "And is this your wife?"

Obviously embarrassed he had forgotten to introduce her, he nodded and said "Yes" without giving her name. He was nervous.

After the introductions, Sam Fitzgerald began to speak, "Sandy let me just say I know how difficult this is and I want you to know that Jeff...," *Oh no you don't. You are NOT going to take control of this meeting.* I cut him off.

"I appreciate that, but I will tell you what *I* expect to happen here today. First, I want you to know I did not come here out of revenge or spite. I am here because I need to heal and begin the process of healing from the pain caused by Jeff Coulier; painful memories I have tried to suppress for twenty-seven years."

Looking at Jeff, I leaned forward in my chair, with my hands clasped holding a handkerchief. Keeping his eyes fixed upon me, I said, word for word, the following:

> *"This is not easy for me. I thought this part of my life was over. The last time I spent any time thinking about you was when Tara, your next victim in Queensgate, called me one day, crying, telling me how miserable she was with you, how she had your baby. I remember thinking; 'I don't want to know any of this. I want this part of my life to be over. I decided then I was going to move forward and not look back.' My life was in order. I had a wonderful husband and I was happy. The only way I knew to survive what you had done to me was to bury it deep within my soul. And for twenty-seven years it's what I did. Every now and then your name would come up but you were nothing more than a fleeting thought.*
>
> *This past March, while driving to one of my daughter's golf tournaments in Greeneville, Tennessee, just outside of Queensgate, all those memories came flooding back without any warning. I was so overcome with emotion. I had to pull to the side of the road and just sobbed."*

At this point he closed his eyes and hung his head. I continued.

> *"I couldn't understand after all this time why I was feeling this pain and emotion all over again, and why after twenty-seven years? Why now? Everything in my life was perfect. I didn't want you back in my life again. I wanted to ignore everything I was feeling. I just hoped it would go away. I wanted to stuff it all back down again, but it wasn't going back. Those feelings were not going away until I faced what you did to me.*

> *For the past seven months I have taken a very painful journey to get to where I am today. I could not have done it without the help of my friends and the support of my husband. In the end, after much soul searching and prayer, I knew the only way for me to resolve this was to face you and tell you what I should have said to you thirty-two years ago when you first kissed me.*
>
> *YOUR BEHAVIOR AND WHAT YOU DID TO ME WAS UNETHICAL, IMMORAL, AND ILLEGAL, AND YOU HAD NO RIGHT TO DO IT.*
>
> *I was sixteen years old. You were thirty, married with two children, and the minister of my church. You took advantage of my youth and innocence and my complete trust in you as my minister."*

At this point I showed him a picture of us taken together at a church retreat just before the abuse began. Without changing his expression, he quickly looked at the picture, turned it over, put it on the table and slid it back to me. I grabbed the picture, held it close to his face and demanded, *"LOOK AT THIS!"*

His expression did not change; I continued.

> *"I was just a kid. Do you remember? You violated the most sacred of relationships; that of a minister and a member of his congregation. You used your position to sexually exploit me. You were supposed to be my moral guide, love me, care for me, and protect me. I was a child of God. Instead, you twisted it and made it all perverse. But even worse, your exploitation of me was deliberate and calculated.*
>
> **You knew exactly what you were doing!**
>
> *You waited that night in my home for us to be alone and then for the next five years you manipulated me, controlled me, and you used me for your own gratification. For the next five years I kept your secret. You lied to me and used my loyalty, trust, and confusion to keep me in the relationship. I survived your abuse but what did suffer was my faith. Because of what you did to me it will never be the same. The church has been contaminated by the memory of what you did to me.*
>
> *The church should have been a safe place for me and because of*

> you, it was not. My mother had every right to expect her daughter would be safe in her own home with the minister of the church. Even now, I am afraid to be left alone with a minister."

I leaned forward and pointed my finger at him, *"That's what you did to me."*

> "While I have faith in God, I have no spiritual connection to the church. It is still unbelievable to me, even after the elders found out what you had done there was still discussion about you remaining at Walnut Branch, and **I was the one told to leave the church! And you stood by and let them!**"

No longer able to hold back the tears, I began to cry.

> "I loved that church. It was the center of my world. I trusted you and I trusted the church and both failed me.
>
> But the real tragedy is you had done this before in Tifton, Georgia at Southwind Christian Church. When Ron Williams confronted you and senior minister, Ben Wilson, at Walnut Branch, instead of dealing with the situation as it should have been, it was swept under the rug. They protected you, and I became your next victim. In less than a year after being confronted with the accusation, which you didn't deny, you were doing the same thing to me. What if someone had only listened to her and ended up doing the right thing by informing the congregation and removing you as youth pastor? But no, protecting you and the church was more important so they didn't and you were transferred to another church, in Queensgate, and onto your next victim.
>
> **You are a sexual predator!**
>
> I have been fortunate. I have a wonderful husband and two great kids. Except for those five years with you, I wouldn't change a thing. I am proud of my life. My only regret is I didn't speak up sooner about you and for that I will always be sorry. I do feel better finally doing the right thing by facing you and holding you accountable for your despicable behavior.

> *I pray your granddaughters never meet a man like you when they are sixteen."*

I felt steadier now and I could sense Bill nodding as I talked.

At this point Jeff Coulier responded, "Everything she said is right on target. I probably should have been shot for what I did. I can only say I am sorry. I didn't know how to make it right. I knew you had married and were happy and I didn't want to interfere. I didn't realize this had been a problem for you. My father was an alcoholic and it impacted my life.

"I've had a history of hurting the people I love. My behavior hurt the church. One such instance, she sued; she had tapes and blew everything wide open. It caused a hurt like I had never known in the church. I never want to see it happen again. Finally, the people around me loved me enough to insist I get help and I did. Thirteen years ago, I had therapy where I was identified as a sexual addict. The therapist told me I had an amazing ability to compartmentalize things. I could function, living my life, separating different parts of it from another. I was required to take boundary classes.

"And I now have safeguards in place. I don't have a private office. I have been faithful to my wife and the church for the past thirteen years. I know I don't deserve it, but for your sake, you need to forgive me."

Pausing, he said, "All I can say is I am sorry."

Everything he said afterwards was about him; he had an alcoholic father, he had hurt churches in his past, he had therapy, he was a sexual addict, he had taken boundary classes, he is faithful to his wife. Not once did he articulate or give any hint of understanding what he did to me. The only time I was mentioned in his response was his statement I needed to forgive him.

I responded by telling him, "Throughout this entire process I have been guided by what my husband has told me, 'Sandy, no one can understand the hurt and pain this man has caused you. Only you can decide what it is you need to get past this pain. Whatever that is, you need to do just that.'"

Then I said, again looking directly at him, "You can never give me back what you have taken from me, and there isn't enough anger in the world to make what you did to me right. There is nothing I can say or do to change what you did to me, and I have considered them all. So, in the end I realized there were two things I needed from you.

"Part of my healing process meant not only facing you, but also facing what the two former elders at Walnut Branch did at the time. The first thing I want you to do is write a letter to the two former elders taking responsibility for what you did. I have a list of key points I want you to be sure you cover in those letters to them.

"You say I need to forgive you. You're right. I do need to forgive you. But forgiveness does not mean I forget or there are no consequences for your behavior. It means I try to let go of what you did to me and turn it over to God. But I cannot forgive you unless you know exactly what you did to me and for all the lies you told me. To say you are sorry does not speak to the pain and hurt you have caused. I need you to articulate, verbalize the things for which I need to forgive you. You degraded and devalued me by what you had me do."

For the first time since I began, I saw him look scared and uncomfortable. He closed his eyes, took a deep breath, hung his head and slowly began to nod. He looked up at me as if to say please don't. He and I both knew *exactly* what I was referring to, the group sex. It was one thing to admit to falling to sin. It was quite another to draw a graphic picture and give the details. It was the most emotion he showed during the meeting, the moment when he feared I might expose something to his wife and Sam Fitzgerald, his boss, something they did not know. Maybe I should have included it on the list. I then continued by telling him, "Of all the things you asked of me, you have never asked for my forgiveness."

So, when I told him I had the list I wanted him to read aloud and then ask for my forgiveness he asked, "May I read it first?" He wanted to prepare himself for how graphic and detailed it was. I told him, "Yes, you may read it, and only read those on the list for which you think you are guilty." I gave a copy of the list to everyone to read as well.

He finished looking at it and asked, "Do you want me to read it now?" He then read the list without feeling or emotion.

> *"Sandy, I was wrong thirty-two years ago when I waited at your house to be alone with you and kissed you. I was wrong when I touched you inappropriately. I was wrong to have sex with you at age seventeen.*
>
> *I was wrong when I used my position as your minister to take advantage of your youth and innocence.*
>
> *I was wrong to violate the boundaries between a trusted minister and a member of his ministry.*
>
> *I was wrong when I broke my covenant to protect and act in your best interest.*
>
> *I was wrong when I made you feel loved and special in order to take advantage of you.*

> *I was wrong when I told you I needed you in my ministry just to keep you under my control.*
>
> *I was wrong to use your loyalty, trust, and confusion to keep you in the relationship.*
>
> *I was wrong when I asked you to lie and keep my secret.*
>
> *I was wrong to hit you after you lied about contacting Kent.*
>
> *I was wrong to let Walnut Branch Church place the blame for my behavior on you.*
>
> *I was wrong to lie to Walnut Branch Church with a "confession" and request for forgiveness I did not mean.*
>
> *I was wrong, after that "confession" to ask you to meet me two days later in a hotel room.*
>
> *I was wrong to allow Walnut Branch Church, a church you loved, to ask you to leave because of me.*
>
> *I was wrong when I took your spiritual life and twisted it.*
>
> *I was wrong to take away your spiritual connection to the church.*
>
> *I was wrong when I contaminated the church for you by what I did to you.*
>
> *I was wrong when I committed adultery.*
>
> *I was wrong to take your virginity when, as your pastor, I should have been encouraging you to preserve it as a special gift for your husband.*
>
> *I was wrong never to have confessed my offense to you and, in repentance, ask for your forgiveness.*
>
> *Sandy, in each and every one of these things, I was deeply and morally wrong. Will you forgive me?"*

His voice was low as he read the list in a monotone, never looking at me. He finished and slid the list across the table back to me.

I answered, "I will try."

He then said, "You deserved to have it read with more feeling and not by rote. I don't remember all of these things, but I don't doubt they are true. "

Bill immediately looked at him, pointing his finger and said, "I've known this woman for twenty-seven years and if she said it happened, IT HAPPENED."

Jeff Coulier responded, "There are gaps in my memory due to the consumption of Halcion and light beer at the time. I am truly sorry."

It saddens me to think he not only didn't remember most of it, but I don't think he quite understood how it affected my life. Not once did he acknowledge the hurt he had caused.

I then brought up Tara, his victim in Queensgate, Tennessee, after leaving Walnut Branch.

"Whatever happened to her and her baby? Did you just leave them?"

He was clearly uncomfortable I would bring her up, probably forgetting I knew about her because he not only bragged about her to me, but also sent me a picture of her. He told me she was angry with him at the time and chose to leave, keeping the baby away from him. She remarried and her husband adopted the little girl and he never saw either again.

Then with a bit of defiance in his voice he said, "I don't feel comfortable talking about her without her permission."

I said, "I have nothing more to say," and I sat back in my chair.

Bill then spoke. He looked straight at Jeff and spoke with the authority coming from years as an attorney. "I do not believe you have changed. What I want to know is why after all of your therapy you have never made any attempts to help your many victims. You are not sorry. You are sorry you are forced to be here. Men like you don't change."

Jeff's wife interrupted him and said, "Oh Bill, he has changed."

Bill leaned toward her, pointed his finger at her and said, "NO, he hasn't, and I don't want to hear another word out of you."

Looking back again at Jeff, he continued, "Let me just tell you, my father was an alcoholic and it is no excuse for what you have done. I grew up with an alcoholic and I don't treat people the way you do. If you cared about anybody but yourself you would have made some effort to think about the people you hurt, including my wife." Bill became teary-eyed at this point.

His voice rising, he said, "It's what you do when you are sorry for your actions. Your words are meaningless. You do the right thing. You have shown no regard or concern for the victims of your actions. The only reason you are here today is because you had no choice. Up until today you gave not one thought to the people you hurt. Neither you nor this church care about the victims. You have made no effort to help them. You may be able to fool the people in your church, but you don't fool me."

Then Su said, "When Sandy told me what you had done, I wanted to shoot you too, and I had an alcoholic father and Bill is right, you are just using it as an excuse. I'm angry with you for what you took from Sandy. Her friends and I could never figure out why she was so active in the school and our community. She was Miss Volunteer of Anderson Township. She was always in charge of some school or community project, yet she never did anything with her church.

We could never figure out why. You took that from her, and you took the talents she could have given to the church away from them. You took away a lifetime of love and service, and it makes me so angry."

Teri spoke next. "Jeff, I have seen the pain you have caused Sandy. I have lived it with her. I don't know if you do realize the pain you caused and the damage done to her spiritual life. You have taken something away from her she can never get back—her trust in the church."

Then Sam Fitzgerald spoke. "First, let me say I admire your courage, but you are describing a man I don't know. This is not the Jeff I know today."

I then said, "I don't want to discuss that. I came here to confront Jeff and it's what I did. I'm finished. I will meet with you tomorrow." With that we stood up and left the room.

As soon as we got in the hallway I collapsed into Bill's arms and began sobbing.

After a few moments, I gained my composure and asked Su and Teri, "Did I say everything I wanted? Did I leave anything out?"

Having spent the last two days listening to me practice over and over, they knew what I wanted to say better than I did.

"You said it all," Su said. "I never had a doubt. I *knew* you would say everything you needed to say. Once you started, I had no doubt. You nailed it."

Bill looked at me and said, "I'm proud of you."

So, the million-dollar question was, how did I feel? I was relieved I didn't fall apart, but much more importantly, I didn't allow myself to feel intimidated by him. He walked into the room and was no longer a big powerful man who could manipulate me. He was exposed. He was nothing more than a fraud. The lies were exposed. For the first time in his presence, I was in control and I felt free. I was no longer held hostage to him or my past.

But did I believe him? He did what I asked. He read the list, agreed to write the letters, and didn't deny anything I said, although he said he couldn't remember it all. There was no admission either. He hadn't seemed sincere. He seemed scared, which was natural I suppose, as he had no idea what I was going to say or ask. He seemed most worried I might demand he resign. Did I really expect him to say anything other than he was sorry?

I certainly didn't expect him to fall to his knees, sobbing, asking me to forgive him, but he showed no emotion other than fear. His goal was to convince me how he had changed, in hopes I would not demand he resign. His statement, "I thought you were happy," gave insight to his complete failure to understand the damage done when a spiritual leader, such as him, crosses the boundaries of his ministry.

What I wanted more than anything, was for him to "get it," to truly understand *my* hurt and not just *his* hurt. He, like many pastors who are abusive and supported by the church, did not truly understand the consequences faced by his victims. He had received therapy, regained his job, and was forgiven by his church and his leaders. Yet, those abused, as I was, are often blamed and not seen as victims. We are left to figure out how to survive, often with a shattered faith.

Bill was correct. Like many abusers, Jeff Coulier never cared about the string of victims he left behind. He didn't care about me twenty-seven years ago; why would I think he would care now?

In the end I felt better for facing him, but I was conflicted as to what it all accomplished. Now what?

SEEKING JUSTICE

Without a doubt, confronting Jeff Coulier was necessary for me to heal, but I now felt an even larger need to confront the church about how my abuse had been brushed aside and kept a secret. Ministers in independent churches, such as Walnut Branch, and the Disciples of Christ, Jeff Coulier's current denomination, could be moved to new churches with no accountability for their actions and no warning for potential victims.

My overwhelming desire was for others to be spared the horror of what Jeff did to me. Often, I thought, if only someone had listened to the young woman from Tifton at his first church in 1970. If only the church believed her words and curtailed his access to other young women then I might have been safe at Walnut Branch. Ron Williams, his boss in Tifton, had tried to change Jeff Coulier's behavior, but even discussing sexual misbehavior was avoided in many churches. No safeguards were in place when I first met Jeff Coulier in 1971, and no such safeguards existed decades later.

In 2004, just two years after the exposure of the numerous tragic incidents of sexual abuse in the Roman Catholic Church, the Catholic Church was beginning to take some action, although not nearly enough, against abusive priests. Protestant and Evangelical denominations had far less hierarchy. Individual churches (or regions) had more autonomy and, as a result, there was less publicity and awareness about clergy sexual abuse. Churches were secretive about their offending pastors.

My first goal was to speak to Sam Fitzgerald about Jeff Coulier's string of victims. His authority could keep Jeff Coulier from abusing others. He should be removed from ministry, although I doubted the action would be taken. Even if Jeff Coulier were to stay in a church, elders and members should know of his past, assign him to a non-pastoral role, and be vigilant in protecting church members.

The day after meeting with Jeff Coulier, Su and I met with Sam Fitzgerald. Bill offered to stay and in hindsight I wish he had. Su went into the meeting absolutely convinced Sam Fitzgerald would ask Jeff to resign now since he knew everything. I, on the other hand, was not so sure. The meeting began by Sam Fitzgerald thanking me for the way I handled things. He then handed me the two letters I requested Jeff Coulier write to the former elders at Walnut Branch, the same men who told me to leave the church.

Before I could say anything, he said, "I know and have seen firsthand the pain caused when a minister falls and steps out of his boundaries." I held my composure but felt fury inside. *"FALL?! Steps out of his boundaries?!"* I was incredulous. He did not fall or step out of bounds. This is not a playground activity or basketball game. He had gravely sinned and exploited a minor, using God to do it. I let him continue.

"Jeff knows he hurt you and he took away your teenage years, and he cannot give those back to you."

After all I said during the meeting, Jeff Coulier's view was he *took away my teenage years*? He took away my spiritual life!

He continued to tell me how Jeff Coulier was no longer the same person and he was no longer a threat. He even said, "I can tell you this, I would leave my fourteen-year-old daughter alone with him."

"Unfortunately, my mother felt the same," I responded.

I then asked him, "How do you know he has changed? YOU DON'T KNOW THAT."

Sam Fitzgerald continued defending him, saying, "I have had the privilege of seeing him and knowing him. He is sincere."

I interrupted him, "That's exactly what he wants you to believe."

"Sandy, he has done some wonderful things here. I do know he had intense therapy for his sexual addiction, and I do believe in the power of God to change people. I believe he has been transformed. He has self-imposed boundaries. He will not counsel one on one or meet at the church with anyone. He does not have a private office."

"So why," I asked, "were you not aware of the number of times he committed sexual misconduct during his ministry in the past? Why do you only have limited knowledge, if you are in charge of him? How do you justify a man with such a history of sexual misconduct is permitted to have *self-imposed* boundaries?"

I continued, "If you don't know his weaknesses and his background, and what he is capable of, how do you know he is no longer a threat or even if you have the proper safeguards in place? Are these the characteristics you want in our spiritual leaders; a man who must be watched for sexual misconduct, an admitted sexual addict, and all the while keeping this information from the congregation and putting them at risk?"

With my voice rising just a bit I asked, "And don't you think Mrs. Smith or Mrs. Jones sitting in your congregation should be the ones deciding for themselves if they feel safe with him? Not you. You have no right to keep his extensive background of sexual misconduct from the congregation."

He responded, "I suppose we differ on that."

It finally dawned on me; Sam Fitzgerald was not just his boss, he was Jeff Coulier's friend. His defense of him and lack of concern for his past behavior told me my words had little sway. He acknowledged he was aware of some problems in Jeff Coulier's past, and there had been some disciplinary issues. He knew he'd been in therapy, but it was the extent of his knowledge. He didn't know specifics nor apparently want to know.

Exasperated, I tried asking the same question but in a different way, "How is it the very people in charge of him, you and his elders, know nothing or very little about his sexual abusive past?" I told him it was of great concern to me how his eleven elders were completely in the dark. If Jeff Coulier was truly transformed, transparency would be a part of his transformation. He was still hiding his past. Fitzgerald confirmed his defense, asserting Jeff Coulier confessed to an elderly female trustee in the church just two weeks after the call from my investigator arranging the meeting.

My anger grew as it seemed Jeff Coulier was simply doing damage control because I had come forward. For years, he kept his life a secret and now he confessed to one female trustee, probably the weakest trustee on the board; someone he could manipulate. Sam Fitzgerald continued, "He has a disciplinary file kept in the regional office in Tennessee with information regarding any incidences."

"Incidences? You mean sexual misconduct and abuse, don't you?" He didn't respond.

"Am I in that file? I am guessing not. My guess is, it is not a very complete file. What about the fact he hit me? Is his violent behavior addressed? Or do they not know about the incident because Jeff Coulier failed to volunteer *that* information? If you don't know what is in his file, how is it you could possibly understand his issues? The fact he has been identified as a sexual addict should be of great concern."

Fitzgerald went on to say, "I don't have access to the file, but I do know the commission on ministry had serious misgivings about his standing. They looked at the risk and then looked at his awareness and the change in him and they determined he deserved a chance. I felt no urgency to know what was in his file. I trusted the commission's decision."

They looked at the risk? Who would accept *any* risk?

Continuing his defense, Fitzgerald replied, "What he did is shameful and a disgrace, but by the grace of God it is not all he is. I see a person who is not playing games."

At this point, I couldn't help myself. My investigator discovered Jeff Coulier owned a red corvette. I then asked, "Do you think it speaks to his character that he drives a Corvette?"

At a loss of words for a moment, stuttering just a bit, "I.. I.. I.. didn't know he still had the Corvette. I suggested to him when he came here he might want to sell it and I thought he had."

I had to tell him my fear. "Look, I understand *you* feel he is safe, but there are too many risk factors. There is always a chance he will do this again. His past behavior proves it."

"Sandy, you are looking at a man you knew from twenty-seven years ago. You don't know the Jeff I know."

"No, Mr. Fitzgerald I don't think you know Jeff Coulier." Unmistakably, he wanted to protect the status quo. He considered Jeff Coulier transformed and obviously believed I was overreacting. The truth from twenty-seven years ago had no validity to him.

I finally said, "My main concern is the fact Jeff Coulier's current elders don't even know of his past issues and history of abuse. At the very least they need to be aware. I became a victim of Jeff Coulier because my church leaders chose to hide his past and it is exactly what is happening now. I have with me a letter I want to send to each of the elders. "

I then showed him the letter.

"This concerns me. I would ask you not to send the letter until I can go to the Commission on Ministry and gather Jeff's file and the region's policy on misconduct. Let me see what is in the file and see what I can find out. Would you be willing to allow me to do that? It may take a couple weeks but by the second week of November I should have it and then perhaps some decisions can be made. I would ask you not to do anything until then. I promise to consider very carefully what I find in his file. I will make no determination as to what, if anything, should happen next until I see his file. Sandy, I take what you have told me today very seriously and I understand Jeff still has work to do. You strike me as someone who genuinely wants to do the right thing. So I am asking you to give me time."

"Yes, I can do that."

The meeting ended. Promising he would look at Jeff Coulier's file, I would give him the two weeks he requested and wait for his response.

"Spotlights that shine light into dark places are seldom welcomed by those responsible for the darkness."

—BOZ TCHIVIDJIAN

OBSTACLES

Sam Fitzgerald's four-page response arrived in less than a week. He had not looked at the disciplinary file as promised. His words stung. He indicated he considered Jeff Coulier a low risk because he felt Jeff Coulier had changed dramatically. He called Jeff Coulier a father figure and asserted his life and words bear witness to the Gospel in the church where he has built the congregation to be "Three hundred members with a beautiful new building." He feared people might leave the church if Jeff's sins were exposed.

The letter ended with him asking me to not send a letter to the elders and the president of the denomination. He had the gall to write, "I would be afraid the damage done to a dynamic congregation, the damage to people's faith, the damage to their sense of security in relationship, the damage to their ability to trust, and the collapse of their spiritual dreams *would weigh upon your spirit*" (emphasis added).

I was relatively new at telling people about abuse, yet I could see in his words, in the implied threat of shame, he was employing a tool used on many victims. The message is to stay quiet; sharing truth will hurt institutions and people, and it is better to hide the truth. It was classic church-response rhetoric.

My view was if I did not send the letter, I would face everlasting regret if there were yet another victim. I wrote him back addressing his points and indicating how even a low risk is still a risk and something they could avoid. I reminded him Jeff Coulier had not been honest and transparent with him so what made him think Jeff Coulier truly changed? Shouldn't a church be built on truth?

Bill also wrote a letter back to Sam Fitzgerald which, in part, read (found, in its entirety, in the appendix):

Sandy and I together read your letter of October 28, 2004. For all the hideous misdeeds that Jeff Coulier has done, the attitude displayed in your letter to Sandy is as hurtful and, frankly, as offending as the conduct of Coulier. Four pages of what a great guy Jeff Coulier is. Four pages of telling Sandy how fortunate she is because Coulier elected for one time in his life to tell the truth. Four pages of "poor" Jeff and what a remarkable recovery. You even tell Sandy how fortunate she is to have the opportunity to face her perpetrator. What a privilege it is to spend thousands of dollars on a private detective to track down a sexual predator.

Bill went on to admonish Sam Fitzgerald for wanting to keep this a secret and for asking me to also keep it a secret.

Within a few days a response addressed to Bill and me arrived. Sam Fitzgerald did not change his views other than he agreed to meet with some of the leaders at the church. He did not apologize for what he said but apologized if he caused offense and hurt. He meant exactly what he said and was sorry I did not agree. He went on to say he trusted the judgment of those who reinstated Jeff Coulier; all this, without having looked at his file, as he had promised. My situation had no relevance because it happened decades prior.

In Sam Fitzgerald's exact words: "If you were to send such a letter, you would know in your heart you may single-handedly veto the experience of God's grace for many, many people. That, to me, would be quite a load to carry. I believe it would create new wounds for you." He continued, "Sandy, I have doubts sending a letter like the one you drafted will bring healing." The message once again: I would be to blame.

He then reminded me again, I had a limited view of who Jeff Coulier was. I should accept the wisdom of those who are able to see more than I am able to see. He ended the letter by once again expressing concern for Jeff Coulier's past being exposed, *"My concern relates to how much information gets to whom and whether those who receive the information benefit from it. I will keep you informed."*

He never kept us informed.

I needed a day or two to think about his letter and allow my anger at Sam Fitzgerald's words to settle before I decided what to do next. On November 1, 2004, the phone call came. It was 2:00 P.M. Sorting and folding laundry on the bed, I stopped to answer it,

"Hello." In a heavy southern accent, a woman refusing to identify herself said, "I have pictures of you nekked."

With the receiver clutched in my hand, I slid to the floor, slumped against the bed, my head between my knees, I could only manage to say in a voice of resignation, "Okay."

"I also know about you and sex and a man and a woman."

My throat tightened as I struggled to respond. "Okay." It was all I could manage to say.

Seemingly disappointed in my response, her voice became louder and more defiant as she asked me, "Did you hear me? I have pictures of you!"

I hesitated; before I could respond, she shot back, "If you don't stop this right now, I will use those pictures. If you send the letter, everyone will know. Stop this right now. You better not send the letter." And then she hung up. Unable to move, I sat on the floor with the dial tone blaring in my ear.

While she didn't identify herself, I had no doubt it was Jeff Coulier's wife, Janet. With my fingers trembling, I called my friend Teri and conveyed the conversation. She tried to reassure me, but at this moment, what words could relieve my fear? Those pictures would turn my world upside down. I had not mentioned those pictures or the group sex episode in either of my meetings with Jeff Coulier or Sam Fitzgerald. So, Jeff Coulier must still have them. How else would she know? What will she do with those pictures? I couldn't let my mind go there. I had never been threatened before and I was shaking. I had to call Bill.

I had not told him about the pictures. I was always relieved whenever I offered to give details about the time with Jeff Coulier and his response without fail was, "If you want to tell me I will listen, otherwise I don't need to know." And he always reminded me, "If it happened before you met me, it doesn't matter."

His assistant answered the phone and said he was in a meeting. Sobbing, I asked for him to call me back as soon as he could. Waiting 15 minutes, I called back, "Please interrupt his meeting."

Barely able to speak, I told Bill about the phone call and pictures. Without missing a beat, he calmly replied, "Sandy, she is blackmailing you. She made her intentions known. She does not want that letter sent."

Hysterically crying I said, "What am I going to do? What if she does something with those pictures?"

"So, what if she does?"

Doubled over and shaking as I held the phone with one hand and my stomach in knots with the other, I felt physically sick at the thought of those pictures being exposed. I let him continue, "First, if he still has those pictures, after all these years, it says more about him than you."

At that moment, I decided the risk was not worth it, I would not send the letters. Then Bill said to me, "Sandy, you are the only one who can decide what to do. I don't want to influence your decision, only to say, it makes no difference to me what she does with those pictures. I don't care if they end up on the front page of the newspaper. I mean that."

Bill offered to come home and wondered if I was OK. I told him not to worry. My final words to him were, "I am not sure I could live with myself if I didn't at least inform those elders, but I *can't* have those pictures be seen."

All afternoon my stomach churned as my thoughts vacillated between sending the letters, risking the consequences or doing what I knew was right. In spite of Bill's pronouncement those pictures made no difference to him, I gagged when I thought of the photos being exposed.

After my phone call to Bill, Bill immediately called Sam Fitzgerald. Clearly upset about her phone call to me, Sam Fitzgerald informed Bill they had an emergency meeting already scheduled with the elders to discuss the situation. Bill then asked, "Will this phone call from Coulier's wife be part of this discussion?"

Sam Fitzgerald agreed he would inform them and then went on to say, "I am not defending Janet, but from her perspective, she has always minimized the situation. She has always believed this situation and all the others were between two consenting adults. She does not see Sandy as a victim. She feels she is equally to blame."

Angrily Bill responded, "Really? Then maybe we should go to a reporter and tell our story and let the chips fall where they may. Then let's see who comes out on the other side."

Sam Fitzgerald interrupted Bill to say he would call Jeff immediately. He made it clear it would not be necessary to talk publicly about the situation.

Sam Fitzgerald's meeting resulted in Jeff's wife initially denying she made the phone call, but eventually confessing. Sam Fitzgerald defended her by saying she was only trying to help her husband who was fearful he could lose his ministry. She did not have the pictures. She only became aware of the pictures on the day of the meeting in Alabama. After the four of us left the meeting, Jeff, fearing I would tell Sam Fitzgerald about the pictures the following day, confessed about the photos and deviant sexual behavior in her presence. He did not have the pictures. He admitted to seeing the pictures in 1999 on a visit to Cincinnati when he visited with the former deacon who had taken the pictures. Jeff assumed he still had them.

When Bill heard this from Sam Fitzgerald he shot back, "And just exactly what is this man, who supposedly had therapy thirteen years ago for sex addiction, doing looking at compromising pictures of my wife as little as five years ago?"

Sam Fitzgerald did not respond.

Disgusted, Bill told him, "Don't tell me this man has changed!"

I was convinced more than ever Jeff was still a potential threat to vulnerable women in his church. He was not "cured." I believed Jeff had the same charismatic hold on his current church. The letters to the elders of Jeff Coulier's current church would now be sent. I suspected a letter to the elders would have little impact, so I decided to mail one to the president of the denomination as well. On November 17, 2004, I sent the letter by registered mail to the eleven elders and the president of the Disciples of Christ denomination in Indianapolis.

No one responded. Not one.

On November 21, I received my last written correspondence from Reverend Sam Fitzgerald. He had finally reviewed the disciplinary file. His letter stated "he was satisfied with the work done by the Tennessee Commission of Ministry back in the early 1990's in giving oversight to the process through which Jeff Coulier regained his ministerial standing."

Their secrecy and silence would continue.

Short of putting a letter on the windshield of every car in the parking lot on a Sunday morning (which some abuse victims have done), I thought I had done all I could to make sure he never abused someone else. I foolishly thought once I confronted Jeff, I'd resume my normal life. It had been a year of exposing the truth and struggling to shed decades of shame. I wanted to be healed. But healing takes time, a lot of time. A deep physical wound requires time to heal, but an emotional wound requires even more. My healing was not complete.

RESTITUTION

It wasn't just what Jeff Coulier did to me, but the response of Walnut Branch Christian Church that altered my life. How different would my spiritual life have been had Milton Crane and Ed Hahn called me to the church to support me as a victim of sexual abuse; instead, they told me I was unfit to worship in the church.

Their response reinforced the incredible notion I was to blame; Jeff Coulier was not. Jeff Coulier could be forgiven. I could not. Jeff Coulier was given a second chance, and a third. I was not. Jeff Coulier could remain in the church. I could not. When the church should have realized their obligation to help me, they instead discarded me.

There are still members of Walnut Branch today who were members when the abuse occurred. Those who were not, have probably heard rumors. I was instructed by the elders in 1976 to remain silent. Now I wanted the full story known to Walnut Branch; particularly, how Jeff Coulier's confession to the congregation was nothing more than a farce. He confessed on a Sunday morning and asked me to meet him two days later in a hotel room. I wanted the elders and those who were at the church at the time to understand who Jeff Coulier really was. I wanted them to know the impact the church's response to his actions had on my life.

For twenty-seven years the narrative had been manipulated by Jeff Coulier and told by everyone else. I wanted to tell my side. I wanted some vindication. I wanted to stand before Walnut Branch Church and say the words I was not strong enough to say the night when I was told to leave. I needed a meeting with the current elders of Walnut Branch.

Confronting Jeff was terrifying, but for me, it had to happen. My intent was clear. I had to hold him accountable to free myself from the guilt. I wasn't looking to shame the two elders who asked me to leave. I wasn't looking to blame the current leadership. I wasn't looking to blame anyone. I wanted the truth to be told and for the current elders to acknowledge what happened to me was wrong. I wasn't seeking to hurt this church. Unlike Jeff Coulier, this was a place which once loved me, a place which provided me the foundation for my faith, a place which held some wonderful memories for me, and a place which had became like my second family. There were members of Walnut Branch who cared for me.

Jeff Coulier's motives were purely selfish, with no regard for the pain he inflicted. It also wasn't entirely true for Walnut Branch. Telling me to leave the church was, without a doubt, *wrong*. My disconnect from my faith for twenty-seven years was the direct result of their actions.

As difficult as it was, I needed to recognize Milton Crane and Ed Hahn were caught in Jeff Coulier's web of lies and deceit. He was a master manipulator. Jeff Coulier's manipulation and control did not stop with me. His ability to con those around him extended to the elders. We were taken in; all of us, but as leaders of the church, the elders had an obligation to do what was right and they failed.

What could Walnut Branch learn from this? I knew my story was powerful. I wanted my story to change how victims were treated by a church. I wanted the church to recognize sex between a clergy and a member of his congregation is not an affair, but rather a way power and position is wrongly used by a trusted spiritual leader.

First, I wanted and needed a meeting with the current elders of Walnut Branch. I was certain if I made my intentions known, the church would be willing to help me arrange a meeting with the two former elders. I wanted so desperately to believe this time they would help me.

On January 24, 2005, I sent the current minister at Walnut Branch, Don Roberts, a letter explaining my journey of healing. I asked if he would be willing to arrange a meeting with the current elders, and the two former elders who had removed me from the church, Milton Crane and Ed Hahn.

I made it very clear in the letter I understood the current elders were in no way responsible for what occurred over thirty years ago. My intention was to address a terrible wrong done to me by the church. I was trying to forgive Jeff Coulier and now I needed a way to forgive the church.

Two weeks went by without a response. His response was *not* to respond. In my usual dogged fashion, I called him and left a message. No response. I called a second time. This time he answered. We spoke at length and he attempted to explain why he felt it did not make sense for me to meet with the Walnut Branch leadership. He didn't see how a meeting would help. His words stung, particularly when he said, "I understand Jeff Coulier was very charismatic. I never heard any of his sermons but heard he was dynamic and had all the qualities that would make you understand why they would want to keep him. So many good things occurred under his ministry while at Walnut Branch. I believe a meeting will only cause additional pain. I am concerned for the welfare of these two men and the pain it may cause."

He made it clear he would not facilitate a meeting with either of the two elders who had caused me so much pain by removing me from the church. He defended their actions, describing them as good men, dealing with a difficult situation.

But what they did was wrong!

These were the same men who allowed Jeff Coulier to remain as our youth pastor after learning of the first accusation of sexual misconduct. When he was found guilty a second time, he was praised, given a going away party and moved to the next church.

Again, I was dismissed. There would be no meeting.

Over the next few months I struggled to let go. Nightmares and painful memories dominated my life. I was not only angry, but also saddened by Walnut Branch's minister stonewalling me. As hard as I tried to let go, until somebody from Walnut Branch church heard me, I was not going to be able to find peace. Deep down I wanted, I needed, someone from this church to say, "You are welcome back to this church." I needed vindication.

When a victim seeks justice, it is not justice from the courts, but justice from the institution which allowed the abuse to occur. The victim wants to be heard. The victim needs someone from the church to acknowledge and feel his or her pain. The victim wants the church to be the church. The safest place on earth should be within the church walls and when the church fails, we want them to own it. I needed the meeting. I *deserved* the meeting.

In November 2005, eleven months after Don Roberts refused to help me, I contacted Charlie and Sadie, members of Walnut Branch. I had known them both from the church since Junior High and I hoped they could help me. Charlie's parents were very active in the church. It was Charlie's dad who took my arm the day at the funeral when other people avoided me. With Bill at my side, I tried as best I could to explain my struggles to them.

Sitting in their living room, I remember thinking, "What if they too respond as Don Roberts did? Was I being unrealistic and selfish to expect such a meeting to take place?" Thankfully, Charlie and Sadie were sympathetic. They indicated they were more than willing to help in any way they could. They knew me. They knew my heart.

On January 24, 2006, I met finally with the current elders of Walnut Branch. Walking from the parking lot, I couldn't help but think of all the times I had entered the church. Thirty years ago, I sat in a room with two former elders as they removed me from this church. Tonight, I would sit in front of the current elders and they would hear the truth. Perhaps then I could forgive my church for what they did.

We entered the room and made our introductions. Along with me were Bill, Zeke and Beth Swift, Teri, and Charlie and Sadie Eger. We sat in a circle with Don Roberts, and the seven elders, including Bill Fudge, the elder who Charlie and Sadie had asked to coordinate the meeting. Bill Fudge's willingness to arrange the meeting showed me his kindness and understanding. Though disappointed it had taken such an effort to finally meet, I was cordial to Don Roberts. One of the elders opened with prayer.

Failing to hold back the tears, I sobbed as I told my story. Unlike my confrontation with Jeff Coulier, where I felt anger, in this meeting I felt grief and pain. I was once again reminded how much I once loved this church. I was reminded of what was taken from me. I was reminded of the devastation of the night I was told I was not fit to be a member. I could not hold back the emotions at the incredible sadness I felt.

I explained how whenever I told my story to others, those individuals would inevitably want to hear what Walnut Branch had done to make this right. I insisted Walnut Branch Christian Church, for the sake of its own spiritual vitality, needed to come to grips with what was done to me and the response. The church needed to seek God's forgiveness for how it handled its minister's sexual misconduct.

I had prepared a list of the errors Walnut Branch made in handling Jeff Coulier and the situation. I handed each elder this list.

It was wrong...
1. It was wrong of Walnut Branch Christian Church to hire Jeff Coulier and retain him, knowing of his past sexual misconduct.
2. It was wrong not to disclose that information to the congregation, and as a result, put them at risk. This church had no right to keep Jeff Coulier's past a secret and put Louise Hofmann's daughter, Sandy Phillips, at risk.
3. It was wrong of this church never to have held Jeff Coulier accountable for what he did and insist he get help.

4. It was wrong of this church, after Jeff Coulier broke the sacred trust of his ministry, not to remove him from ministry.
5. It was wrong of this church to be a part of moving him to the next church.
6. It was wrong of this church not to be open and honest with the Walnut Branch congregation about the incident when it happened, but instead, doing everything possible to keep it a secret.
7. It was wrong of this church to ask Sandy to participate in this cover-up.
8. It was wrong of this church to blame Sandy for the actions of Jeff Coulier.
9. It was wrong for this church, in action and words, to tell Sandy she was not worthy of God's grace and forgiveness.
10. It was wrong of this church, in all the years since this happened, to never have made any attempt to make amends to Sandy... at the very least to tell her she is welcome in this church.

I concluded by emphasizing the importance for me, for the church, to acknowledge what happened was wrong.

I then explained my involvement in The Hope of Survivors ministry and my speaking before the Ohio House regarding Senate Bill 17 in my role as a victim advocate. In some ways I shared this because I still felt the need to show I am a good person, trying to convince them I was not the sinful person who had been exiled thirty years ago.

The meeting was near completion when the chairman spoke. He was very kind and thanked me for sharing this obviously painful story. Each elder then spoke. In some form or another, each expressed how sorry they were and thanked me for coming.

I once again asked if a meeting could be arranged with Milton Crane and Ed Hahn. There was a concern since both men were elderly and this occurred so long ago it may not serve a useful purpose. My heart sank.

A couple of the elders began defending Ed and Milton, "These are Godly men who have been faithful to the church and I don't think their intent was to do anything they didn't feel was right."

"I think, if given the situation today, they might respond differently."

As the next elder began, "I think it's important to understand Ed and ..."

Without hesitation, Zeke cut him off. "What they did was wrong. It may have been a different time, and regardless of their motives, it does not change the fact it was wrong. What they did to Sandy was wrong."

Then the discussion became a concern for Milton; his health and his advanced years. A couple of the men worried this might be too much for him.

One described him as being frail. Then Charlie, who is a doctor, spoke up. "I have been with Milton and he is in good health. He is anything but frail. I expect he will be around another ten years. I don't see his health as an issue nor is Ed's."

After more discussion it was decided they were unsure about contacting Milton Crane for a meeting with me, but Don Roberts and one other elder would be willing to talk to Ed Hahn.

The meeting ended with the chairman telling me I was welcome in the church anytime. I appreciated his words but I wanted to hear those words come from Milton Crane and Ed Hahn.

How did I feel after the meeting? Good. I accomplished what I wanted. I appreciated their willingness to meet me and contact Ed Hahn. I received a follow-up letter thanking me and encouraging me to worship there. This was a significant step in my healing. I was grateful. Their letter is included in the appendix.

Now I would wait for Ed Hahn's response.

THE ELDERS

As promised, Don Roberts and the chosen elder met with Ed Hahn. Afterward, Bill Fudge came to our home to relay the results of the meeting. Don Roberts said he was "pleased with how openly Ed discussed the whole event." Don Roberts' assessment was Ed gave the facts as he remembered them. However, not only did Ed deny he had asked me to leave the church, he said he did not want to get into the middle of something he had nothing to do with.

When Ed was told Jeff Coulier had written a confession admitting what he had done, Ed said it could be mailed to him. Because of Ed's response, Don Roberts felt a meeting with me would be counterproductive. Moreover, Bill Fudge relayed Don Roberts said he had a genuine concern for me and worried what a meeting would do.

I was furious! It was not Don Roberts's place to decide how to proceed. They'd promised to ask for a meeting. Instead, he had made me a victim again by assuming he knew what was best for me and denying me the opportunity to be heard. I decided to mail Jeff Coulier's letter of confession to Ed Hahn, along with a letter from me. Writing in third person about my past gave me perspective. It heightened my understanding of how debilitating it was to be asked to leave the church.

Dear Ed,

One Sunday evening thirty-four years ago, a charismatic youth minister, just barely a year into his ministry in Cincinnati waited until the other youth left a YAC meeting at the home of one of the girls in the youth group, and then he put his arms around her and kissed her. He was thirty and married with two children. She was a minor and a virgin. Startled by his advance, "What is he doing?" she thought, but reassured herself, "This is my youth minister. He wouldn't do anything he shouldn't."

It was a moment that changed the course of her life forever.

My letter, which can be found in its entirety in the appendix, went on for three pages describing what Jeff Coulier had done to me and how he had covered his lies. I ended the letter asking to meet.

He did not respond.

I decided I would contact Milton Crane on my own, without intervention from the elders or Don Roberts.

I sent Milton Crane a letter requesting we meet, along with the letter from Jeff Coulier. If he was in frail health, I assumed he would not respond. I wrote to him saying,

Dear Milton,

In the early 70's, I was a member of the youth group at Walnut Branch Christian Church. Jeff Coulier, the youth minister at the time, initiated a sexual relationship with me and took advantage of my confusion and trust to control my life for nearly five years. It was a very difficult and painful time.

In October 2004, I located and confronted Jeff Coulier with his offenses against me. He asked me to forgive him and I did so. In the same vein, last January I met with the senior minister and current elders of Walnut Branch. Though none were in leadership at that time, they expressed deep regret over what had happened to me at the hands of Jeff Coulier.

There is one last step in this process and that is for me to meet with you and Ed Hahn, the Chairman of the Board, and Chairman of the Elders at the time.

I will contact you shortly to set up an appointment or feel free to call at the number below.

Four days after sending the letter, Milton Crane called me. "Dear, I was so glad to get your letter. I have thought of you many times over the years. I have prayed for you."

We agreed to meet but the friendliness of his tone told me he did not understand the purpose of my request. Could it be he thought I was coming to him to finally confess my sins and ask for forgiveness? Should I tell him why I wanted to meet with him? The irony did not escape me. Thirty years later I was requesting *him* to meet me and he did not seem to know what the meeting was about or consider he may want to have someone in attendance with him. Our roles were now reversed.

We set a date and time. A few days later he called and asked to reschedule because his theater group would be practicing the same day for a production to be performed the following week. I was not longer worried about his frail health.

June 30, 2006, I went to meet Milton Crane at the retirement home. My husband Bill, Zeke and Beth Swift, and Charlie and Sadie Eger accompanied me.

We made introductions and his first comment to me was, "You're just as pretty as I remember you."

Finally, I said, "Milton, I would like to tell you why I am here."

After reading to him the facts of what actually took place at Walnut Branch, Jeff Coulier's grooming, manipulation, and control of me, his violent behavior and sexual abuse, I told him of my confrontation of Jeff Coulier. He seemed surprised and said,

"Good for you."

I continued by saying, "It was wrong of Jeff Coulier to take away my innocence and my virginity, but the response of Walnut Branch Christian Church was also wrong. At the time, you were Chairman of the Board and Ed Hahn was Chairman of the Elders. It's why I am here and why I've also asked to meet with Ed Hahn.

"As a teenager, you'll remember, I was very active at Walnut Branch. I sang in the choir. I taught Sunday school. I led youth retreats. If Walnut Branch's doors were open I was there, spending time and energy on something I loved so much and growing in my faith and my relationship to God.

"When Jeff Coulier violated me all that changed. The church became contaminated for me because of what he did to me. A place where I once found joy and peace, now brings me only conflict and pain. Walnut Branch's response to the situation contributed significantly to those feelings.

"Walnut Branch never held Jeff Coulier accountable or disciplined him for what he did to me, what he did to his wife, what he did to his children, or what he did to the members of Walnut Branch. To the contrary, he was sent off with a celebration including gifts and a letter signed by you and Ed saying, "How grateful many parents will be for the influence Jeff Coulier had on their young people."

I continued with the facts about the night he and Ed asked me to leave the church. He sat straight up and looked at me and said, "Honey, I don't remember any meeting with you and I would NEVER tell anyone to leave the church."

"Well, whether you remember or not, it is *exactly* what happened. Milton, you did not take my innocence or my virginity, Jeff Coulier did that, but what you and Ed took from me in the meeting on that night in 1976 was a lifetime of love and trust of the church."

When I finished, he then went on to disparage Jeff Coulier, and how bad he was. Again, he repeated he never liked or trusted him.

"I blame him totally."

"Milton, it wasn't just Jeff Coulier to blame. Walnut Branch was wrong as well." Sitting there looking a bit stunned, he now seemed to understand the purpose of the meeting. I continued, "Even after knowing what Jeff Coulier had done, there was a vote among the elders and you as chairman, to try and keep him on staff and keep his actions hidden from the congregation!

"Not only was Jeff Coulier not disciplined, he was given a going-away party by the congregation and invitation came to me and my mother, from you and Ed!"

He interrupted me, "Oh no! I wasn't even on the board then."

So, both Ed and Milton used the same defense. *"Couldn't have been me, I wasn't on the board."*

He then began to tell me how wonderful I was, what a fine young person he remembered me to be. "You were a beautiful girl and smart too. I'm trying to remember the last time I saw you."

"It was in 1976 when you told me to leave the church," I said and looked directly at him, amazed about his denial.

Again, he repeated, "Now honey, I was not a part of that. I wasn't on the board then."

Looking at him squarely in the eye, while holding the letter from 1976 inviting the congregation to Jeff Coulier's going away party, with his name at the bottom I said, "You weren't on the board at the time?"

"No, I was not."

I then handed the letter, signed by him and Ed Hahn to him.

"I am flabbergasted. I have never seen this letter. I did not write this letter. I did not authorize this letter."

"It clearly shows you were not only on the board; you were the chairman."

"I did not authorize this letter. I have never seen it."

Bill spoke up, "So, you are sitting here expecting us to believe someone else from the church deceitfully, without your knowledge, just put your name on this letter, sent it to every member in the church and you knew nothing about it?"

"All I know is, I did not have anything to do with that letter."

"So, you don't remember telling me to leave the church *and*, in spite of what is on this letter, you were not on the board?"

"Dear, what happened was a terrible thing. I am a minister and a counselor and I know how you feel."

Bill leaned forward and looked at him squarely in the eye and, with disgust, said, "NO, YOU DON'T. You couldn't possibly know that."

Charlie then said, "I think a lot of people looked at it as an affair. I too thought that, until I heard what actually happened. I wasn't aware of Sandy's age or the deviant behavior."

"Milton, I am here to try and heal from what was done to me. I don't know what else I can say," I added.

Zeke then spoke, "I think what Sandy needs is for someone who was at the church at the time to acknowledge what happened to her was wrong."

"Of course, it was wrong, but I blame him!" was Milton's response.

Charlie then asked if he had read the letter written by Jeff Coulier to him. "Yes, and I don't believe a word he said. He's a liar."

Looking at Milton, I said. "I don't have anything else to say. Is there anything else you want to say to me?"

"I think you are a fine young lady and you have come out of this okay and you are to be admired for what you have done."

In a disappointed tone and with resignation I said, "Okay I guess that's it then."

"What else do you want me to say?" he asked.

"I want you to say you are sorry for…"

He interrupted me. "I have NOTHING to apologize for. Jeff Coulier is the one who needs to apologize."

And with that the meeting was over.

Whether he was hiding the truth or had genuinely forgotten and rewritten history in his mind, it was time for me to let go of the past.

Meeting with the elders reminded me of Mr. Wilson. I often wondered over the years, how Mr. Wilson felt learning about Jeff Coulier and what he had done at Walnut Branch. Mr. Wilson, the senior pastor, who along with the elders, allowed Jeff Coulier to continue in ministry. He mentored and praised Jeff Coulier even with the knowledge of Jeff Coulier's prior misconduct in Tifton. I would later learn, when Mr. Wilson was asked about Jeff Coulier, he replied.

"That man is evil." Now it was finished. I had accomplished what I set out to do.

I confronted Jeff Coulier, I exposed his past to his elders, I met with the leaders of Walnut Branch to tell my story, and now whether they accepted the truth or not, the two elders who judged me and discarded me also heard the truth. Yet, I still felt unsettled. The need to do more took hold; a responsibility to do more.

"I never knew how strong I was until I had to forgive someone who wasn't sorry, and accept an apology I never received."

—UNKNOWN

PART THREE
ADVOCATE

"Telling a victim that they are worthy of protection and have a right to speak up about abuse is one of the clearest messages about human value a pastor or church leader can give to their congregation members."

—SHANNON THOMAS

SILENT NO MORE

Just as I knew I could no longer remain silent about the abuse in my own life, I knew I would now give a voice to help other victims, to raise awareness, and to work toward prevention. I wasn't sure how I would accomplish all of this, but I began to understand my story and my experience would now have a purpose.

I worried I might be overwhelming my friends with my unquenchable need to talk about the abuse. I felt so fortunate to have friends with an unending supply of patience, love and Kleenex. But I also needed to learn more and not keep burdening them. I spent time Googling clergy sexual abuse.

Fortunately, or unfortunately in some sense I suppose, I found an abundance of material. One particular site seemed to offer the kind of help I needed. It was a faith-based organization, which felt right to me. I didn't want to bash the church. I wanted to learn how to trust it again. The Hope of Survivors website mentioned I could personally contact them. I contacted Samantha Nelson, who founded the ministry with her husband, Steve. We talked many times and they offered knowledge, support, and encouragement.

Within a few months, I started volunteering for The Hope of Survivors ministry, sharing my experience and story with other victims and participating in awareness campaigns at various venues across the country. Through their ministry, I began to find my voice. Sharing with other victims opened my eyes to the widespread problem of clergy abuse in every faith and denomination.

Where once I believed I was the only victim and Jeff Coulier was the "only bad apple in the barrel," I now sadly understood this was not the case. I learned firsthand the power one survivor has in helping another. "God comforts us in our affliction so that we may comfort others." —2 Corinthians 1:4. After seeing my testimony on The Hope of Survivors website, I was invited by Barbara Blaine, co-founder of SNAP (Survivors Network of those Abused by Priests), to speak before the Ohio House of Representatives in Columbus, Ohio regarding Senate Bill 17.

The Bill, if passed, would change current Ohio law which required victims of child abuse to sue within two years of their eighteenth birthday. SB 17 would extend the statute of limitations. To expect a child abuse victim to file legal actions within two years of the child's eighteenth birthday is totally unrealistic.

This requirement leaves a victim no recourse years later, when they are finally able to come to terms with abuse suffered. In my case, it was twenty-seven years before I could speak of what Jeff Coulier did to me. At the State House, many courageous men and women abused by a trusted spiritual leader surrounded me, each telling his or her story of pain and devastation, each trying to convince a body of uninformed, and for the most part, uninterested legislators.

With opposition of the bill from the Catholic Church, one priest declared the passage of this Bill would bankrupt the church. If he meant financial bankruptcy, I wondered if that may not be an appropriate result for the world's biggest cover-ups. I was sure the actions of the abusive priests had occurred over and over for all those years, to which the church turned a blind eye, had more to do with the moral bankruptcy of the Catholic Church than this Bill.

The Bill failed.

Early in my recovery, I did not have a clear understanding of the dynamics of sexual misconduct. I failed to realize an adult minister kissing me at sixteen years old was sexual misconduct. In my mind at the time, sexual abuse meant intercourse. In truth, abuse begins when a person with power crosses the boundaries. It would take me another year *after* my testimony to finally comprehend how his waiting for me in my hallway and kissing me was not only morally wrong, it was an abuse of his position.

Through meetings with other victims I've learned the steps to healing are highly individualized. Each person's wounds and recovery are unique. Factors such as the age at which the abuse begins, prior sexual abuse, their emotional state at the time, and available support systems all play a role. Some victims benefit from therapy; others share their stories in journals or with their friends.

I had loved standing in front of a crowd of teenagers leading YAC gatherings. Public speaking was a natural path for me. God had given me the ability to speak publicly. I should use my gift. Speaking out not only gave meaning and purpose to my journey, but each time I shared my story it helped me to heal further.

With a sense of urgency, I wanted to address the clergy and administrators in the Disciples of Christ denomination. It had been nearly seven months since I wrote the letter to the president of the denomination, and I had never received a response to my letter from any of the elders of Jeff Coulier's church or from the president of the Disciples of Christ denomination. Once again, the response was no response.

The stonewalling infuriated me. Whether their lawyers told them not to respond or they simply hoped I would disappear, I did not plan to stop. I could not let go of my nagging feeling to do more. I didn't expect them to remove Jeff Coulier, but perhaps I could help influence policy change. If the president wouldn't answer my letter, perhaps a phone call would elicit a response.

Sitting in my kitchen I dialed and he answered. Nervously but calmly, I shared my history and my concerns about the church's lack of controls on pastors. I told him I wanted to speak to someone in charge of discipline and policy making. He told me he wasn't sure to whom he could direct my concerns. He explained, "Each of the thirty-three regions are responsible for hiring its own ministers and operate independently. My office has no jurisdiction." He directed me back to Sam Fitzgerald. *Been there, done that*, I thought.

I was done taking no for an answer. I responded by saying, "I understand from your website you have something called a General Commission on Ministry that seems to have some input in this area. Is there someone there I could talk to?" Relieved to be able to pass me on to someone else, he was more than happy to give me the number of Reverend Brad Devidsen.

On July 26, 2005, I sent a letter to Reverend Devidsen requesting a meeting. After talking on the phone, he agreed to allow me to speak at their General Commission on Ministry meeting on August 22, 2005, at their headquarters in Indianapolis.

Accompanying me to the meeting was my husband Bill, and Zeke and Beth Swift. With the help of Zeke, a long-term elder at his church, I was prepared!

I believe I had an impact. Whether it was enough to make policy changes I recommended, I will never know. I have learned over the years churches are not only slow to address the issue, they prefer to avoid it all together.

A major concern of mine was the lack of information being passed from region to region. A pastor who committed sexual misconduct in one region could move to another of the churches in one of the thirty-three regions in this denomination without his record following him. In addition, the regional minister had total control over what information was disclosed to the congregation. In Sam Fitzgerald's case, he chose not only to keep Jeff Coulier's past hidden from his current congregation, but he himself only had limited information on a file kept two states away.

I did what made sense. My solution was to write all thirty-two of the thirty-three regional ministers! (I figured Reverend Fitzgerald had heard enough from me already.) I expressed my concerns regarding policy and safety. I sent Reverend Sam Fitzgerald a copy of the letter. Of the thirty-two regional ministers, only four and the president responded. Twenty-eight ministers ignored my plea.

Of the four who responded, all expressed in some form or other their sorrow for what was done to me and commended my work with The Hope of Survivors ministry. Although each voiced concern about the issue, no real interest was indicated in creating such a policy to share information among the regions regarding a pastor's sexual misconduct. As stated in one of the letters, "We have little say over whom a congregation calls as its pastor."

Due to a lack of hierarchy and an established chain of command, many of the independent, evangelical churches set their own rules and answer to no one. There is no universal policy, making it easy for an offending pastor to be moved to the next church, oftentimes without exposing his misconduct. Sadly, as seen by the cover-up in the Catholic Church, even having an established hierarchy does not guarantee those in charge will do the right thing. The crux of the matter is church leadership will not, and should not, police itself.

My dining room became my research library, filled with books and piles of articles from the internet. Binder after binder was filled on subjects such as church response, victims' stories, healing, legal issues, church policy, and related topics. The amount of information required a new bookcase.

During this time I realized this array of paper and books, along with my increasing volunteer work with The Hope of Survivors ministry, was bound to raise questions from my kids. Beth was still in college and Bob had just graduated. I needed to tell them and now I could tell them with my emotions in check. More importantly, I wanted them to see me as a survivor, not a victim. Not unexpectedly, Beth's reaction included tears and concern I was okay. Bob was stoic. Both were very supportive. I explained to them I wanted them to know, in part, because I had been speaking out publicly about my abuse in order to help others. Bob said, so importantly, "Go for it Mom."

"When you finally regain control of your life's story from abusers who have held the pen for so long, it can take time to get the courage to write again, to say in effect: 'You are no longer the author of my story and I do not need your approval to write the next chapter.'"

—WADE MULLEN

DEEPER UNDERSTANDING: PASTORS

After my meeting with the Board of Elders at Walnut Branch, one of the elders, Jerry Adams, asked if I would be willing to speak to the seminary students at Cincinnati Christian University (formerly, Cincinnati Bible Seminary). He believed I had a powerful story and it would benefit those who were entering the ministry.

I thought, "God, if this is a test, forget it." How could I could sit in a room full of men who planned to enter the ministry? Why would I return to the campus of Cincinnati Christian University after all these years?

It took a year before I found the courage to contact Professor Mike Shannon, D.Min. and request to speak to his class. When we set up the speaking engagement, I decided not to name Jeff Coulier or Walnut Branch because of the many connections between Cincinnati Christian University and Walnut Branch. I decided never to use actual names when I spoke. I didn't want my message to be misunderstood. My purpose was to raise awareness about clergy sexual abuse and to prevent future abuses. It was not about revenge.

In a follow-up phone call, I reminded Dr. Shannon I would not name my abuser. He offered, "I believe I know who he is and as a matter of fact, you and I met years ago when he was your minister. Is his name Jeff Coulier?"

I concurred with a simple, "Yes."

He continued, "You may not remember, but back in the early 70's he arranged a lunch with the three of us one day. I got the distinct impression he was trying to fix us up. We never went out, but I remember the lunch, and thought it was odd at the time."

I didn't remember the lunch but of course the scenario was all too familiar.

In March 2006, I spoke to Professor Shannon's class, over a year after Jerry Adams' invitation. I returned to campus feeling more self-assured about my life now. I believed I was doing what I was called to do; offer a voice to a difficult and painful topic. I spoke in both Professor Shannon's class, *Practical Ministries,* and Steve Yeaton's *Leadership Class.* I began each presentation with my story, followed by key points on the dynamics of clergy abuse, power imbalance, consequences and, most importantly, how to maintain proper boundaries in the clergy/congregant relationship. Most pastors are faithful to their calling, and I am grateful for their service. Unfortunately, some are not and, therefore, discussions on the topic, no matter how uncomfortable, are necessary.

I stressed those in leadership needed to understand the power imbalance that exists between a pastor and a member of his congregation. Any physical relationship between a pastor/congregant is not consensual. When a power imbalance exists, the ability for the person with less power to fully consent is compromised. A power imbalance can exist in social status, job position, economic condition, age, or as in the case of a pastor, spiritually.

The website of The Hope of Survivors defines the four major imbalances within the pastor/congregant relationship: 1) authority, 2) knowledge, 3) experience, and 4) responsibility. I shared a slide visualizing the weight of responsibility on the pastor. Heads nodded. I hoped these young men recognized their future responsibility.

thehopeofsurvivors.com/4_major_imbalances.php

In the *Practical Ministries* class, I shared the scenario of what can happen in a counseling relationship. When a woman comes to her pastor seeking help, she comes in a vulnerable, emotional state. The power imbalance that exists does not allow for a true consensual relationship. In some ways, a person in crisis gives up a part of herself to the one offering help. She may no longer trust her own judgment. It is precisely why she seeks help. She would not enter the relationship with the pastor with the tools needed to evaluate the situation. She puts an inordinate amount of trust in the pastor. The greater the trust, the easier it is to be manipulated. Initially, she feels validated.

I explained to the students any time professionals take on the role of helping another, whether as a teacher, counselor, physician, social worker or pastor, it is *always* their responsibility to maintain the proper boundaries. It is a reasonable expectation to trust a pastor will stay within the boundaries of his profession. A woman seeking counseling should not have her problems compounded by her counselor's sexual advances. In the rare case where a woman is flirtatious or comes on to her minister, he must remain "the professional" and understand her actions as a cry for help, not an invitation to go to bed.

Laws are now being passed to protect adults from sexually abusive clergy and counselors. I found the website *Psapartnersagaisntsexualabuse.org* to be a valuable resource and urged church leadership to become familiar with it. More and more states are now recognizing the professional violation of pastors; making such relationships illegal.

> *"If a minister is having sex with a member of the congregation, that's not consensual any more than an attorney having sex with his client or a psychiatrist having sex with his patient."* –LINDA OXLEY

An affair is between peers or equals. By calling the abusive relationship between a pastor/priest and a member of his congregation an affair, we fail to recognize these imbalances and unfortunately, blame is equally placed. Other euphemisms like sin of the heart or fallen pastor or, as Jeff Coulier called it in his letters to my two elders, a debacle, sanitizes the sin of the clergy.

My presentation echoed much of the learning and research from Dr. Martin Weber, D.Min., a former law enforcement chaplain who worked within police forces. He has written several books and currently serves as a hospice chaplain. His words are direct and concise.

> *It's terrible to be raped by a stranger and worse to be assaulted by*

one's own biological father. In some ways it is most damaging of all to be the sexual victim of one's spiritual father—a trusted pastor, supposedly a man of God.

Here's why. Reasonable people are outraged at a sexual predator who drags a jogger off the trail into the bushes. Society springs to the defense of such victims. As for incest, everyone except enabling relatives is furious about paternal predators. But when it comes to clergy sexual abuse, congregational sympathy usually gravitates to a popular, powerful preacher. Ironically, victims of clergy sexual abuse often must go outside the church to find a sympathetic heart. Tragically, they lose not only their trusted spiritual father figure but also most, if not all, of their faith community—even close friends.

Dr. Weber works with The Hope of Survivor network, a lifesaver for many lonely victims who suffer in solitary shame because a pastor abused them. In Dr. Weber's view, whether a pastor was a confirmed predator who had a pattern of abuse OR a previously fine clergy member who fell into a sexual relationship inadvertently, in both cases the pastor MUST be removed from ministry. God will forgive him if he repents but he cannot remain in a position of authority in the church. He is no longer fit to shepherd the flock.

M. Garlinda Burton, writings from the book "When *Pastors Prey*" says:

Remove errant pastors. Period. Being ordained or licensed as a minister is not a right—it is a calling and a privilege. Ordination is the church's imprimatur on our representatives, who are not perfect, but who are called and set apart by God as servant leaders. Clergy (and lay people serving ministerial roles) who use their parishes as their harems, who exploit children and vulnerable adults and who operate out of a sense of maverick entitlement, harm the church and its members. They are not effective ministers of grace, they cannot be trusted to represent the Gospel of Jesus Christ in a hurting world, and they have no place teaching and preaching in the name of our church. Errant clergy are, of course, recipients of God's love, redemption, and forgiveness. Removing pastors who exhibit bad behavior and offering them redeeming love and pastoral support are not mutually exclusive."

When my elders and Mr. Wilson agreed to allow Jeff Coulier to remain as our youth pastor after he admitted to sexual abuse in his first church, they were telling me and every teenager and woman in our congregation, "We are willing to risk your spiritual life and emotional health so this man can have a second chance to keep his ministry." I do not believe God meant for me or anyone else to be collateral damage in order for Jeff Coulier to have a second chance. To remove an offending pastor or priest is not just for punishment but also for the safety and integrity of the church.

The young students at Cincinnati Christian University seemed interested as we talked about pastoral trust. It was important for them to understand the trust implicit in their role. I stressed they must never abuse that trust. It is always *their* responsibility to maintain the proper boundaries. They have an oath and a covenant to act in the best interest of the people they serve. Sexual misconduct destroys their integrity and trust, and if trust is destroyed, there must be consequences.

A period of questions and answers followed my presentation. I found their questions to be insightful and asked with a true desire to understand more about this issue. I continued as a regular speaker to the students and appreciated being asked to return. My first few presentations were, to say the least, a bit rough around the edges.

Professor Shannon's and Steve Yeaton's patience gave me the encouragement to continue. Each time I improved my presentation. I was grateful for their understanding of the importance of addressing this topic and giving me the opportunity to share my story. More importantly, each presentation brought healing.

"It is easier to prevent evil than to recover from it."

—PASTOR MARK ROWLAND,
ANDERSON HILLS UNITED METHODIST CHURCH

DEEPER UNDERSTANDING: VICTIMS

Shortly after I started volunteering for The Hope of Survivors ministry, I wrote a piece for their website entitled "Long Awaited Hope." At the time, I began to understand how my experience impacted others. After one victim read my story, she wrote: "I read Sandy Kirkham's story on your website and I could so easily relate to her, as I had a similar experience as a teenager. I've never known anyone else who went through this, and I was wondering if I would be able to contact her?"

Speaking at a conference in New York, I watched as those who had been victimized listened intently as I talked. I shared my story and spoke about the dynamics involved in clergy abuse. Women in the audience leaned in and nodded. The room was so quiet I barely needed the microphone. When I finished and took my seat, one woman looked over at me with tears in her eyes and mouthed the words, "Thank you."

In addition to the victim conferences and large conventions, I've spoken to church elders on church safety and policy. I've conducted talks with church members to help educate them about clergy abuse. More than once I've had someone approach me and thank me for my presentation because it allowed them to understand what their own mother or a friend had experienced.

The Hope of Survivors ministry often has a booth at large denominational conventions to spread awareness about clergy sexual abuse. I've been privileged to volunteer at the booth and share information about the ministry and talk one on one with victims. Whether to a crowd or an individual, sharing my story is a way to put a face to the horrors of abuse. Sadly, there were many of us whose stories were strikingly similar. I began studying clergy abuse as a way to help me understand what had happened to me and enable me to heal. I now realize how helpful my work is to others. After an abusive relationship, victims find themselves in an abyss, wondering what the hell just happened. Broken, discarded and ashamed, we find ourselves with no answers. Yet, when I learned about the stages of victimization, it brought some clarity to how the abuse occurred.

Now my desk overflowed with information. I set about organizing it so I could use my knowledge in lectures and conversation. There is often a pattern that will be used by abusers with set stages. There is terminology of the psychological tactics used by abusers which I've highlighted in bold. In workshops the participants and I would go through the stages of victimization and how these stages fit with Dr. Michael Welner's research on the stages of grooming (from Survivor's Manchester). I've consolidated this learning below:

- First, the relationship begins by targeting a victim with praise and attention which often makes her feel she is special to the abuser. This is called **love bombing**. An abuser uses false affection to suck in the victim. There is a reason for the analogy of the wolf in sheep's clothing. The wolf disguises himself with kindness and false love. What is striking is the patience an abuser has as he slowly lures in his victim.
- Next, the pastor or abuser often exploits the victim's vulnerabilities as part of the **grooming** process to gain the victim's trust. A false trust is established for the sole purpose to violate the very same trust he will get her to confide in him, showing concern, so he can use those vulnerabilities and weaknesses to exploit her. The victim rarely sees how she is being manipulated because it feels so good to be heard and understood. The clergy will be filling a need in her life. From here, Dr. Welner says the grooming offender will isolate and develop a special relationship where he is alone with the victim. At a stage of sufficient emotional dependence and trust, the offender can now sexualize the relationship.
- Third, eventually the abuser will replace praise with subtle criticism, often done in a joking way as to disarm the victim. He will become less attentive or overly attentive to extreme jealousy. Because the victim has become dependent upon his attention, she will do whatever she can to please him. His yo-yo erratic emotions are done purposefully to keep her off balance. Dr. Welner says this is when the abuser has control of the victim and **trauma** begins. Any attempt to question his behavior or motives is met with denial and responses such as "you are overreacting," or "you misunderstood," or even "you are

crazy." This convinces the victim she is the one with the problem. It is a term called **gaslighting**. The victim looks inward to see what she should do to fix the problem instead of looking outward to the real culprit; her abuser.
- Finally, on the occasion when the abuser pushes too hard, or the victim attempts to stand up to him in any way, he is crafty enough to adjust. Knowing his victim (a predator always knows his prey's weaknesses and habits), he will either push even harder or beg forgiveness, and for a short time, give her affection and attention. Most abusers are classic **narcissists**; people with a lack of remorse or empathy (although they pretend to have these qualities). They lie and manipulate to hurt others with a sense of entitlement, power, and superiority. Often, narcissists have a deep need for admiration and loyalty.

> *"I have a new understanding of people in toxic, or abusive relationships. The abused individuals are groomed slowly to accept the person's abuse or misbehavior. It is a slow process where the person manipulates them and gets them addicted to them, by giving them positive attention, and then taking it away, in a way that leaves people confused and off center. Slowly that it makes that person doubt themselves, and it chips away at their self-esteem, leaving them in a constant state of confusion, sadness, and crippling their ability to function normally and protect themselves."*
> —MARIA CONSIGLIO

In church settings, much of the congregation may be blinded by the narcissist's charismatic personality, resulting in defending him at any cost. Martin Weber says churches often scorn and blame the abuse victim while either denying the pastor's responsibility or attempting to "restore" who they see as an upstanding man of God.

To explain how a narcissist works I often share a quote from Carol Allred (a Survivor/Advocate):

> *"...the narcissist adjusts tactics as the relationship goes along and over time, the love bombing behaviors happen less and less, while the withholding occurs more and more. This is referred to as the mask coming off. Victims describe this as being jerked back and forth, or feeling like the relationship is a rollercoaster, or feeling like they are walking on eggshells. It's exhausting and one day*

the victim notices he/she hasn't been happy in a while, but when they bring it up, the conversation gets turned around so they are to blame, leaving them shaking their head in confusion. There are equally confusing double standards, things not adding up, strange silent treatments, criticisms where they used to be perfect, etc. These are all nothing more than mind games, but the victim has no idea. Psychological abuse is subtle. The abuser will throw bones of love bombing whenever they need to distract the victim from seeing their tactics. This is called intermittent reinforcement, which is a bona fide brainwashing tactic."

The additional horror to the victim is the **trauma** which happens. Trauma interrupts the cognitive thinking process from making rational decisions and rewires the brain's ability to think clearly. It can be sudden or systematic over time.

For a long time, researchers described the response to trauma as either fight or flight. It is now understood there is a third, more common reaction: freeze. Instead of responding to fear by fighting back or fleeing, the mind and the body freeze, preventing the victim from taking action. For me, healing occurred every time I spoke to a group or to an individual. Whether I shared information on abuse with PowerPoint presentations or simply listened to one person's story, I grew stronger. Shame for my actions was replaced by compassion.

Thankfully there were resources and groups that offered support. Certainly, conferences and The Hope of Survivors network were a lifeline for me. And, after being invited by the co-founder of SNAP (Survivors Network of those Abused by Priests) to speak before the Ohio House on Senate Bill 17, I attended their weekly support group. I will be forever grateful to Christy Miller and Dan Frondorf, co-leaders of the group, for allowing me, a token Protestant, into their fold.

> *"Sometimes God redeems your story by surrounding you with people who need to hear your past so it doesn't become their future."*
>
> —JON ACUFF

SETTING THINGS RIGHT

I wanted to apologize to the people I had hurt, particularly my best friend Chris. Once Jeff Coulier began to control my life, he created a wedge between us as another way to isolate and control me. I knew I could never explain to Chris what happened to me at the time and I hurt her deeply. After Jeff Coulier left Walnut Branch Church, Chris learned what had happened.

Chris and I kept in touch over the decades, but it was never the same as before. After I confronted Jeff Coulier, I invited her to dinner to try and explain why our friendship fell apart. We talked about the night she hit Jeff's car. She did see him kiss me, but she was too upset about the car. Thinking about it later, she brushed it off, just like I did. Trusting Jeff, she thought she just misunderstood what she saw. As we cried and hugged each other, she said, "All these years I wondered what I had done to cause you to pull away from me."

My story both saddened and angered her, because Jeff hurt me and destroyed our friendship. Her fury was explosive. She too was used by him. "I want to go down there and confront him." Initially I asked her not to do so. I didn't want to stir things up again. But as time passed, I realized she had healing to do as well.

Soon thereafter I told my story to both of my sisters. They too were enraged, not just for what he had done to me but how he had remained in ministry. How could it be they asked, even after his confession he could continue as a pastor? They were appalled he continued as a pastor. Perhaps more frightening, his current congregation was clueless about his past.

On a Sunday morning in 2006, my sister Jackie and Chris went to Faith Christian Church unannounced, sat in the third row and listened to Jeff Coulier preach. Waiting for him after the service, he began walking toward them. First though, he stopped and retrieved their visitor cards, before anyone else saw them, and slipped them into his pockets. Attendance numbers may have been important to him, but he didn't want these visitors to be known.

Chris was surprised he recognized her, and he gave both a hug. Chris talked about all the people he had hurt. He apologized for severing her relationship with me and blamed his behavior on his alcoholic father. Chris replied, "I don't want to hear your sob story, you need to be gone. Out of the ministry. Vulnerable women are not safe with you here."

Jackie doubted his understanding of the hurt he caused and asked him directly how many women there had been? "Oh many; I was a predator," was his response.

Jackie then assumed the leadership of his church knew about his past when they hired him so she pointed to a woman nearby and asked, "So, if I walk up to that woman right now, she would not be surprised by our discussion?"

He responded, "I have spared them some of the details."

"So, you continue to hide who you are."

The conversation lasted about a half hour with Chris asking him why he continued as a pastor. He indicated he was tired of it all and would probably retire and go somewhere where no one could find him. He said unmistakably, "Sandy won't be able to hurt me anymore. I'll not be able to be found."

Chris replied, "It is exactly what you should do. Go away and stay out of the ministry!"

"What makes you the judge? I don't owe you any explanation."

Before leaving, Chris handed him information on clergy sexual abuse.

The next day, Jeff Coulier called me. His voice shook with anger as he accused me of sending Chris and Jackie to intimidate him. "What are you trying to do to me?" He accused me of emotional blackmail and lying about forgiving him.

Infuriated, he asked, "What are you trying to do to me? What do you want from me?"

"Nothing," I replied.

"You lied to me!" in a tone I remembered from so long ago. "You haven't forgiven me or you wouldn't keep doing this to me and continue to talk about it. You are only trying to hurt me more."

I hung up.

Hearing his accusatory tone brought back so many horrible feelings and memories. I began to shake. Bill, as usual, was there to steady me. Bill immediately called Sam Fitzgerald and told him; Jeff Coulier was **never** to contact us again. "I never want to hear that man's voice again!"

Sam Fitzgerald agreed and said it was a stupid thing for Jeff Coulier to do and totally inappropriate, but the visit from Chris and Jackie had upset him.

Bill then informed him there was a new sexual predator law in Ohio. He explained we were looking at our options and Jeff Coulier's call was not helping. Bill ended the phone conversation with the statement, "Jeff Coulier is clearly a predator."

A new sexual predator registry, which replaced the failed Senate Bill 17, was now in place in Ohio. The Registry was a Declaratory Judgment, which has no legal standing and provides no monetary damages, but it creates a registry of sex offenders. Some saw it as a way to appease those abused in the Catholic Church who were upset by the failure of SB 17.

The statute of limitations prohibited me from taking any legal action against Jeff Coulier. Laws vary from state to state. In many states, the law requires a victim of sexual abuse to file a claim within two years of turning age eighteen. Those who work with victims know it is highly unlikely a young person would be capable of naming their offender within that time frame. Moreover, rarely does a young person have the financial means to take action.

Beginning in August 2006, a victim of sexual abuse as a minor could file a Declaratory Judgment to put an abuser on an Ohio internet registry. The victim must present enough evidence to show the abuse more than likely occurred. Again, due to the statute of limitations, the accused is not held criminally responsible nor does this action allow for any financial recovery. No legal action may be taken against the accused; it would allow only his name to be put on a list in the state of Ohio.

Jeff Coulier's actions after our meeting convinced me he had not changed and Sam Fitzgerald's assertion that, "He is a low risk," horrified me. I had done all I could to alert the Disciples of Christ denomination of the danger of allowing a man such as Jeff Coulier to remain in good standing.

On January 10, 2007, Jeff Coulier received notice from the Ohio Attorney General's office investigating my claim of abuse. The following day, January 11, he abruptly announced his retirement to his congregation. My goal was the Disciples of Christ prohibit him from ministry. It did not occur. While retirement had not been my purpose; it did remove him.

After providing information to the Ohio Attorney General, I was informed in a letter dated November 28, 2007, that while I was a minor, the age of consent in Ohio at that time was sixteen. Therefore, my allegations did not constitute abuse and no crime was committed. The year after my abuse began, 1972, the age of consent was raised to eighteen.

He did not rape me nor have I ever claimed he had. However, if Jeff Coulier had been my teacher, and not my pastor, I would have had a claim. Under

Ohio law, students cannot give consent to an instructor or teacher as they are in a position of authority and could take advantage of the teen. In a response through his attorney, Jeff Coulier denied ever being my teacher. From my perspective, teaching at camp and leading Bible studies was indication of holding a role as a teacher and he certainly had authority. Jeff Coulier, with his history, could not get a job anywhere in this country teaching in a high school, but he remains in good standing as a spiritual leader.

The letter ended from the Ohio Attorney General with, "We thank you for your correspondence; however, our office is unable to take legal action in this case." Jeff Coulier received the same letter.

He returned to the ministry, ending his retirement of six months.

BACK IN THE PULPIT

Less than a year after coming out of retirement, Jeff Coulier was recommended by Sam Fitzgerald to fill the position of interim minister in another small church in Alabama. One of the assurances Sam Fitzgerald and Jeff Coulier gave to me in our meeting was safeguards were in place for him. More importantly, he did not have a private office. Yet, for the summer while pastoring this church, he would be given an apartment to live in while his wife remained home.

A painful aspect of my healing was the realization had the Walnut Branch leadership removed Jeff Coulier from the ministry or, at the very least, informed the congregation of his past behavior, I might have been spared the life-altering effect of his abuse. They *knew!* They *knew!* And they did *nothing* to stop him.

I acknowledge clergy who have broken their ordination vows, committed adultery, and used a member of their flock for his own sexual needs, can be forgiven by God. But by their *own* actions, they should lose the privilege of ministry. They deserve the love and grace God gives us all, but love and grace should be given to them while sitting in a pew, not standing in the pulpit. The goal of restoration of these men should be to restore them back to Christ, not back to their jobs.

Equally painful was the realization my silence over the years contributed to him continuing to prey on women. Since the disclosure of past sexual abuse is not required by denomination policy when considering the hiring of a minister, my conscience would not permit me to remain silent. I sent a letter to each of the eight leaders of the church where he was now serving as an interim minister informing them about Jeff Coulier.

A couple weeks later, on July 1, 2008, I opened my computer to respond to my emails. It was a hot muggy day and it felt good to be in an air-conditioned room. Opening an email from a fellow survivor of clergy abuse, I read about her pain and struggle to regain her faith in God. We'd met at a conference in April, and we had exchanged emails on occasion since then. She too had been sexually abused as a teenager by her youth pastor.

Being able to share my story to help other victims was rewarding. It was a way to take a horrible experience and make some good from it. As I was drafting a response to her, a new email popped up on my screen, with the AOL chime, "You've Got Mail."

I immediately recognized the name and the subject line, "Jeff Coulier". It was a response to my letter from the church moderator where he was now serving as the interim pastor in Alabama. I became physically ill when I read it. Her words were harsh, cutting, and accusatory. I sat there dumbfounded.

> *From: ------*
> *To: Sandy Kirkham*
> *Subject: Jeff Coulier*
>
> *I am truly sorry you have suffered from such a terrible injustice. I hope one day you will find the peace you are seeking and deserve.*
>
> *But I have to tell you in your campaign to destroy Rev. Coulier, you are not helping anyone but yourself! What you are doing is driven by evil not by love. You don't want to help others who have suffered as you, you want to hurt someone who hurt you.*
>
> *Your actions to help others has caused more harm and pain than you could possibly dream. Your hateful, selfish actions have accomplished nothing but to cause great hardship for a tiny church struggling to keep our doors open. I pray you can live with the fact your actions, and yours alone, may well be the cause of a church closing.*
>
> *God grants forgiveness. If you don't want to forgive Rev. Coulier, that is your choice.*
>
> *What you are doing is driven by evil, not by love. For you to choose to hurt hundreds of people with this hate campaign of yours is just plain evil. I sincerely hope you are happy and pleased with your evilness. Yes, we now know Rev. Coulier made some serious judgement mistakes in the past. It is a shame you will not be able to enjoy your life, now or ever. I feel the deepest pity for you. You have hurt more people with your hatred for one person than Rev. Coulier ever thought about hurting. May God Forgive You!*

Her words were so spiteful they did not seem credible and yet this response is all too common toward victims. Her emotional response came from anger or, perhaps, Jeff Coulier was behind the words, manipulating the leadership to believe he was martyred for his sins. Who knows what lies he told!

"People don't want to hear the truth because they don't want their illusions destroyed."

—FRIEDRICH NIETZSCHE

WHAT THE HELL JUST HAPPENED?

Healing is hard work. Waves of depression often engulfed me. I mourned for the loss of my spiritual life, knowing it would never be the same. Where once I could sit in church and block out the reminders, those memories were now ripping at my heart. It took everything I had to make it through a Sunday morning. There were days when I simply stayed in bed. SNAP meetings and The Hope of Survivors network became my lifeline. While I never sought professional help, I think I would have benefited from it, as many victims have.

One of the hardest parts of moving forward after clerical abuse is forgiving the perpetrator. The message of the church is to love and forgive. But the idea seemed outright impossible to me. How could a man who violated so many women, who stole my teenage years and who caused me to be thrown out of a church deserve forgiveness? Yet, in church settings, we are taught and told to forgive and even to love. Sometimes I thought about abuse victims in secular situations and wondered if they were expected to forgive their abuser, or if their abusers were worthy of forgiveness? No victim should ever be told they must forgive.

In the meeting with Jeff Coulier when he asked if I would forgive him, I responded, "I will try". Time had passed but I was still angry at what happened and wondered how God had let it happen. I never blamed God, but I certainly doubted his presence during those years. Where was he and was my anger justified? Occasionally I would open a Bible and look for some healing. One afternoon, I Googled "shepherd," a term I'd always associated with church leadership. The following verses came up:

> *"Care for the flock God entrusted to you. Watch over them willingly, not grudgingly, not for what you can get out of it, but because you are eager to serve God. Don't lord over the people assigned to your care, but lead them by your good example."* —I PETER 5:2-4

I stopped when I got to the words *"Don't lord over the people assigned to your care"* and thought how Jeff Coulier had violated God's words. He had not done what was commanded!

More helpful was a verse from Jeremiah.

> *"Woe to the shepherds who are destroying and scattering the sheep of my pasture declares the Lord. I am about to attend to you for your evil deeds declares the Lord. And they will no longer be afraid."* —JEREMIAH 23:1-2

Woe is a heavy word and means affliction, misery, and wretchedness; powerful words. Could it mean God too was angry at how Jeff had betrayed me as one of his lambs, and betrayed God as one of his shepherds?

I knew I needed to forgive Jeff Coulier to move forward, but doing so seemed impossible given my emotions. For months, I struggled internally with what forgiveness meant; its connotation was weighted with so many meanings.

Forgiveness is NOT about condoning behavior. Abusers have committed evil acts and should be judged as such. No excuses.

Forgiveness is not forgetting. People often say forgive and forget as though what happened is meaningless.

Forgiveness is not foregoing consequences or justice. There are consequences to all behavior, good and bad. One of the consequences of clergy sexual misconduct/abuse is removal from the ministry. James 3:1 talks of stricter judgment for spiritual leaders. These men have demonstrated by their behavior they are no longer fit to be shepherds of the flock. As in any profession, there are lines and boundaries not to be crossed and when they are, the privilege of the position is lost. Church teachings will often say, "It's not our place to judge," foregoing true consequences.

Neither does forgiveness mean I will remain silent. Speaking about our abuse helps us heal. As victims, we are often told, "You hurt the church by talking about this." Jeff Coulier accused me of lying to him about forgiving him because as he put it, "You said you forgave me so why do you continue to talk about it?" Courageous survivors willing to speak out should be celebrated as they can help others.

> *"When victims ask the church to hear them, it demonstrates their faithfulness and their trust in the church. Disclosure and willingness of victims to talk about their abuse is a gift and should be valued and affirmed,"* —MARIE FORTUNE

So, what is forgiveness? For me, forgiveness is letting go of the hurt and anger. Some victims prefer to use the words "they are going to unburden themselves of the offender," instead of using the words "forgive the offender." In my case, as long as I held onto the suffering and anger, I remained trapped with him. It prevented me from living in the present; from healing.

For the first twenty-seven years following his abuse, I allowed the shame and guilt to eat away at me. After confronting him, anger and pain ate away at me. I decided to let go of the anger to allow me to channel my time and energy toward affecting change in the church and helping other survivors. I had to let go so I could begin to heal.

None of this means there cannot be justified anger that looks to change the culture of blaming the victim. The culture which twists scripture to allow for easy forgiveness, and cheap grace of returning offending pastors, wolves in sheep's clothing, back to the pulpit. This practice has to stop!

Forgiveness was difficult because I wanted some kind of justice or consequences for what he did to me. Legally, I had no recourse and Jeff Coulier suffered little or no consequences for his actions. But I asked myself, "What could happen which would be enough for me to feel better?" Jeff Coulier felt little or no remorse and never sensed the pain he inflicted. Nothing would change. There may have been some consolation had I been able to take some legal action, but I had to accept it would not happen. Forgiveness meant letting go of the hope of a different outcome. He still continues in ministry and remains in good standing in the Disciples of Christ Church.

I also worried by forgiving him I was being "unfaithful" to my pain. Letting go would somehow diminish what he did to me. I wanted to remind myself and never forget.

Most importantly, I wanted to live the life I was meant to live, **not** the one created by the damage done by Jeff Coulier. I wanted to go from victim to survivor. It took time, but finally I was out from the burden of his shadow. I was able to let go of the burden of the atrocities of his guilt. This is what worked for me. Each victim/survivor must find his or her own journey of healing.

Where once I fully embraced my church life, it is now at arm's length. Instead, I embraced my spiritual life. Most of the time I no longer find it difficult to attend church, but I do so without the trust many church members have. I miss that. I still experience flashbacks when in church. They are neither as frequent nor as intense, but they remain. Many victims never return to church. That's what spiritual abuse does. It robs many of the joy once known within the church. Not only have these men robbed us of the love of the church, it has robbed the church of our gifts and talents.

Prayer now provides for me the reassurance of God's faithfulness and promise for the future. However, I still cannot pray in public and whenever a prayer is offered I want to leave the room and sometimes I do. Perhaps with time this will change.

At one of my very first conference speeches in 2005, I tearfully shared how difficult prayer had become after his abuse. I felt sad and regretted never having a bedtime prayer with my children. After the conference, one of the attendees took my hand and said, "It is my hope the prayer you never had with your children you will someday have with your grandchildren." Neither one of my children were married at the time, but her words filled me with optimism.

Twelve years later, for the first time, I felt safe enough to pray. As I sat at lunch with my four-year-old granddaughter, I suggested she pray.

"What do I say Grandma?"

"Abby just thank God for your family and for the food we have." As she clasped her chubby hands and squeezed her little blue eyes shut, she prayed. I too shut my eyes while she prayed. It was my first prayer in twenty-seven years. No prayer ever meant more than the one she just said.

REFLECTION

In 2018, Su hosted a birthday party for one of our friends on her screened-in porch. It was a steamy July day and Su's backyard pool looked inviting. I lingered for a moment on the same porch where I told my story for the first time fourteen years ago as my friends went inside to load their plates with salads and desserts. How grateful I felt for their love and support. It was this very spot where I started to deal with the most painful chapter in my life. It was here where I first stuttered those words to Su, "I was sexually abused by my youth minister." It was then where my healing began.

With the healing came my need and passion to speak out about clergy abuse. Through the years, I've continued to work with The Hope of Survivors ministry. I now serve on the board of the Council on Child Abuse (COCA). I've spoken to many groups and churches on the topic of prevention and I have met courageous survivors. After one such presentation, several of the attendees remarked, "You should write a book."

I began to understand my story could have an impact. Over the years the same suggestion came from many of my friends. It took thirteen years before I felt strong enough to consider allowing a much larger audience see my pain and struggles. When I spoke to groups, I could see their faces. I was comfortable in front of a crowd. Writing a book seemed scarier. Eventually, I realized the wound I once protected was now but a fading scar. Perhaps I *could* share my story in a book.

But before I could do so, there remained one aspect of this journey to complete. I needed to contact Nancy, Jeff Coulier's first wife.

I knew I was not responsible for the pain in her life; Jeff Coulier was. But I wanted to acknowledge her pain. She too had been a victim of Jeff Coulier. I had thought of her many times over the years. Would contacting her cause her even more pain? I knew my heart was in the right place, but would she see it that way? My investigator provided her number. I called her.

Nancy could not have been more gracious. Her kindness and understanding lifted a burden from my heart. Our conversation revealed she and her current husband lived forty minutes from my daughter in Charlotte. We ended the conversation with a promise to meet.

A few days later a note came from Nancy expressing concern for the guilt and pain I had carried all these years.

> *"When you come to Charlotte for a visit, give me a call. I can't wait to see you. I'm sure you are just as beautiful inside and out. You are a good person and I know God is looking down on all of us knowing we are doing the best we can."*
>
> Love, Nancy

We've met several times and Nancy encouraged me to live my life without regret.

As the result of the willingness of the Walnut Branch elders to meet with me in 2006, and their response, I helped organize a Youth After Church reunion at Walnut Branch. Many old familiar faces and former youth group leaders filled the Fellowship Hall. As we sang the old VBS and camp songs, the memories returned. Only this time they were good memories. I had conquered my demons.

Now stronger, and with a clearer understanding of clergy abuse, I realize there are things I would have done differently if I were to again begin this journey I started in 2004. But looking back, in the midst of my pain and healing, I did the best I could. At age seventy-seven, Jeff Coulier is semi-retired and remains in good standing with the Disciples of Christ denomination.

I've thought a lot about my mom and dad while writing this book. I had good parents and I loved them, and they loved me. They just didn't know how to do divorce. In 1962, there was no such thing as "co-parenting," "how-to" books on how to talk to your children about divorce, Oprah, or the internet. It wasn't a matter of forgiving my mom, dad, and Chuck, but rather coming to understand they did the best they knew how. After I was blessed with children, my relationship with my dad grew closer. Even Dad and Chuck buried the hatchet as they found themselves together at family functions and shared holidays. My dad and I remained close until his death in 2015 from Alzheimer's.

Mike, Wendi, and I were at his bedside. I never told him about the abuse. I knew he would feel guilty for not being there and doing more.

My sister Wendi lives in New Hampshire and we keep in touch.

Losing Mom at such a young age was a profound loss. My brothers and sisters and I get together every year on her birthday to remember her and celebrate her life. I miss her dearly.

How would Mom feel about this book? I think my forty-seven-year-old Mom would not have understood my need to share, but my eighty-four-year-old Mom, if she were with us, would be proud of me.

Abuse forever changes a person. Healing takes time. But there can be joy again.

And fortunately, the years have erased much of the sadness, allowing me to embrace joy in my life. My daughter was married in May 2010. The day was perfect and Bill and I felt such happiness for her and her husband. The reception was a time of celebration and I couldn't have enjoyed myself more, surrounded by friends and family.

As the music played and people danced, I found myself laughing with one of the guests. Bill stood beside me as he had through all these years. He put his arm around me and said, "Don't you just love her laugh? She has the greatest laugh!"

Survivor Psalm

I have been victimized.

I was in a fight that was not a fair fight.

I did not ask for the fight.

I lost.

There is no shame in losing such fights.

I have reached the stage of survivor and am no longer a slave of victim status.

I look back with sadness rather than hate.

I look forward with hope rather than despair.

I may never forget,
but I need not constantly remember.

I was a victim.

I am a survivor.

—GIFT FROM WITHIN—PTSD

EPILOGUE: USING HIS NAME

One of the most agonizing decisions in writing this book was whether to name the pastor who abused me. For years I lived with the shame caused by this man; didn't he deserve to be shamed? In keeping his identity a secret, was I complicit in keeping his actions a secret? Over the years, I never revealed his identity when lecturing, speaking with victims, or in my work with survivor networks. My goal was always to expose the horrors of clergy abuse, not to make it a personal vendetta.

Writing allowed me to tell my story. My story is backed up by hundreds of pages of materials verifying what took place: his signed confession, written correspondence with his ministry officials, letters and taped recordings of everything from conversations, his sermons, and meetings. I am a packrat. For years, boxes of memories from church sat unopened in my basement. Once I began to search for explanations, I had the courage to look through the boxes. In this book, I have changed the names of the pastor, the church leaders, including those who allowed the abuser to continue in the ministry (and to continue to sexually abuse women) and the name of the church where the abuse occurred. I have chosen to use real names of those who were supportive and kind to me through this process.

My story is told not as much about shaming my abuser publicly, but to explain how clergy abuse happens. My story shows how a charismatic leader (and a church full of such people) can thwart the word of God and create massive harm. The church elders who hid his actions to save his reputation, while removing me from the church, deserved to be "outed." However, they are no longer living and I saw no benefit to visit the sins of the fathers on their children.

While I was writing this book, the #MeToo movement, and the lesser known, but growing, #MeTooChurch movement were born. These groups provide so many victims a voice. My hope is those who have been abused are now heard and believed, and perhaps books such as mine and organizations such as The Hope of Survivors and SNAP will bring light and better understanding to the topic of clergy abuse. Our goal is to provide hope and healing to victims.

To my fellow survivors, you are not alone.

APPENDIX A

Resources: Healing and Understanding

ADDITIONAL READING

Baptist News Global, "Don't call it an affair. Call it abuse of power"
Diana Garland, Baylor University, School of Social Work

Broken and Beautiful (2017)
Kristal Chalmers with Eileen Peters

Healing From Hidden Abuse: A Journey Through the Stages of Recovery from Psychological Abuse (2016)
Shannon Thomas, LCSW

Is Nothing Sacred?: The Story of a Pastor, the Women He Sexually Abused, and the Congregation He Nearly Destroyed (2008)
Marie M. Fortune

The Subtle Power of Spiritual Abuse: Recognizing & Escaping Spiritual Manipulation and False Spiritual Authority Within the Church (2005)
David Johnson and Jeff Van Vonderen

Victim to Survivor: Women Recovering from Clergy Sexual Abuse (2009)
Foreword by Marie M. Fortune
Edited by Nancy Werking Poling

ONLINE RESOURCES

Advocate Web
Provides information and provides understanding of the issues involved in the exploitation of persons by helping professionals
www.advocateweb.org

David Pooler
www.facebook.co/dkpooler

Faith Trust Institute
Resources, learn basic facts about abuse by clergy FAQ's
www.faithtrustinstitute.org

Godly Response to Abuse in the Christian Environment (GRACE)
Their mission to empower Christian Communities to recognize, prevent, and respond to abuse.
www.netgrace.org

Jimmy Hinton
www.JimmyHinton.org

Survivors Network of Those Abused by Priests (SNAP)
A self-help group that supports people who have been victimized by clergy.
www.survivorsnetwork.org

Tamar's Voice
A religious non-profit organization that ministers to those who have been sexually abused by members of the clergy.
www.tamarsvoice.org/

The Hope of Survivors
Help for adult women abused by clergy
www.thehopeofsurviors.org

APPENDIX B

Research on Clergy Abuse by David K. Pooler

What follows are the things that may help you frame your own healing journey or that of a loved one.

Churches and congregations have a responsibility for people's wellbeing by teaching spiritual principles, forming character, creating opportunities to serve others, and helping people contribute to the greater good (Gushee, 2017). People involved in congregational life expect safety, nurturing, and freedom to grow and flourish in that environment and should have a right to trust anyone in leadership. However, reality is such that not all leaders can be trusted and not all congregations provide a safe milieu for people who are vulnerable. In the United States and around the world, children, adolescents, and adults in congregations are sexually abused by trusted leaders.

Clergy Sexual Abuse (CSA) happens when a person with religious authority uses their role, position, and/or power to sexually harass, exploit, or engage in sexual activity with a vulnerable person. This involves sexualizing conversations (including on the phone, through social media or email), transmitting sexual images, touching or hugging women who do not want to be touched, pushing for sexual involvement, creating pressure and hostility when boundaries are set, using sexual language and jokes, pressing or rubbing up against a woman, or purposely invading personal space. The sexual activity can include, but is not limited to, touching sexual organs (over or under clothing), kissing, oral sex, masturbation, intercourse, and rape. The hallmark of clergy sexual abuse is the misuse of power by the perpetrator to exploit and control the victim and the inability of the victim to provide consent (Pooler & Frey, 2017).

The fact is that religious communities have been helpful and healing as well as oppressive and hurtful and, if we are honest, some of both at the same time. The knowledge that there have been children sexually abused by priests and church leaders and that the institution of the church has attempted to obfuscate it, has made its way into public consciousness over the past fifteen years through watchdog groups, media reports of abuse, the growth of advocacy groups, and support networks such as SNAP, Hope of Survivors, and Faith Trust Institute and recent films such as Spotlight and The Keepers. In the current news and social media are stories of priests, pastors, and other leaders who abused vulnerable people and even more problematic is how the institution of the church covers and hides the truth. Society and its religious groups understand that sexual exploitation and abuse of children is morally wrong and there is a basic awareness of the devastating consequences to victims. Society has laws to hold perpetrators of child sexual abuse accountable.

What is just as important is the growing awareness of church leaders sexually abusing adults in congregations (cf. Bill Hybels at Willow Creek), which highlights a problem that has always existed (Fortune, 1989; Werking Poling, 2009) and has not been discussed much. Frequently, religious institutions and society call it an affair and fail to understand the underlying misuse of power and complex structural issues that often further harm victims and, unfortunately, few states have laws that criminalize the sexual abuse of adults, but the good news is that there are some (cf. Minnesota, Texas). Religious institutions often try to sanitize this egregious misuse of power and the harm done by labeling the offense as a moral failure (marital infidelity) or moral slip that ought to be forgiven. That is skirting reality and the truth. It is indeed abuse, it is not an affair, the harm is incalculable, and in most cases should preclude the ability for the perpetrator to ever continue in ministry.

Another fact that must be acknowledged is that most perpetrators of clergy sexual abuse are men and heterosexual; therefore, most victims are women because of the patriarchal structure of so many religious institutions. While we know that perpetrators can be women and victims can be men, clergy sexual abuse is primarily an issue of female victimization by men in positions of authority.

The following is a common broad outline of how sexual abuse of adults happen (Garland, 2009; Pooler & Frey, 2017). A woman in a congregation seeks pastoral support because of a personal problem (recent loss, marital problems, past abuse, depression, etc.). The pastoral leader will identify the problem and suggest that they address it together. It is also possible the pastoral leader may be the one to initiate more interaction and remark to a woman that he notices she seems depressed or he wonders what is wrong, or he may just begin to show heightened interest in her wellbeing. They might meet in a formal counseling relationship, but almost as often the interactions happen informally and are framed as discipleship, spiritual advisement, or even a caring friendship. As the relationship progresses and deepens, the leader sexually advances, but slowly.

The path to explicit sexual activity is frequently months and sometimes years in the making. Perpetrators know that most women in a church will stop any overt boundary violations so they are very strategic and use the religious context, power/authority, their shared spiritual life and its language to manipulate her and slowly cross boundaries. The leader might use scriptural principles, bible verses, religious or spiritual language, spiritual admonitions, sexual talk, and touch (e.g., frequent hugs, prolonged hugs), or invitations to be together to break down barriers and boundaries and to persuade the victim that she is important, their relationship is special and unique, and that sexual touch is acceptable (or even sanctioned by God) in the relationship. Many perpetrators do this even when the victim has a spouse and the spouse is aware of the time spent together. The pastor uses many encounters of gradual boundary crossing and blurring before engaging in sexual activity with her, and convinces her that it is somehow not the big deal that people think it could be, or that they are just human and can be forgiven.

Once sexual activity starts most women know something is very wrong, but feel trapped, and partially, if not totally, responsible. If the victim voices her concern, the perpetrator often points out how they are in this together and the victim is told to "think of the greater good," or "let's not harm the church or my reputation," and "if this becomes known and people leave the faith it will be your fault." The perpetrator uses fear and guilt of harming the church to keep her silent and persuade her to not report or say anything. By using shame and persuasion to pacify the victim, the perpetrator maintains sexual access to the victim and is able to keep her silent. This abuse cycle is as much about power and control than it is any kind of sexual gratification.

This cycle may last a long time and is very challenging because victims experience the conflict of feeling special and important to the pastor and being in his inner circle, to feeling confused and perplexed and unable to trust oneself, and feeling trapped. This cycle eventually ends with them being caught or the victim speaking out or reporting. Unfortunately, making it known can end up further traumatizing the survivor. And the experience of most survivors in trying to find help and support within the church is not good (Pooler & Frey, 2017).

Lest anyone fall for the misconception that a congregant is still somehow partially responsible, let me say right here that it is always the responsibility of the person with more power to delineate and maintain appropriate professional boundaries that keep people safe, especially vulnerable people (those who are youth, those with trauma, or pain, etc.). There is no profession, not medicine, psychology, social work, law, or nursing that would ever tolerate the excuse that the client or patient was to blame for sexual misconduct; never! It still baffles me that in 2018 churches and trained clergy are willing to let perpetrators blame victims or point to a victim as being responsible.

When clergy sexual abuse happens, churches are often ill equipped to be helpful or supportive to victims because of their misguided need to protect their image or reputation. The need to protect and fortify against threats and look good to both insiders and outsiders becomes the priority and is an immediate obstacle to providing support. Organized religious bodies use their power or prestige to create a place of significance within a community. But these same strengths are the Achilles heel of religious institutions in that if there is failure in a leader, the need to protect the image or the influence they have becomes a hindrance to being vulnerable, accountable, or responsive. Churches are rarely nimble or flexible or able to respond effectively which further harms survivors.

About a decade ago, Chaves and Garland (2009) wanted to better understand the prevalence rates of clergy perpetrated sexual abuse of adults. In that landmark study they wanted to know the percentage of women who regularly attend church (at least once a month), that had experienced a sexual advance from a church leader since they were 18. In that study they found about 3% of women report that this had happened to them. This equates to about 7 women in the average church size of 400 people. The study also found that about 2% of women had experienced a sexual advance from a leader in the church they currently attend. This is profoundly disturbing. The results of this study are methodologically sound and there is high confidence in the results.

A few highlights from the survey of 280 survivors from 2015:
- 75% Agree or Strongly Agree that the congregation felt safe before the abuse started
- 8% Agree or Strongly Agree that their church supported them after the abuse occurred
- 15% Agree or Strongly Agree that their church/denomination thoroughly investigated the report
- 80% Agree or Strongly Agree that their experience with the church after the abuse negatively affected their spiritual life
- 33% Agree or Strongly Agree that when the reported the abuse they were believed
- 8% Agree or Strongly Agree that the perpetrator apologized to them
- 78% Agree or Strongly Agree that they are healing or getting better

- The abuse lasted on average 4 years
- The average age difference between the perpetrator and victim was 15 years

A survivor named Cambrielle captured her experience with the church well when she said, "I know that they haven't ever walked this way before, and they didn't know what they were doing, and that's been a real source of my forgiveness… just Father forgive them they don't know what they are doing… the way they have shut me down and shut me out, relationally, and emotionally, and every other connected way… has been pretty devastating…. arguably as devastating or more devastating than the actual abuse… I don't believe that my church meant to re-victimize me, but that is what they did, because they didn't understand what happened."

People who have been abused by church leaders do heal and they know how they healed. They recover their voice, reclaim their lives, and often work to make change in the very areas where they have been wounded most. When I asked the 27 survivors what had been most helpful and healing to them the following is how they responded. I included the number of quotes from the 27 transcripts in descending order just to give you a sense of the frequency with which the survivors talked about what was most helpful to them.

- **Support** (206 quotes): Survivors talked about social support, spousal support, and support from other believers and friends as instrumental to their healing and recovery. Churches that surrounded the survivors with support were most healing.
- **Believe and validate** (201 quotes): Survivors talked about the value of their story and account being believed and the magnitude of the pain and trauma being validated by another person. Survivors stressed over and over to me that this is critical and that being believed the first time is so healing and that not being believed is devastating.
- **Professional counseling** (79 quotes): Survivors described the value of professional help, especially having a trauma specialist to help them work through the betrayal trauma. They were clear that therapists who fully understood the power dynamics and knew that it was not an affair were the ones most helpful.
- **Perpetrator accountability** (52 quotes): Holding the perpetrator accountable was very important for survivors and not holding him responsible is unjust and part of the larger problem. They reported that churches who removed the perpetrator from ministry felt most safe.

- **Human Church** (48 quotes): The survivors described that oftentimes churches were so focused on image and people as objects that there was a monumental failure to see everyone as human (as actual people) and to see the church as flawed. People described churches that were willing to deal with human brokenness and trauma, and acknowledge their failures were better able to provide support, help, understanding, and accountability. The churches that understood they were flawed actually understood the betrayal and trauma the best.
- **Communication** (39 quotes): After they reported the abuse, survivors said that churches that were willing and able to be direct and clear in their communication and were willing to keep lines of communication open were most helpful to them.
- **Transparency and Truth** (37 quotes): Survivors said they needed a safe place to talk about what happened and that churches that were most helpful to them owned the truth publicly and were transparent with other members about what was happening and publicly owned their failures.
- **Boundaries/Safety** (33 quotes): Lastly, survivors talked about creating safety and the need to help pastors understand professional boundaries and about how to use their power for good and for healing.

David K. Pooler is associate professor at the Diana R. Garland School of Social Work, Baylor University, Waco Texas. Dr. Pooler serves on the Clergy Misconduct Task Force.

APPENDIX C

Documentation and Letters

Volume 26, No. 27   Cincinnati, Ohio   August 23, 1973

By Their Fruit Shall Ye Know Them

"With one mind they kept up their daily attendance at the temple, and, breaking bread in private houses, shared their meals with unaffected joy, as they praised God and enjoyed the favour of the whole people. And day by day the Lord added to their number those whom he was saving."

God in His wisdom and grace continues to add strength to His church and kingdom. He has given us depth spiritually as He allows us to grow in number. He constantly gives vitality and love to His people. May we continually be open to the spirit as God transforms us into His image and leads us to where we should be.

See you Sunday.

New Year – 1974

Where did Christmas go? "Gone is the rustle of the wings heard in the watch serene – The Golden Hour of God is past."

The old world is in labor. The New Year is being born. God has blessed His church here in 1973. We've had over 100 new members, many joys, some tears. God has used it all as a fabric of faith to more fully establish His people.

Now 1974 breathes upon us. Let's leap into the New Year! The past is in smoldering ruins. What are your resolutions? What are you planning of eternal significance? What does the New Year hold for us? Only what we let it. It's an empty vessel waiting to be filled.

There's something refreshing about new beginnings. A New Year comes bringing new lives, new faces, new horizons, new hope. Resolutions for the religious should include a new priority – a new ultimacy – a new commitment to the Lord and His church. Elton Trueblood says, "A new man for our time – the Christian."

"Therefore if any man be in Christ, he is a new creature: old things are passed away; behold, all things are become new."

A Happy New Year – – – A Happy New You

Two Walnut Branch newsletters written by Jeff Coulier

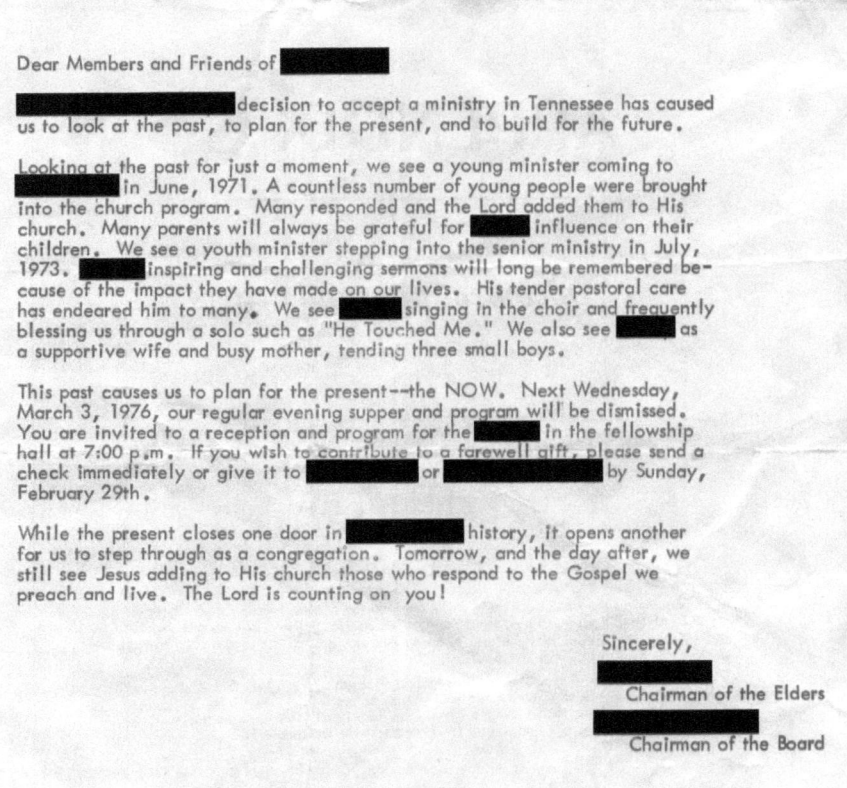

Letter from the board of Walnut Branch Church announcing Jeff's acceptance of ministry in Tennessee, 1976

October 28, 2004

Sandra L. Kirkham
███████████
Cincinnati, Ohio ████

Dear Sandy,

I give thanks for your courage and for your strength in facing a very painful part of your past. I admire you for no longer suppressing those wounds from your formative years and for choosing to be healed, really healed. I believe you will find a freedom due to these steps you have taken, and I pray that you will be able to release any and all negative feelings and fears that are common in those who have been abused by ministers.

Facing the perpetrator who has given you so many painful memories and who took away your God-given innocence as a teenager was a significant step. Many wounded victims never have such an opportunity, but you did, and I am thankful. I am also thankful for the fact that this face-to-face encounter came at a time when your abuser already had an understanding of what he did to you and was able to ask for your forgiveness. Imagine how much additional pain could have been caused by a perpetrator who was unrepentant, or who sought ways to blame you or others, or who even tried to deny the facts of what actually happened. As hard as Sunday's meeting was, it could have been almost unbearable ha ¹ ███ brought those qualities to the meeting.

Your visit to ███████ allowed me to know a part of ███████ past that I had not known before. I want to thank you for providing me with added insight. I intend to respond appropriately and professionally to the new information I now have about ███. For example, at my recommendation, ███████ has already begun a regular regimen of de-briefing with me about relationships in his ministry. As a way of knowing he is in an accountable relationship with me, I intend to discuss regularly with ███ matters related to boundaries, temptations, and secrecy. I honestly do not expect that ███ encounters these struggles to a great degree in his ministry (he is much more a "father figure" to most of the parishioners, and I think he enjoys this), yet I am insisting that he and I visit this subject regularly, about twice a month. I have also encouraged him to get re-established with a therapist in ███████ whom I have recommended, and will expect that relationship to begin immediately. Your words of caution to me were appropriate, and I do, indeed, want to do my part to help ███ maintain his health for his own sake and also for the congregation.

I hope you can also appreciate the fact that there is a gap of 27 years between your tragic

Letter from Sam Fitzgerald four days after meeting with Sandy and prior to ever looking at Jeff Coulier's disciplinary file (page 1)

experience with ▮▮▮▮ and today. Due to your missing all of the real events that ▮▮ has gone through in the intervening years, you understandably cannot really appreciate the person ▮▮ is today. Imagining myself in your shoes, I understand your vantage point. Knowing that in his earlier adulthood ▮▮ had a habit of playing games, of failing to take responsibility, and moving on to the next place seemingly unscathed, I would expect you to feel, almost instinctively, that ▮▮ remaining in ministry is evidence that this pattern of behavior continues to this day. I would expect you to conclude that just as the "church" failed to address the issue long ago and continued to find places of ministry for ▮▮ so also the church is continuing to look the other way on ▮▮ behavior. But I want to assure you that is not the case.

▮▮ definitely had a problem that resulted in unspeakable hurt to many people. No one can deny that. ▮▮ doesn't deny it, and I certainly don't. But ▮▮ bottomed-out with this pattern of behavior about 13 or 14 years ago when he was guilty of misconduct once again. This time he was not in the ▮▮▮▮▮▮▮▮▮▮▮▮▮▮▮▮ where each congregation maintains its own version of accountability and where unethical ministers can run from trouble. Instead he was in a congregation of the ▮▮▮▮▮▮▮▮▮▮▮▮▮▮▮▮▮▮▮▮ which meant that his ministerial credentials were subject to regular review and that a Commission on Ministry had the power to strip him of the authorization to do ministry. ▮▮ ministerial standing was removed by the Commission on Ministry in Tennessee, and he lost the opportunity to do what he believed God had called and equipped him to do. It must have been a painful, yet defining moment in ▮▮ life.

Fortunately for ▮▮ he was blessed to have some key individuals in his life who cared about him, which didn't mean simply singing his praises. Instead, they declared emphatically to ▮▮ that he needed help. ▮▮ spent some significant time in therapy where he confronted his abusive and addictive behavior. He made a choice, I don't know how, but he made a choice by the grace of God to be something else. Although he would always be the person who had sinned, hurt people, and lied to himself and to the world, he saw that this did not have to be the ONLY thing that can be said about him. He realized that he could now be an authentic person, and that being authentic is not something one has to fear. He realized that God can still use a person who is healing. He learned all of the lessons about appropriate and ethical behavior for those in ministry, lessons that reinforced for him just how badly he had violated persons who had trusted him.

At that point in ▮▮ life, he did not believe he would ever be in ministry again. He worked in a secular field and carried the burden of having wasted something very sacred to him, the privilege of serving God through ministry in the church. He knew he could never again fool anyone about his past, and he understandably assumed that he was "finished" as a minister. Yet he continued the healing process and those close to him saw that he had made a dramatic turn in his life. His self-understanding had matured and his sensitivity to the pain of others had sharpened, largely, I believe, out of his own experience with pain and failure.

▮▮ was encouraged by others to come back before the Commission on Ministry in Tennessee and present himself as one who had a new understanding of himself and others and who was seen by mental health professionals as a man capable of carrying out the functions of ministry with highest integrity. Not taking their task lightly, the members of that Commission on Ministry chose to believe that God can still transform human lives and that ▮▮▮▮ had experienced such a transformation. Many things were different in ▮▮ He had a system of support and accountability in friends who knew

Letter from Sam Fitzgerald four days after meeting with Sandy and prior to ever looking at Jeff Coulier's disciplinary file (page 2)

all about his past and who could regularly engage him in conversation about his continued journey into health. He married ▇▇▇ and displayed a commitment to total honesty about every aspect of his past and present life. He had an awareness of boundaries in relationships that showed he could be trusted to serve with integrity.

Of course there was/is a risk. Anyone that is approved for ordination or who is given ministerial standing can go astray and make Commissions on Ministry appear incompetent. But in the last analysis, that committee determined that the good that can come from ▇▇▇ future in ministry outweighs what they believed was a small risk. They didn't believe there would be any more victims in ▇▇▇ ministry. So ▇▇▇ was given a second chance, one he was determined not to ruin. With a new humility ▇▇▇ began to care for people and draw them into the truth of God's amazing, undying grace. ▇▇▇ life–not just his words–began to bear witness, to the wonderful good news of the gospel. And churches grew–not primarily because of ▇▇▇ but because of the authenticity of the message ▇▇▇ preached and lived out.

Now we have the benefit of 13 years of ▇▇▇ ministry AFTER he bottomed-out and dealt with important issues. He has served with highest moral integrity and openness. There has been no hint of misconduct or even coming close to the boundary lines. I believe that ▇▇▇ finally "got it" 13 years ago.

▇▇▇ would say that he knows he doesn't deserve to be in ministry, yet God has somehow continued to give him an opportunity to serve. ▇▇▇ has been a good steward of that opportunity. The church where ▇▇▇ was pastor in ▇▇▇ Tennessee, grew from three persons to 150 in just four years. The church in ▇▇▇ where ▇▇▇ now pastors, was also a new church–not even yet chartered when ▇▇▇ came to serve with them. Now there are 300 members, a beautiful new building in a rapidly growing area, and an energetic young membership that loves their church, their minister, and their future. ▇▇▇ could very likely become the largest congregation in the Alabama-Northwest Florida Region within a few more years.

Please don't misunderstand me, Sandy. If I believed ▇▇▇ would abuse even one person in his ministry, then none of the good things about ▇▇▇ would matter. I would want ▇▇▇ removed from ministry. Protecting people from abusers is a priority for me and for this Region. The issue for me is the lack of integrity around taking action against ▇▇▇ doing untold damage to hundreds of people, simply due to the hypothetical thought that "he might abuse again" when there is solid evidence that he is "low risk." The people at ▇▇▇ believe in God's redeeming power, as well they should. Do you realize the kind of hurt and conflict that would be caused over taking punitive action against ▇▇▇ for something done 27 years ago and, more importantly, AFTER his time of rehabilitation? The bitterness against the larger church that a majority of members would express is not a pleasant thought. Most of them would probably leave the church, severely jaded about whether the church really believes and practices what it proclaims.

So the draft of your letter addressed to ▇▇▇ and to me, copied to the officers of ▇▇▇ is a great concern to me. You impress me as a thoughtful person who intends on doing the right thing. And yet I am appealing to you to recognize that your frame of reference about who ▇▇▇ is today is quite limited–much too limited to justify an act that would damage a dynamic congregation that has done nothing to harm you and that has had no experience with

Letter from Sam Fitzgerald four days after meeting with Sandy and prior to ever looking at Jeff Coulier's disciplinary file (page 3)

███ that even closely resembles your experience with him.

I appeal to you to make peace with your past by realizing that you have forgiven ███ as you said on Sunday, and by realizing that you have shared your story—an important story—so that those responsible for ███ ministry can have a better understanding of ███ past. You have done the right and responsible things to insure your own healing. I ask you, now, to recognize that the church must weigh all the information it now has and determine the right response for all involved. I ask you to trust me to do that, with professionalism and with integrity.

Sandy, I have doubts that sending a letter like the one you drafted will bring you healing. Instead, I would be afraid that the damage to people's faith, the damage to their sense of security in relationships, the damage to their ability to trust, and the collapse of their spiritual dreams would weigh upon your spirit. Even through your pain you would have to recognize the possibility that ███ has, indeed, experienced transformation and that he has conducted his ministry with highest integrity. Yet, if you were to send such a letter, you would know in your heart that you may have single-handedly vetoed the experience of God's grace for many, many people. That, to me, would be quite a load to carry. I believe it would create new wounds for you.

If ███ were unrepentant, it would be entirely different. If he had not been in therapy and been able to confess his sins, name each of them, and put himself at the mercy of others, it would be different. There is no place in ministry, in my strong opinion, for anyone who doesn't honor boundaries or who minimizes the effects of sexual misconduct in the ministerial relationship. So please, please do not understand me to be a judicatory official who just wants to side with the minister. I care deeply about victims. But in this case, I believe ███ restitution for his behavior with you can only come with the sincerity of his repentance. I do not believe a disciplinary action as a result of his abuse with you is appropriate. His pattern of exemplary conduct for 13 years and the damage that would be caused to his current congregation simply outweigh, morally, whatever satisfaction you might get from seeing him shamed and removed from ministry.

I am very sorry if this offends you in any way. What I pray for is that you will come to understand that your vantage point about who and what ███ is today is limited, and therefore, that you will accept the wisdom of those who are able to see more than you are able to see. In accepting this, I hope you will continue to forgive ███ to release him to God's providence, and ask God to use him in wonderful ways to impact lives only in positive ways.

I would appreciate some response to this letter, either phone or e-mail or regular mail. I am obviously interested in where your pursuit of healing is taking you and how a letter such as this fits into that process. I am certainly open to having more conversation with you about my thoughts and also about your thoughts.

Sincerely,

███
Regional Minister

Letter from Sam Fitzgerald four days after meeting with Sandy and prior to ever looking at Jeff Coulier's disciplinary file (page 4)

Sandra L. Kirkham
Cincinnati, OH ▮

Reverend ▮
Regional Minister, ▮
▮

Dear Reverend ▮

I am responding to your letter of October 28, 2004. I respect the pastoral concern you express for the people at ▮ You suggest ▮ is a low risk to others. I disagree – any risk is too great and easily avoidable.

The rest of your letter reflects an incomplete view of Christian restoration on several fronts. First, the fact that our discussion unearthed for you parts of ▮ past that you had not known indicates that ▮ has not taken the path of transparency and vulnerability with even his closest associates and those to whom he might hold himself accountable.

Second, if you believe most of the members of the church would leave if this aspect of ▮ past were known, it is clear that his message and life within the congregation have not been characterized by authenticity and openness, but that he has, naively or intentionally, continued to "fool others about his past." Thirty two years ago everyone looked at ▮ as a "father figure," just as you described.

Third, I conclude from our discussion that I am not the only one of ▮ victims with whom he has failed to make amends. I came to him as one offended, after the pattern of Matthew 18:15-17. For his own restoration and that of his victims, ▮ needs to go to the others, following the pattern of Matthew 5:23-24, to acknowledge his offense and seek forgiveness. If you do, as you say, care deeply about ▮ victims, you will require him to devote himself quickly to this important work. It is admirable that ▮ dealt with his own character and behavior 13 years ago, but by that measure, he is at least 13 years late in dealing with the consequences of his behavior in the lives of others.

To be clear, I am not seeking or expecting that you or the officers of ▮ Church violate your integrity by taking action – punitive, disciplinary or otherwise – to remove or shame ▮ The shame bestowed upon him has been and should be the result of his actions, and no one else's. I have never asked that ▮ be removed from the ministry or stripped of his credentials. I do believe, however, he should serve in another capacity, where he is not given to the temptation of his sexual addiction. As stated by both you and ▮ he is never cured and there will always be a risk for him to repeat this behavior. I, too, believe in the power of God to transform people with the deepest of problems. And I believe the grace of God is manifested most clearly when we lay ourselves open before the body of Christ, starting with its officers, and are both accepted in their failures and affirmed in their restoration.

Sandy's letter written in reponse to Sam Fitzgerald's letter
after her meeting with Jeff Coulier (page 1)

Reverend ■
November 3, 2004
Page 2

Though the matters above are of importance, as your letter anticipates, I am deeply offended by your thoughts and innuendoes. You assert that by the victim speaking up, by breaking the veil of secrecy, I will be guilty of damaging a dynamic congregation, damaging people's faith, damaging their sense of security in relationships, damaging their ability to trust... that I, the victim, would single-handedly veto the experience of God's grace for many, many people. On the contrary, Reverend ■ If the congregation is damaged – and it need not be if the restoration is complete, the damage will be because of more than 20 years of sexual misconduct as a minister on ■ part, and the actions of the Commission on Ministry, other church officials, and ■ himself to hide this aspect of his life from the officers and members of his current congregation. I do not believe he is being honest and authentic when he has failed to address the damage done to his victims and he continues to deny a child of his when stating how many children he has.

As I hope I have communicated by both my circumspection in dealing with this and in our discussion, this is not about "satisfaction," it is about commitment to biblical processes of healing, restoration and honesty. I find it confusing that you can assert that being truthful in any situation will cause hurt and damage. Telling the truth is not the problem, hiding the truth for 27 years caused the damage. Why do you want to help to enable him to hide this part of his life? Members of your congregation will not be disappointed in the truth, but rather disappointed that they have been deceived about who ■ was and is. He is a sexual addict with a despicable past, who has had therapy, but will always have this problem. You appear to suggest that this hideous conduct is less egregious because of the passage of time. I assert that the passage of time has nothing to do with right or wrong or that it is ever too late to right a wrong. That is my only satisfaction.

You said that if I were to send the letter to the officers of the church, "it would weigh upon my spirit." On the contrary, failing to send the letter will result in everlasting regret if anyone is ever again the victim of ■ despicable misconduct. I was a victim because those who knew failed to protect me. In that vein, as means of providing a more complete picture of ■ recent history, I will be happy to include a copy of your letter and this response in my correspondence to the officers of ■ Reverend ■ and the Disciplinary Minister.

Sincerely in Christ,

Sandra L. Kirkham
■

cc: Officers, ■
     Reverend ■ General Minister and President ■
     Disciplinary Minister
     Reverend ■

Sandy's letter written in reponse to Sam Fitzgerald's letter
after her meeting with Jeff Coulier (page 2)

William N. Kirkham
Cincinnati, OH

November 3, 2004

Dear Reverend ▓▓

    Sandy and I together read your letter of October 28, 2004. For all of the hideous misdeeds that ▓▓ has done, the attitude displayed in your letter to Sandy is as hurtful and, frankly, as offending, as the conduct of ▓▓. Four pages of what a great guy ▓▓ is. Four pages of telling Sandy how fortunate she is because ▓▓ elected for one time in his life to tell the truth. Four pages of "poor" ▓▓ and what a remarkable recovery. You even tell Sandy how fortunate she is to have the "opportunity" to face her perpetrator. What a privilege it is to spend thousands of dollars on a private detective to track down a sexual predator who attacked you in your own home during your childhood. Perhaps Sandy should write ▓▓ a thank you note for taking time out of his busy schedule to see her.

    You go to great length to praise ▓▓ for his good deeds and "highest moral integrity and openness." When did you become aware of the extent of ▓▓'s actions? Were you aware that Sandy was removed from her church because of his lies? If not, then perhaps Mr. ▓▓ does not have the "highest moral integrity and openness." If you were aware of his actions, then why were you, like ▓▓ totally indifferent to the well-being of the string of victims that ▓▓ has left behind? Is it just your job to heal the transgressor? What about the victims? Obviously, ▓▓ made no effort to seek out those who suffered the consequences of his appalling conduct. But since he was so honest and open with you and your church, why did not you and the church seek to help the victims and require ▓▓ as part of his "choice by the grace of God to be something else," to try to help my wife and the others? The answer is simple. Until October 24, 2004, neither ▓▓ nor the church cared about his victims. Sadly, based upon your letter, I am not certain how much you care today.

    "He learned all of the lessons about appropriate and ethical behavior for those in the ministry, lessons that reinforce for him just how badly he had violated persons who had trusted him," you say. Appropriate and ethical behavior? My mother taught me that ethical and appropriate behavior would include telling those you have harmed that you are sorry. ▓▓ has had 13 years to help erase the disgrace and suffering of his victims, but no one, until October 24, 2004, heard one word from him. Imagine a young

Bill's letter written in reponse to Sam Fitzgerald's letter after Sandy's meeting with Jeff Coulier (page 1)

November 3, 2004
Page 2

lady being thrown out of church because of a lying, perverted minister. And you want to tell Sandy what a great guy he now is although he was perfectly content to let Sandy live forever with the pain and suffering that she endured by being told that she was unfit to worship with her friends and family. Clearly, you have a different definition of appropriate and ethical behavior.

The fact is, ▓▓▓▓ never intended to tell you the truth; and he never intended to help anyone who has suffered because of his reprehensible conduct. You speak of his wonderful "friends who knew all about his past." Do you mean that people knew he was responsible for Sandy being thrown out of the church, yet no one said to him ▓▓▓▓ you should write that church and make things right for Sandy Kirkham"? Those friends did not know about this and ▓▓▓▓ was not about to tell them. He told Sandy he was sorry because Sandy had the resources to track him down and the courage to confront him, but for no other reason. That is not, Reverend ▓▓▓▓ the conduct of a repentant man or a man of "highest moral integrity and openness."

But for all of the insensitive things you have said, nothing can match your statement that ▓▓▓▓ "is much more a father figure to most of his parishioners, and I think he enjoys this." I'll bet he does. That is exactly what ▓▓▓▓ was 27 years ago, a "father figure" to a 17 year old girl when she met him at her home alone and was sexually abused. Who would ever suspect a "father figure" of committing such a hideous act? And who would ever expect that same father figure would lie about those sinful acts in order to have his victim dismissed from her church? Yes, a "father figure," that is just how ▓▓▓▓ wanted everyone to see him 27 years ago and how he wants everyone to see him today. But now Sandy has the power to dispel this myth. Before the next parent leaves his or her 17 year old alone with ▓▓▓▓ that parent should know what ▓▓▓▓ did as a "father figure" 27 years ago. That parent should know the suffering of those left in the path of ▓▓▓▓ sexual foray. Then that parent, and that parent alone (not you and not some church commission), should make the decision of whether ▓▓▓▓ will be his child's "father figure."

However, keeping ▓▓▓▓ secrets is not enough for you. You want Sandy to play the same game; unfortunately, the same game that churches around the world have played the last 27 years. Don't tell anyone. A victim of ▓▓▓▓ may cause "hurt and conflict" and "bitterness against the church" if she tells the true story. Please do nothing, you ask, because you may cause someone to leave the church and become "severely jaded about whether the church really believes and practices what it proclaims." Reverend ▓▓▓▓ that is exactly what you and your parishioners should contemplate. Does your church practice what it proclaims? What do you believe and practice when you find it more important to have a minister who has a church with a "beautiful new building" and the "largest congregation" rather than someone who has lived his or her life by the word of God. ▓▓▓▓ did not care about the children of your church 27 years ago. Your letter tells me an abundance about your church's priorities. It may not be a bad idea if your parishioners question "whether the church really believes and practices what it proclaims."

Bill's letter written in reponse to Sam Fitzgerald's letter after Sandy's meeting with Jeff Coulier (page 2)

November 3, 2004
Page 3

I told you at our meeting that I would consider your response to our meeting before I decided if any other action on our part is necessary. I will take your letter as your response. If I am nothing else, I am a man of my word. Sandy and I will respond accordingly.

Sincerely,

William N. Kirkham

WNK/dlh

Bill's letter written in reponse to Sam Fitzgerald's letter after Sandy's meeting with Jeff Coulier (page 3)

Sandra L. Kirkham
███████
███████

January 24, 2005

Reverend ███████
███████
███████
Cincinnati, Ohio ███

Dear ███████

Almost 30 years ago I was sexually abused by Reverend ███████ Associate minister, then Minister at ███████ I was subsequently asked by Elders, ███████ and ███████ to leave the church.

In the intervening years, I felt the best thing to do was to simply try and put this painful chapter of my youth behind me. Early last year I realized that I could not be fully healed and restored unless, consistent with the process described in Matthew 18:15-17, I both confronted those who offended me and forgave them.
In late October, I did so with ███████ While there is no way to erase the pain, I have been able to forgive and surrender the effect on my life to God.

There is one last aspect that remains—speaking with ███████ and ███████ the elders responsible for the matter at the time. One aspect of the discussion will be to provide a letter of confession to each of them from ███████ Would you please arrange a meeting at the church that includes you, a current elder, ███████ and ███? I will be accompanied by two friends who have walked with me through this process over the past year.

If you have any questions before we meet, please feel free to contact me.

Sincerely in Christ,

Sandra Kirkham
███████

Sandy's letter to the current minister of Walnut Branch,
Don Roberts, requesting a meeting

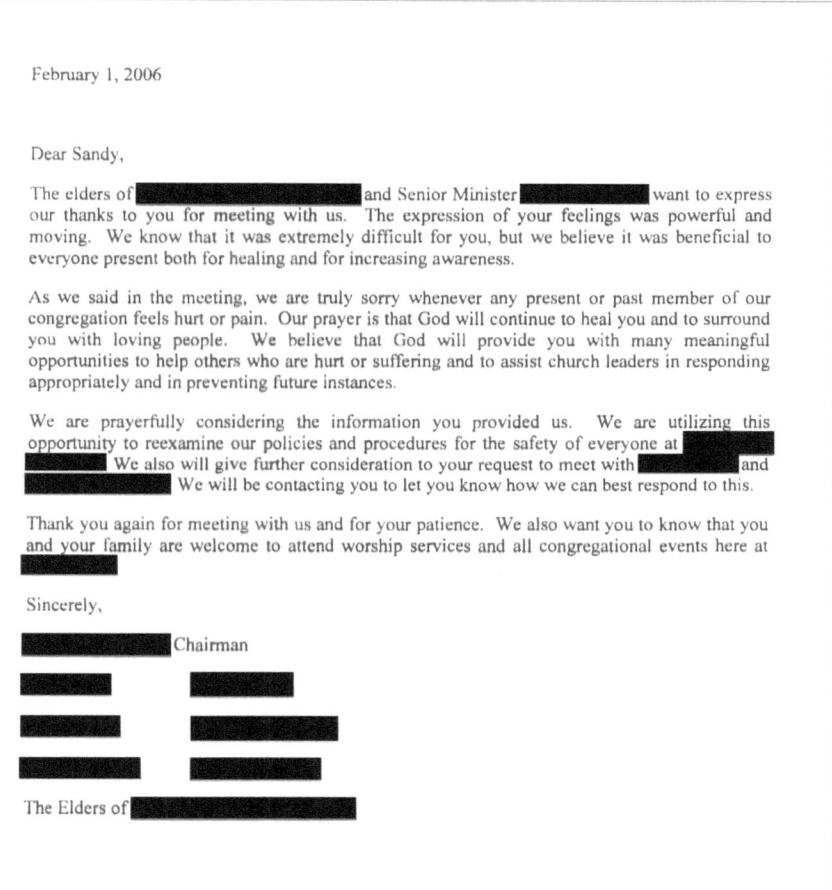

Response from Walnut Branch Church after Sandy's meeting in 2006

Sandra Phillips Kirkham
Cincinnati, OH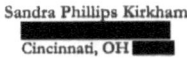

June 11, 2006

Mr.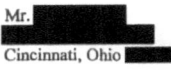
Cincinnati, Ohio

Dear

One Sunday evening 34 years ago, a charismatic youth minister, just barely a year into his new ministry in Cincinnati waited until the other youth left a YAC meeting at the home of a female member of the group...and then put his arms around her and kissed her. He was thirty, married, and the father of two children. She was a minor and a virgin. She was startled by the advance. "What is he doing?" she thought, but reassured herself, "This is my youth pastor. He would never do anything to hurt me."

It was a moment that changed the course of her life forever. Shortly after his first advance, the minister initiated a sexual relationship with her in his home while his wife was at work and the teen had been hired as babysitter. For the next three and a half years, the minister took advantage of the teenager's naiveté, confusion, and trust to control her life. On one hand, that meant sex at his whim—at his home, in his church office, in hotel rooms, even group sex with one of the church's deacons. On the other hand, it meant the minister isolated and controlled her by dictating what she wore, the friends she saw, who she dated...and above all what must be done to "keep our secret."

When the teenager tried repeatedly to end the relationship because of her unhappiness and guilt, the minister prevailed on her, at times saying he needed her because she was the reason he was successful in ministry, at times warning he would lose his job if anyone found out, and at other times becoming physically abusive. In the midst of his adultery, the minister was promoted from youth minister to senior minister.

The minister's wife and the church's Christian education director eventually discovered the relationship. Despite efforts to contain the truth, word began to spread in the congregation. The minister confessed to the congregation that he had sinned against God and against his wife, and asked to be forgiven. The elders and board permitted him to remain in ministry and hosted a sendoff celebration, along with a substantial cash gift, as the minister and his family departed for a new church in ▓▓▓▓ Tennessee.

But despite the public confession, the minister continued the relationship. Just two days after the confession to ▓▓▓▓ the minister insisted the young woman meet him in a hotel room to have sex. Even from ▓▓▓▓ he continued to call, write and insist that the young woman come to see him.

This was not the minister's first sexual predation. Shortly after his arrival in Cincinnati, a teen in the youth ministry at his former church in Atlanta confessed to a sexual relationship he initiated. He was confronted by his former and current senior ministers and promised it would never happen again. Nor was it his last predation. After arriving in ▓▓▓▓ the minister initiated a similar relationship with a young woman in his new congregation, this time with more dire consequences—the woman became pregnant and bore the minister's child. His wife left him and he left the ministry for a time, but was subsequently hired by a church in another denomination. Not long thereafter, he initiated a sexual relationship with a young woman in his new congregation. When this relationship was uncovered, the minister was removed from ministry by the denomination to complete a year and a half of therapy for sexual addiction.

Letter to Sandy's former elder Ed Hahn requesting a meeting (page 1)

After three and a half years, the young woman in Cincinnati found the courage to break free of the relationship, married a loving husband and raised two children. Though she attended church, it was no longer a place of joy and service, but a place of conflict and pain. The energy she devoted to the church in her youth, she diverted to her community and her children's schools. For more than 30 years she bore the guilt and shame of those three and a half years alone. Then, during a trip that took her close to ▓▓▓▓▓ the memories and emotions she'd suppressed erupted without warning. After several months of depression, anxiety, counsel, study and prayer, she located and confronted the minister with his wrongs against her. The minister confessed his offenses and asked to be forgiven…and the woman forgave him.

Though the minister took the teenager's innocence, her virginity and her ability to embrace the church for life, it was not only the minister that wronged her. The leaders of her church wronged her as well. Instead of assuring an environment of safety, they permitted an environment of risk by retaining a known sexual abuser to lead the church's youth program, by failing to notify parents and the congregation of the minister's past behavior, and by failing to monitor the minister's contact with youth, especially young women.

More grievous still, a few months after the minister's departure, the Chairman of the Elders and the Chairman of the Board called the young woman alone to an evening meeting in the church's Fellowship Hall. They did not say what the meeting was about. They did not suggest the young woman bring her parents or a friend for support. There, in an otherwise darkened church, two church leaders dismissed a shaken, disillusioned young woman from the church she had grown up in, loved and so vigorously served. They asked no questions…not what happened or how. They offered no biblical counsel. They asked nothing of how she was doing, or who she was able confide in, or whether she needed help. They just said she must go…and the young woman did.

The church, of course, is ▓▓▓▓▓▓▓▓▓▓▓▓▓▓▓ The adulterous minister is ▓▓▓▓▓▓ The victim of ▓▓▓▓▓'s predation at ▓▓▓▓▓▓▓▓▓▓▓▓ was I. And the two men who summarily dismissed me from the church were you and ▓▓▓▓▓▓▓▓▓▓.

▓▓▓ in the course of my counseling, I was exposed to Jesus' process for dealing with wrongs between people:

"If your brother sins against you, go and tell him his fault, between you and him alone. If he listens to you, you have gained your brother. But if he does not listen, take one or two others along with you, that every charge may be established by the evidence of two or three witnesses. If he refuses to listen to them, tell it to the church. And if he refuses to listen even to the church, let him be to you as a Gentile and a tax collector." Matthew 18:15-18

I followed this process in locating, meeting and forgiving ▓▓▓▓▓▓▓. The outline of his confession and his letter to you taking full responsibility for what occurred is attached. I followed this process in meeting with the elders and senior minister of ▓▓▓▓▓▓▓. My request through the elders to meet you is in the same vein: to discuss the wrongs committed in the past for the purpose of confession, forgiveness and restoration. Meeting with you and ▓▓▓▓▓ is the final step in the healing process for me. I believe it is a necessary step for ▓▓▓▓▓▓▓▓▓ Church to fully be released from this affront to God. And it may be an important step of spiritual healing for you as well.

I appeal to you, on the basis of Christ's instruction, to meet to me at ▓▓▓▓▓▓▓▓ at a time convenient to you. Please feel free to bring along others you'd like to have present. Let's bring to a close this painful chapter in the church's history and my own. I will contact you shortly to set up an appointment or you may call me at the number below.

Sincerely in Christ,

Sandy Kirkham
▓▓▓▓▓

cc: ▓▓▓▓▓▓▓▓▓▓▓▓▓▓▓▓▓▓▓▓▓▓▓▓

Letter to Sandy's former elder Ed Hahn requesting a meeting (page 2)

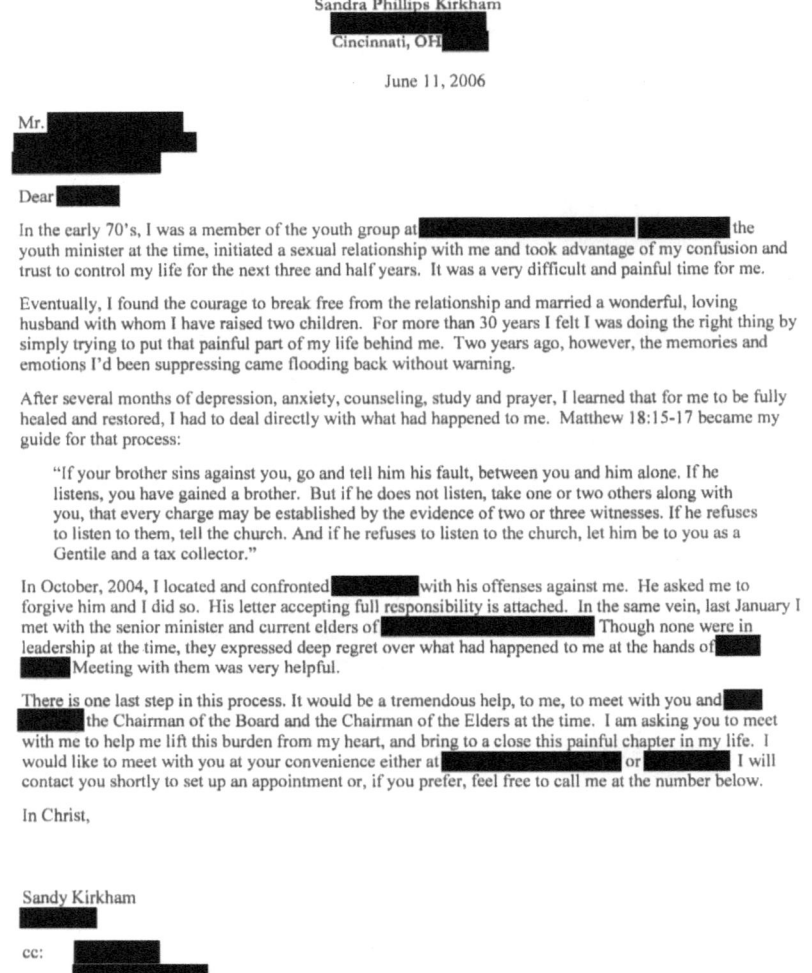

Letter to Sandy's former elder Milton Crane requesting a meeting

ROBERT F. SPADA
Assistant Majority Floor Leader

Senate Building
Columbus, Ohio 43215
614-466-8056

OHIO SENATE
24th District

COMMITTEES:
Ways and Means and Economic Development
   Vice Chair
Energy and Public Utilities
Environment and Natural Resources
Rules
Controlling Board

November 28, 2005

Sandy Kirkham

Dear Sandy:

I appreciate your courage and strength in testifying before the Ohio House Judiciary Committee last week. Your support of Senate Bill 17 is valuable to the passage of this important legislation. With your continued help, we will protect children and prohibit past offenders from continuing their crimes against Ohio's youth.

Again, thank you for the information; should you have any questions, please do not hesitate to contact me.

Sincerely,

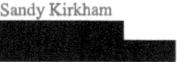

Robert F. Spada
State Senator
24th District

ROBERT F. SPADA
SENATOR
24TH DISTRICT

STATEHOUSE   FAX 614-466-4250
ＩＵＳ, OHIO 43215   HOME 440-230-2868
-466-8056   rspada@maiIr.sen.state.oh.us

Letter from Ohio Senate, 2005

APPENDIX D

Photos

My parents

Dad's college graduation, 1964

Counterclockwise: Vickie, Jackie, Sandy, Chuck, Randy, Mike, Christmas 1969

Sandy, Cindy and one of the Gardner twins. Camp 1970

Teens for Christ Convention, 1971

Mike and Sandy in 1971

Family in 1975

APPENDIX D | PHOTOS **253**

Mom and Sandy, age 16, 1971

Mom and Sandy, Christmas 1980

Teri and Sandy, 1978

Sandy and Teri, 2019

APPENDIX D | PHOTOS

Chris and Sandy 1972 and again in 2019

Chris and Sandy 1972 and again in 2019

Bill and Sandy 1980

Christmas 1993

Dad's 70th birthday: Sandy, Herb, Mike and Wendi, 2003

Bill and Sandy, current

APPENDIX D | PHOTOS **259**

Sandy with David Pooler and Mary Jo Noworyta from the Victim's Conference in Buffalo, New York

www.ingramcontent.com/pod-product-compliance
Lightning Source LLC
Chambersburg PA
CBHW020522080526
44583CB00013B/704